"J. P. Bone's novel *Illegals* is a rarity in contemporary literature — a story which boldly and vividly presents a piece of contemporary history, told through characters who cannot fail to move you with their anguish and their courage. I am reminded of Upton Sinclair and John Steinbeck, who did not hesitate to confront the most urgent issues of their day through their fiction. *Illegals* is a novel that touches the heart. I hope it is widely read."

Howard Zinn, Historian,
author of *A People's History of the United States*

". . . a rare uplifting literary work . . . cites chapter and verse the details of the exploitation of working people from Latin America by the corporate colossus up north. It paints a bleak picture of immigrants' plight, yet offers inspiring hope for those who dare to work together in solidarity."

Studs Terkel, Pulitzer Prize Winning author, historian

"J.P. Bone has not only produced a novel worthy of reading on its literary merits, but his *Illegals* is also an extraordinary story which captures the human drama of the everyday struggles experienced by Latino immigrants in their quest for survival and social justice."

Carlos Muñoz, Jr. Professor Emeritus, U. C. Berkeley

". . . accurate and moving description of a good old-fashioned union organizing campaign, as seen from the inside. This makes it, along with other strengths, a valuable handbook for those who want to rebuild the labor movement." **Steve Early**, Labor Journalist

" . . . . I encourage you to read *Illegals* not just for its powerful commentary, but because it's a damn good read!"

Michael Moore, Academy award winning director, author

"*Illegals* is a powerful story of humanity, hope, and faith from the hearts of the exploited Latino poor in their struggle for justice."

Martin Sheen, Actor, humanitarian

Long before the Dream Act Movement came into being, J.P. Bone's novel, *Illegals*, presented the compelling story of a group of undocumented immigrant factory workers who risked deportation in order to demand better treatment as workers . . . . the novel chronicles the genesis of a group's collective coming to courage at a time when most undocumented immigrants remained silent about the abuses they experienced . . . . the book is prophetic and revealing . . . . ahead of its time in the way that it depicted a pan-Latino and cross-ethnic coalition of workers striving towards a common goal. Readers will enjoy the story as much as the characters. **Alberto Ledesma**, artist, writer

ILLEGALS

A NOVEL

by J. P. Bone

Mindfield Publications
Berkeley, California

For information, contact:
MINDFIELD PUBLICATIONS

www.Illegalsthebook.com

Library of Congress Catalog Card Number: 96-094555
ISBN 0-9651921-0-5
First edition cover and book design by John Heisch
Cover Photo by Dennis Galloway
Second edition interior and cover formatting by D. Bass
inspired by the original work of John Heisch.

For María Dolores, Christopher Omar and Iliana Louise.
Los quiero mucho

1

Santa Ana, El Salvador, 1980

It was quiet that afternoon. There were no explosions, no gun battles, no soldiers patrolling the streets. And though it was not easy, the people of el barrio Colón tried not to think about the war, the death squads, or those who had disappeared. After all, it was Sunday, the day of rest — even in El Salvador.

In the shade of a tamarindo tree, an old man played his guitar, strumming the chords of a cumbia as the men around him tapped their feet. The old man paused for a moment and smiled, his tired eyes gazing out beyond the dirt street, beyond the brick mesones painted blue and yellow and red, and beyond the children playing among las flores de fuego — the flowers of fire.

Throngs of people jammed the outdoor market that afternoon. They bought beans and rice, tomatoes and onions, and, as a special treat, sweet bread to eat with their coffee. Many could not afford to buy coffee, though they had worked all week in a processing plant sorting the beans into superior and inferior classes. They would make their own brew at home out of toasted corn and cinnamon.

On the street corners, small groups of men gathered, smoked cigarettes and talked quietly. Indoors, women made tortillas in the cavernous shadows, fed crying babies and gossiped.

Manuel, a lanky young man, carried his infant son on his shoulders down the dusty street, the child's inquisitive eyes protected from the glaring sun by a peasant's straw hat. As

Manuel crossed the street, a small barefoot boy ran past him, weaving and growling like an automobile as he clutched a broken plate, pretending it was a steering wheel. The men on the corner laughed quietly and Manuel smiled, thinking how soon his son would be running in the streets and playing.

An army jeep raced recklessly around the corner, wheels spinning, blankets of dust rolling as National Guardsmen flaunted arrogant grins and M-16's. As the soldiers bounded down the street, people searched frantically for their children and yanked them indoors. Manuel grabbed his son around the waist, jumped a low wall and hid. The jeep skidded to a stop in front of a small brick house and the soldiers burst through the door brandishing automatic rifles, turning over tables and chairs. Manuel heard a long piercing scream. He peered over the top of the wall and saw the soldiers yank two teenage boys out into the street, knock them down and curse them. Then, for a moment, everything stood still; there was no wind and no sound—not even a breath. The old man watched from his spot beneath the tamarindo tree, his eyes glassy, his lips pursed.

A plump woman—the boy's mother—stumbled into the street in pursuit of her children, pleading with the soldiers, holding her head in disbelief and sobbing: "Por favor! Ellos no han hecho nada! Please! They've done nothing!"

"Callate, mujer!" one of the soldiers shouted. "Shut up, woman! If they've done nothing, then they have nothing to fear!" Jabbing his M-16 into the younger boy's ribs, he ordered the brothers to put their hands behind their heads and climb into the jeep.

Their mother fell to her knees and begged: "Please! They're just children! Don't take them! They are all I have left!"

The soldiers sneered and climbed aboard their jeep, intoxicated by the terror they had unleashed. As they raced down the dirt road of el barrio Colón, their vehicle careening from side to side, the guardsmen laughed, amused by their young prisoners who huddled together trembling with fear.

The boys' mother sobbed in the middle of the dirt street, teardrops drawing lines in the dust on her cheeks.

Manuel's boy began to cry and he held him tight. "It's all right, mi hijo," he said, though he knew better.

As the dust settled, the old man began to strum his guitar, the chords drifting across the dusty road. He sang a corrido, making up the words of the song as he went along. It was a sad song about two boys who never lived to be men.

2

Los Angeles, California, 1980

A taxi blared its horn as it screeched to a stop. But the sound was lost in the drone of a thousand voices, the blare of a dozen radios on display in open-air shops, and the omnipresent roar of car engines, all echoing off walls of aging theaters, department stores and tall dark hotels where desperate people slept and slipped into oblivion.

Clouds of exhaust plumed from rows of pushing automobiles jammed bumper to bumper. Men leaned out of car windows and shook their fists in rage, blood and cracked skulls just a gesture away. And the aroma of tacos de carnitas, fresh coffee and pastry merged with the oozing stench of garbage and urine dripping from stains on buildings that towered over the street and blotted out the sun. Smoke and voices and odors tumbled in dirty clouds, blown back from the street by endless traffic, blown back and flattened by the footsteps of ten thousand people.

Rosa—a tired but lovely Mexican woman with high Aztec cheekbones, bent over her four children, holding them close to her side as she waited for the traffic light to change. When the signal turned green and the last cars raced through the intersection, she cautiously led her children across the street, trusting no one, well aware of the danger there.

On the corner, a prostitute paced back and forth, searching the eyes of men as they drove past, licking her lips with feigned lust. The young mother quickly herded her children past the woman on the corner, dodging a man hustling hot jewelry, his voice as cold and vaporous as dry ice.

Rosa led her children into an open-air market, aisles brimming with fresh vegetables, fruit and nuts. As they strolled past the aisles of produce, two policemen strutted down the street like gunslingers, examining the eyes of every person they passed as if to measure the nature of their crimes. It wasn't long before they spotted the hustler, conspicuous in his overcoat. He made a hasty retreat and vanished in the crowd. The cops laughed cynically and gave their weapons a reassuring pat. He was not worth the trouble, they reasoned—after all, in their eyes, most of the people on the street were criminals. Rosa weighed a bag of tomatoes on an overhead scale and calculated its price. She counted the money in her purse, wrapping a strap firmly around her wrist to discourage any would-be thieves. As she reviewed her weekly budget and estimated the bus fare home, her youngest child set out to explore the bright colors and shapes of the marketplace—a learning experience he would have to do without. Rosa gently yanked him by the collar to her side. She took inventory of her children and returned one tomato to the display, checking the weight of those that remained on the scale.

Outside the market, just beyond the zucchini and acorn squash, shoppers began to move with unexpected haste. A voice cried, "La migra!" Women gasped for breath. They snatched the hands of their children and pulled them down the street, tiny heels drawing lines on the sidewalk. The street instantly cleared as two green vans bounded over the curb and jerked to a stop.

Rosa herded her children around the aisles of produce as immigration agents burst into a cafe next door. She could hear screams and the crash of broken glass as Latinos trapped there searched frantically for an escape. There was nowhere for them to go.

"Andenle!" Rosa cried as she corralled her children down the street, glancing over her shoulder, biting her lip. "Hurry!"

A bus stopped near the corner, its door flying open with a gush of compressed air. Without checking its destination, Rosa lifted her children aboard, climbed the steep steps and rummaged through her purse for change.

"Come on, lady!" the bus driver said as he veered into traffic. Rosa frantically dug through her purse, talking to herself, hands trembling as she struggled to pick out quarters and nickels and dimes.

The driver glanced at Rosa and shook his head.

"Yo tengo!" Rosa assured him, though her response only made him angry.

The driver rocked back and forth impatiently, steering with one hand and tapping the top of the fare validator with the other. "If you want to play, you got to pay. I need *dinero*. Comprende?" he said, glancing at her derisively. Rosa dropped all of her change into the machine, well aware it was more than what was required. She struggled frantically to reach her children at the back of the bus and fell into a seat beside them. And as she drew her children close together, Rosa bit her lip with such intensity it nearly bled.

As the bus lumbered down the street, immigration agents shoved a dozen handcuffed men into green vans, their prisoners stumbling, eyes glazed in disbelief. "Andele!" an agent said in a jaded North American accent. He paused to adjust his sunglasses then slammed the van door shut. Horns honked and babies cried and radios blasted cumbia and salsa and rock 'n roll. The tide of street noise drew back like a spent wave, gathering itself together for another assault. The prostitute leaned into the window of a car and bargained with an ashen-faced man, while the hustler, back in business, sold a watch. And inside the marketplace, Rosa's bag of tomatoes bobbed on the overhead scale, red and shiny and ripe.

3

The driveway leading to Rosa's place was blocked by a weather-beaten station wagon with two flat tires, rusted bumpers and a tailpipe that clung to the ground like a root. Tomatoes, peppers and corn grew to the left of the driveway, the right side bordered by a small wood-frame house, flakes of paint peeling off like yellow flower petals. The splintered windows of the house were wide open and two young children stood there and watched as a stranger passed by.

Antonio, a young Chicano built like a running back, made his way down the driveway toward Rosa's flat out back. He moved with cool deliberation, his arms and shoulders cut like a man who had done time. His walk was not natural—it was the walk of his barrio, learned and perfected years before on the sweltering streets of East Los Angeles. And there was something about his eyes and the steady clap of polished shoes on pavement that frightened the children as they stared from the windowsill.

As he approached the house in the back, Antonio considered his plan: She could be a key person, he thought. Rosa could be key. She works in the cutting department. That's strategic. We've got someone from every department in the organizing committee *except* cutting, and it's at the center of everything. If I can organize *her*, we'll have the factory wrapped up tight!

A dog barked and chickens cackled. The long dusty leaves of a corn stalk stretched leisurely in the warm autumn sun.

Man, it's true what they say. . . . Echo Park, Frogtown, Temple Street—they're all the *same*! Simón! El barrio es el *barrio.* . . .

Antonio took a long drag from his cigarette. Man, this sure looks like home. Mom used to grow corn—and tomatoes and cilantro and peppers. And our yard—it was as fucked-up as *this* one. I'd come home from school and she'd be in the kitchen cooking and ironing somebody else's clothes. Trying to make a few extra bucks—sweating and cooking and ironing, taking care of my brothers and sisters. Damn! And she would still manage a smile when I walked in that door. She would still smile. Then she'd ask me about school. What could I do? What could I say? And she'd give me that look and ask if I'd been fighting again. She was on to me, man. I'd tell her I'd been playing football and that's why I was all messed up. But she knew better. She knew. "Oh, los hombres, como les gusta la guerra. Oh, men, how they like war." She could not understand that sort of thing. Pues. I guess she was right. Fighting all the time over nothing. But then she'd sit me down at the table and serve me up a big plate of her enchiladas, with refried beans and rice. ¡Orale! They were the best in town!

Antonio climbed around the abandoned station wagon, taking care not to scuff shoes polished like black mirrors. Man, *look* at this place! Just like home. Dogs barking and kids crying. I don't know how she did it. Then Pop would come home—when he *came* home—and she'd wait on him hand and foot. Like if she wasn't even tired—worried about what kind of day *he* had. Damn. She'd do anything for me and my old man. Eso. She'd do anything. One of these days I'm gonna buy her a house of her own. For real! Maybe with this job with the union, I'll be able to save some bread. At *least* so she can retire. At least so she won't work herself to death like Pop did. . . . Man, I can't wait to sit at the negotiation table with that son of a bitch Mersola. Sit eyeball to eyeball with the bossman. People working their asses off so they can live like *this*!

As Antonio approached a battered wooden gate, the children from the front house abandoned their vantage point at the window and raced toward the back door, anxious to get another glimpse of the stranger. In their minds, he looked something like an outlaw from the Old West gunning for the sheriff. When he swung the gate open like the door of a saloon, the children gasped in astonishment. Antonio turned toward them and grinned. Frightened and excited, the two boys ran to their mother for protection, crying in Spanish, "Mamá! Mamá! The man is in the back now!"

Antonio walked around a garage at the end of the driveway, where a middle-aged Mexican in a soiled sleeveless undershirt labored away, stapling new fabric to an old chair. Sweating profusely from his work and weight, he used the inside of his right arm to wipe away the puddles of salty moisture that had gathered around the hair of his eyebrows and the pores of his cheeks and nose. Pausing to size up the situation, he, too, was troubled by the unexpected presence of a stranger.

Antonio recognized the laborer's apprehension. "Cómo te vá?" he asked. "How is it going?"

The man nodded and reached for his cigarette. He took a long, deep drag, exhaled and leaned back into his work. He squinted his eyes against the white curling smoke of his cigarette perched on a workhorse close by. No, he's not from the immigration, thanks to God, the man thought as he pounded another staple into the chair. Not a pinche cholo. Pues. Not from the government, neither, I don't think so. He didn't look around, didn't look at my bed or my stove. Thanks to God, he didn't come here to tell me I can't live in the garage anymore. Ah, I think I understand: I think I know what is happening. He's going to visit Rosa!

The sweating man straightened up, scratched his large belly and smiled. I see. . . . Well, he's a real man, that's for sure. Still. I don't think she will have him. Pobrecita! She'll wait forever for her husband to come back home.

Antonio rounded the corner of the house, worked the latch of yet another dilapidated gate and made his way across a dirt yard, pounded smooth by child's play, fractured by cracks like fault lines. He stepped carefully to avoid broken toys scattered about and ducked a low clothesline until he reached the stairway leading to Rosa's flat.

Man, they don't have to worry about a prowler snooping around *here* at midnight, Antonio thought: he'd bust his ass before he ever got *near* the place. As he climbed the steps, gray splintered boards creaked beneath his weight.

At the top of the stairs, Antonio rapped three times on a battered screen door that kept things in but nothing out. Two young boys answered in the middle of the third rap.

"Está tu mamá?" Antonio asked. "Is your mother home?"

"Mamá!" they cried, though Rosa was only a few feet away slicing an onion and dropping the pieces into a pot of boiling pinto beans.

Rosa carefully laid down the knife, wiped her hands on her apron and leaned around the corner of the apartment's only door.

"Buenas," Antonio said with a grin. Rosa returned the greeting politely, wondering who he was, what he was selling. Then she noticed the scar over his eyebrow and her mind began to spin as she quickly paged through her memory to recall where she had seen him before. There is danger here! she thought, though she could not remember why. This man is someone to be avoided! Instinctively, she pulled her sons away from the doorway. Antonio talked fast.

"I'm a friend of Sonia and José. Tú trabajas en la fábrica de Mersola, verdad? You work at the Mersola Shoe Factory, right?"

"Sí," Rosa answered, still guarding the door and her two boys.

Antonio laughed at himself and glanced at his shoes. Take it easy, man, he thought. She's scared.

"I'm sorry, Señora. I should have introduced myself. My name is Antonio Rodriguez. I'm an organizer for the Shoeworkers Union, Local 305. We're organizing a union at your factory, and your friends, Sonia and José, suggested I come and talk to you about it. They said you might want to hear what we're trying to do."

Eso, she thought. That's it. At the factory gates—that's where I've seen him. Talking with the people about the union—right in front of the factory!

"Could I come in for a few minutes and talk with you? It won't take long."

"Well. . . ." She hesitated.

"I only want to explain to you what we're trying to do with the union. We're trying to build a future for our children, no? That's all. No one will ever know I spoke with you. Don't you have a few minutes?"

"Pues. . . ." Rosa bit her lip. "Well. All right. Come in."

Antonio entered the kitchen just as a pot of beans boiled over, white foam and water sputtering into the stove's burner. As Rosa extinguished the flame and cleaned up the mess, Antonio kneeled down on the kitchen floor so he could talk to her two little boys.

"Cómo están, niños?"

"Bien," they replied, dropping their eyes to the floor.

"Que bueno," Antonio said, patting them affectionately on the shoulders.

As Rosa hurried to flip handmade tortillas on a griddle before they burned, she asked Antonio if he would like a cup of coffee. He accepted, though he'd already had three cups at two previous house meetings.

Rosa's two girls peered around the doorway from their self-imposed exile in the living room, one head atop the other. They giggled and blushed and covered their mouths with their hands, then ducked back around the corner.

"María. Ven aqui, mi amor," Rosa called to her oldest. "Come here, my love." María obediently stepped into the kitchen, her hands behind her back, doing her best to disguise her shyness. "Mija, would you please prepare some coffee for our guest?" María nodded and immediately set to work filling a saucepan with water, though she could barely reach the faucet.

"María, mucho gusto," Antonio said formally.

"Igualmente," she replied stiffly. "It's nice to meet you, too."

Antonio smiled. "And how old are you, muchacha?"

"I am ten years old," María replied with confidence, though her eyes betrayed her.

"Ten years old! Well, you are the prettiest ten-year-old I have ever met!"

María grinned and buried her chin into her shoulder. Rosa looked up from her work and smiled. Rosa reached for a tortilla, dipped it in a pan of chile salsa, then wrapped it carefully around grated Mexican cheese.

Antonio lit another cigarette and reveled in the warmth of a kitchen filled with steam, the scent of chili and the voices of small children. He felt very much at home there.

"Well, let's see. I count four children. Is that right?"

"Yes," Rosa smiled patiently. "There are four of them."

"That's a lot of work."

"Yes, it is. But María helps me a lot. Anyway. They are my life. But going to the factory. That is different. That is a lot of work!" Rosa said, hoping her remark would get Antonio down to business and speed his departure.

"Yes, I know. I used to work in a shoe factory in El Monte. That's how I got involved in the union. I used to be fighting with the bosses all the time. They used to treat us real bad. Until we brought the union in. Then their attitude changed: They were more careful. You know, before we had the union, they paid us less than the minimum wage. They didn't pay for overtime, and we didn't have any benefits. None at all. Except Christmas.

They gave us Christmas Day off. That was it. Just like at Mersola's, no?"

"Yes. It is the same."

Antonio measured her response. He sensed she was anxious for him to leave. But that was part of the job and he was used to that sort of thing. Still. There was something about the kitchen and the steam and the home-made tortillas.

"Señora, I know you are very busy. I don't mean to impose on you. But let me ask you one question: What do you think about forming a union where you work?"

"Well. I don't know very much about it. My husband used to be involved in a union in México. He was very active in it. It would probably be a good thing for the people. But I can't get involved."

"Doesn't your husband think you should join?"

"He probably would. I don't know. He disappeared two years ago. After he went to visit his mother in Chihuahua." Rosa stared into the pot of beans as she stirred them. "His mother was sick, and he went to visit her. He said he was coming back. But . . . I don't know. Maybe something happened to him when he was crossing the border."

"I'm sorry, señora," Antonio said as he took a drag from his cigarette. As Rosa shook off the thought of her missing husband, Antonio was reminded of his mother. That's what *she* does when someone mentions Pop, he thought, watching Rosa rub both sides of her face as she would if reassuring a child, somehow managing a smile. Incredible! he thought. It is the same! Exactly the same mannerism as Mom! What a *trip!*

María carefully poured Antonio a cup of hot water, then, with a sense of formality, placed a jar of sugar, a tin of instant coffee and a plastic white spoon directly in front on him, each in its own appointed space.

With an avuncular nod of his head, Antonio thanked her and turned back to Rosa. "It's a lot of work to support a family—

even when you have help."

Rosa smiled gently. "Why don't we go into the living room. It's cooler there. Don't you think it's hot in here? María, please take Señor Rodriguez's coffee into the living room, would you please, mija? And would you bring him some pan? Some sweet bread?"

As Antonio moved to the back of the flat, he passed the apartment's only bedroom. From one wall to the next it was nearly filled-up by a queen-sized bed covered with blankets, dolls and coloring books; a mirror with photos tucked in the corners sat propped upon a particleboard dresser—a luxury that, combined with the bed, occupied so much space that Rosa's children had to climb over the bed when they needed something.

In the living room a twin bed became a couch during the day. Antonio was led past it to a chair covered with plastic that stuck to him whenever he tried to move—the best chair in the house.

There were pictures and ornaments attached to the walls with scotch tape and thumbtacks—finger paintings and year-old Mother's Day cards, snapshots of confirmations and family portraits from K-Mart. A crucifix bore witness to Rosa's faith, palm fronds tucked between the cross and the wall. And then there was the calendar, a gift from the local carnicería, it depicted an Aztec warrior cradling a woman slain by an unknown enemy. A beam of sunlight shined down upon the warrior from high in the heavens. If Antonio didn't know better, he would have thought it was a portrait of Rosa.

María brought Antonio his coffee and a pastry served on a small plastic Ronald McDonald plate. Antonio could see that Rosa let nothing go to waste.

"Señora. I appreciate your time and hospitality," Antonio said. "Again, I understand you are very busy and have many things to do. Entonces, con su permiso. I'll get right to the point. There are a lot of people at Mersola's who want to bring in the union. People like Sonia and José."

Rosa listened but betrayed no feelings.

"You work in the cutting department, no? So you make, at best, the minimum wage. I don't see how you can survive with four children."

Rosa arched her eyebrows. "Es bien duro. It's very hard. Especially when one of them gets sick."

"Pues, sí. I can imagine. Now, if you had a union and the people were together, you could get a health plan that would pay a lot of your medical bills. Not all of them, but most. And you'd make more money. You'd make more per hour and you'd get overtime pay. They tell me they don't pay you extra for overtime. You know, the law in this state is that if you get the minimum wage, and if you work more than forty hours a week they have to pay you time-and-a-half. See? They don't even do that, do they?"

"No," Rosa admitted. "That's true. They don't do that."

"Well, see? They couldn't get away with that if you were in a union."

"But . . ." Antonio waited for her to continue, but she only stared at the floor. "Those things would help, wouldn't they?"

"Yes. They would be very nice. But right now, I just have to be working and paying the bills. Life is hard and I don't need any more trouble. And some people say if we bring in the union, the immigration will come. The bosses would call in la migra. And they would deport me to México. That's what they say. Who would take care of my children?"

"Señora. La migra could come at any time, whether there's a union or not. What we're trying to do is more than just vote in a union. We're trying to organize the people. We're trying to bring everyone together. We have a plan for how to deal with the immigration if they ever come. But we have to be organized first, see? That's the important thing."

Rosa watched Antonio carefully, getting a sense of him. She'd been conned before. Could she trust him? He seemed sincere, she thought. But there are so many dangers! The immigration downtown! They were so close! And my children!

"My husband used to say that the sindicatos—the unions—are different in this country. He said here the representatives wear suits and ties, sit in business offices and use fancy words—that they look and talk like los patrones—like the bosses."

As Rosa and Antonio talked, María sat quietly with her hands folded in her lap. Ramón, the youngest child, climbed up on the back of the armchair where Antonio sat. María leaped up, arms and legs swinging, grabbed his shirt and carefully dragged him back to the floor. Once he was safe and out of harm's reach, she sat back down as though nothing had happened.

"What your husband said is true in a way," Antonio said, not distracted by the children. "Even though I'm in the union, I have to admit, in a way, with some unions, it's true. That has to change. But you see a lot of people who are in unions aren't *organized*. They're in the union, but they don't really *have* a union."

Rosa blinked and tried to make sense of his seemingly contradictory words.

"See, they pay dues and that's *it*. They have union cards and their officials send them letters and newspapers. But the *people* are the union, no? Pues, la union hace la fuerza! When we're united, we're strong. When we're *organized*. That's what we need."

"Sí, claro," Rosa answered politely. She glanced at her children and sighed. Ramón was chewing on the windowsill. María, ever mindful of her mother, followed her eyes to Ramón, jumped up instantly and led him to a toy in the corner.

"Hay Dios mío," Rosa sighed again. "I'm sorry. I don't need any more problems than I already have. I hope I haven't wasted your time."

"No, señora. You haven't. Maybe you'll change your mind. I

understand how you feel—but we have to think of the future, too." Antonio reached into his pocket, pulled out a business card, and handed it to Rosa. "Look, if you ever have any questions, or if there's ever anything the union or I can do for you, please don't hesitate to call me."

"Gracias, señor," Rosa smiled.

"De nada, señora. And please call me Antonio."

"Thank you, Antonio. And please call me Rosa."

"Okay, Rosa," Antonio grinned. "Well . . . thank you for the coffee. And the pastry."

María was concerned that he was leaving so soon. She searched her mother's eyes for any hint of disappointment, and though none was evident, María was troubled and her expression showed it.

Ramón sat in the corner quietly dismantling the toy provided by his older sister. Still he, too, felt something was wrong. As Antonio stood to leave, Ramón raced toward him, his hard leather shoes clapping against the wood floor. He grabbed Antonio around both legs and hugged him, his eyes closed tight. What's *this*? Antonio thought. He lifted both hands, not knowing what to do, uncomfortable with the unexpected display of affection. The little boy let go and Antonio slowly made his way toward the kitchen, Rosa and the children following close behind.

"I'll come back again some time and visit," he assured them.

María watched as Antonio opened the battered screen door. Unfazed by its decrepit condition, María was, however, terribly concerned about her mother's state. Her brother came to the rescue.

"El no va a comer con nosotros?" Ramón asked innocently. "Isn't he going to have supper with us?"

Rosa was embarrassed and her brown face turned deep red. She gazed down at the buckling linoleum kitchen floor, with its curled edges and worn patches, bare floorboards smeared with dried black glue. But the condition of the flat was the farthest thing from her mind.

Gathering her courage, in an effort to avoid any hint of rudeness, Rosa asked: "Would you like to stay for dinner? We're not having anything fancy. Just beans and enchiladas."

A wonderful vapor escaped the confines of the oven, carrying with it the aroma of roasted chilis, melting cheese and toasted corn tortillas. Antonio bobbed his head up and down and his eyes sparkled. He felt very much at home in Rosa's kitchen.

4

In another part of town, a gaunt old man with sun-worn skin, white hair and a carefully trimmed mustache held up a crystal glass and said, "More wine, please!" But his request was ignored. The old man stared at an arc of candlelight and waited patiently for a reply—for a word of acknowledgment—for *any* response. But there was none.

The dining room where the old man sat sparkled with silver and china, wine and champagne glistening like the Mediterranean Sea at dusk. Silver brackets held candles that burned with the steady intensity of molten glass.

The old man grew impatient. He pounded a clenched fist against the white linen tablecloth and searched the eyes of his family, gathered together for a special dinner.

There was his son, Amerio Mersola, his graying hair slicked back. He ate with his mouth open, detached and confident. Flanking him were his two sons, filling their chairs like bodyguards, mimicking their father's every mannerism. Their wives in turn sat dutifully beside them, quietly picking at their food, nervous and uneasy.

As the old man glared across the table at his son, his daughter-in-law, Mary, swung into the dining room with a deep dish of homemade lasagna, adding to the feast she had made with a mother's love—and a little help from a maid and a cook. The table was laden with roast turkey and stuffing prepared with Italian sausage; there were platters of pasta and antipasto, steamed fresh vegetables with hollandaise sauce, and a tossed green salad with watercress and croutons. At each end of the table were baskets of hot rolls and tiny dishes stacked with cubes of sweet butter.

The old man listened to the ringing of forks on china. When he could bear it no longer, he asked, "Can I please have some more wine?" His grandsons cocked their heads as if they heard a faint sound in the distance. They returned to their meals, which they quickly devoured.

Mary, humming softly to herself, poured her father-in-law another glass before her husband could object. The old man smiled and winked in appreciation.

Amerio looked up from his plate and glared across the table at his father. "That's all for you!" he barked, scooping up a forkful of turkey and shoveling it into his mouth, washing the half-chewed mixture down with wine.

The old man muttered a few choice words to his son in Italian—nothing but meaningless garble to the Mersola boys. And though Amerio could hear what he said, he had forgotten his Italian many years before. Or so he claimed.

Quite accustomed to the situation, the younger son turned to Amerio and asked, "Well, Dad—have you got things under control at the shop?"

"No!" grumbled his father as he wiped his mouth and poured himself another glass of wine.

Hesitating long enough to show the proper respect, Amerio's son asked, "Don't you think it's time you called that legal firm I told you about? I have lunch with one of their attorneys once a week. He tells me they really get results."

"I don't need to spend a lot of money on lawyers to keep a bunch of illegal aliens from bringing in a damn union! Excuse me, girls."

The old man objected, speaking again to his son in Italian. Amerio waved his hand next to his ear as though an insect was buzzing about and annoying him.

22

"Besides," Amerio continued, "in a few days there won't be any more trouble."

"Trouble!" the old man snorted. The young women were shaken by the outburst.

"Don't pay any attention to him, girls," Amerio said in a tone more a warning than an apology.

The old man leaned forward and pointed his nose at his son. "You might be a big shot now—but I'm still your father! And I don't care how old or rich you are, you speak to me with respect!"

Amerio arched his eyebrows, but otherwise ignored the speech. He took another sip of wine and turned to the young women. "Would either of you care for some more champagne?"

The old man stormed out of the dining room, cursing under his breath.

As he watched his father leave, Amerio shook his head with disdain. "Sorry, girls. He's getting old and senile." His sons continued to eat as though nothing out of the ordinary had occurred. But their wives were clearly shaken.

"You see, years ago, my father used to be in the Longshoreman's Union—back when he was young and worked on the docks. In those days, they needed unions. They were a pretty good thing. But nowadays, things have changed. They're just a bunch of crooked bastards, if you'll pardon my French. Troublemakers. At my factory, they're coming around trying to get everyone all worked up. Hell—most of the people working for me aren't even from this *country*! They're all Mexican, or whatever. You know. And they're damn happy to have a job, believe you me!"

"Dad pays them more than they ever dreamed of making in México," the older son asserted. "They're all wetbacks."

Mersola winced, but nodded his head in confirmation. The young women, eager to be convinced, nodded submissively as they digested their lesson in labor relations.

"My father lives in the past—he doesn't know any better. He was a good man, and a good father, and—well, I love the old cuss." Amerio paused and shook his head. He laughed softly as he remembered his youth, thinking about his father. He had taught him how to throw a baseball, how to fish and how to fight. "Yeah, I suppose there's nothing I wouldn't do for that old man . . . well, practically nothing, anyway. I know he sounds like some sort of radical. But, believe me, he's not. That's all just for show. You just have to ignore him when he gets like that. Like I said, he's getting kinda senile."

The young wives turned to their husbands to gauge their reactions. Both were staring at their father in awe, as if they, too, shared secret memories of the old man's youth.

Mary pushed open the swinging door from the kitchen with her hip, carrying a silver coffee set given to her on her wedding day. A wisp of steam rose above the sterling silver pot. Lost in another world where there are only family gatherings and baked bread, she asked with wide eyes and the utmost of devotion: "Has everyone had enough to eat?" Amerio Mersola glanced up from his plate, wiped his mouth and belched.

5

Manuel hurried down the street of his barrio, past the blooming scarlet jacaranda, past brick walls where hastily painted slogans declared: LIBERTAD O MUERTE! LIBERTY OR DEATH! A breeze kicked up clouds of dust and carried dead leaves from mango and orange trees growing in the patios of los mesones— the brightly painted apartment buildings where poor workers lived. In the distance, a long green line of parrots babbled madly across the sky as if escaping a holocaust. How strange! Manuel thought. Usually, the parrots appear in April or May. There must be a battle nearby. Yes, they must be fighting again. Well, they will know tomorrow. Tomorrow, they will know. If the vultures appear.

Manuel rounded the corner and approached the meson where his cousin Ana lived. Yes, he thought, they will know tomorrow. And tomorrow, I will be on my way to the United States—the patron of the vultures. How strange life is! I've walked down this dusty street a thousand times. But after tomorrow, it will be only a memory. This barrio where I've spent my whole life. My friends, my wife, my son—all will be only a memory. But there's no choice, is there? There is no alternative. I have to work. My family has to eat. And it's no longer safe for me here. It's no longer safe. What good will I be to my wife and my son without a head?

An iguana sunned itself from its perch on a high wall made of dirt and cement. It blinked its eyes as Manuel passed.

Well, it doesn't matter. One must do what one must do.

That's it. When I'm working in North America and sending money home, my boy can drink milk. Milk! He barely knows how it tastes. Maybe next Christmas I'll be able to send him a present. Maybe a toy and a new pair of shoes. It's best for everyone. But it will be hard. How I will miss them—my wife and my son. I'll miss them more than my home, this dusty barrio—more than this land and the mango trees and the volcanoes, more than the thunderstorms and the warm clear sea, more than dancing cumbias beneath palm trees in the moonlight. My wife, Dolores—I will miss her soft eyes and the way she smiles when she is beside me. And my son. What will it be like without him? How will I sleep without putting him to bed, knowing he is safe and well? If I return—no! *When* I return—he will be so much bigger! He'll be talking and playing with the other children in the street. Will he recognize his father? Will he run up to me with his arms open, smile and cry "Papá! You are back! You've come home at last!" Will he? Anyway, I must go. I must.

As Manuel thought about his son, he spotted what appeared to be two large gray worms on the street. There was something about the way they lay there that made him stop. They seemed to be pointing at him. He squatted down for a closer look. There, lying in the dirt, gray and stiff, were two fingers—two small fingers—the fingers of a child. Oh God no, he thought, the vision of his son's face still before him. No! What madness is this? What sort of man would *do* such a thing?

Manuel rushed toward Ana's home. She must not know. Ana must not know of this thing. Maybe I should have buried those fingers. What if a child finds them? Should I go back and bury them? What if someone sees me? What would they think? What would they say? No. I can't do anything. Nothing! Damn it . . . *I can't do anything*! Those sons of bitches! And I can't tell anyone. Especially Ana. Not the day before we leave. She has seen enough. Enough! The men who did this. ¡Que barbaridad! Some day they will get what they deserve! Someday. . . .

Manuel reached the brick apartment where his cousin lived. He took a deep breath and stepped out of the bright light of the street and into the cool darkness. Two women washed clothes in a double cement sink shared by all the tenants. They scrubbed clothes against the slanting sides of the basin, dipped their bowls in la pila and rinsed each item clean. When they spotted Manuel, they wiped the sweat from their brows with their aprons and smiled.

"Qué pasa, Sanbumba?" they asked, laughing at his barrio nickname. Manuel smiled, amused by the greeting. "Aren't you going to kneel before the barrio saint?"

"Puta! Sí vos sos santo, entonces yo soy virgen!" cracked one of the women, her hand on her hip. "If you are a saint, then I am a virgin! Anyway, where did you get a name like that? San-boom-ba! What, did you used to play the drums or something?"

"No, niña. I think it was something else he used to do," the other woman joked, hiding her teeth with her hand as the three of them laughed.

As the laughter died down, they fell into a heavy silence. They dropped their eyes and thought about what all wanted desperately to forget. Finally, one of the women spoke up. "Manuel. Did you hear about los cipotes? About the children?" she asked softly.

"Yes," Manuel said. "I saw la guardia take them away."

One of the women swallowed hard. "But did you hear what happened to them? Pobrecitos! They found them in the street this morning." She began to weep. Her neighbor wrapped her arm around her and dabbed the tears from her eyes. She turned to Manuel and completed the story. "They'd been mutilated. Their fingers and ears had been cut off. And they'd slit their throats."

Manuel fought back the pressure he felt in his throat. My son! It could have been my son! He leaned over and patted the sobbing woman gently on her back, though it was a struggle for him to move. What kind of men would do such a thing? he thought. What kind of men? Men who should not have to wait until the judgment day to be punished!

Manuel took a long deep breath. He forced the air from his lungs through his throat, out into the open, carrying with it the sounds of words barely audible: "And their mother?"

"She is at the church. Just crying and praying, praying and crying. I don't know if she is going to make it this time. She seems fine for a while. She is like herself. And then, she starts to talk crazy. She thinks she is talking with her husband. Poor thing! He has been dead for so long!"

He *has* been dead for a long time, Manuel thought. For a long time. Back when the people were marching in the streets: that was when it happened. That was when it all began. And he was one of the first. One of the first to dream—one of the first to die.

"She will be all right," Manuel said, though he did not like to say things that were not true. "She is a strong person."

The sobbing woman blew her nose on her bandana and wiped the tears from her eyes. It was not good to think too much about things one could not control. That much she knew. "I must look like an old cow, standing here, crying."

"Yes, and you've got enough milk to feed all the children in the barrio!" her friend teased.

Manuel and the women laughed again softly. They listened to the sound of water as it dripped into the pila—a basin that sat nestled between two sinks. And the water dripped slowly, following the inner dimension of the faucet as it might the contours of a stalactite in a limestone cave, reluctant and oblivious to time.

Manuel finally broke the silence. "Well, I have to go now. Ana and I are leaving tomorrow, you know. And we have a lot of things to get ready."

"So, you are going to the United States, eh?" one of the women teased. "Going to eat hamburgers and drive around in big red automobiles, no? Pues. If you meet Erik Estrada—tell him you know the perfect woman for him."

"Okay," Manuel laughed. "If I meet Erik Estrada, I will tell him that."

"Oiga, Manuel," the other woman said. "Would you mind doing *me* one little favor when you get there? There is just one thing I would like you to send me, if it won't be too much trouble."

"Of course! If I can do it, you know I will! What is it you want?"

She smiled mischievously. "Send me one of those big blond men with the blue eyes—like the ones in the movies. A big gringo! Okay?"

"Oh, sure. No problem. But what are you going to do with him once he gets here?"

"Bueno, that's easy. I'm going to give him as much pupusa as he wants."

"Aguantas!" the other woman said, blushing. "Do you believe that!"

Manuel laughed. "All right, señora. I will see what I can do. Well. I have to go talk to Ana now, you know. Nos vemos! Bye!"

"Sí no nos vemos mañana, que tengas buena suerte! Good luck!"

"Gracias, mujeres!"

"De nada, Sanbumba!" the women laughed.

Manuel stepped out from the shadows of the laundry room onto the patio at the center of the meson. He strolled past the orange and mango trees that grew beneath a framed sky there, past clotheslines laden with blankets and clothing. Then he slipped back into the shadows, following a long corridor with a line of small wooden doors, bruised and battered by forced entry, warped by years of rain. Behind those doors lived El Salvador's trabajadores—those who built the buildings, sorted the coffee beans, spun the cotton, cleaned the homes of the rich and worked in factories owned by wealthy North Americans, Europeans, and Asians. Some of the tiny apartments had no doors at all in the daytime, their occupants propping up pieces of sheet metal in the thresholds at night to keep out intruders.

At the end of the corridor lived Ana, her door secured with a thick wooden barricade. Manuel knocked three times and waited.

"Quien es?" Ana asked, as she peeked through the slit between the door and the threshold.

"It is only me, Manuel."

Ana unbolted the barricade and turned a medieval key as large as her hand to unlock the door.

Her apartment was a shambles. There were clothes scattered everywhere and stacks of things organized in a system only she could understand.

"What happened?" Manuel asked.

"Nothing, hombre! I am just trying to decide what to bring, what to give away and what to leave at my mother's house."

"Púchica! You can't bring a suitcase, you know!"

"I know that, hombre! Do you think I don't know that? But I can't just leave everything, you know, as though I were going away for the weekend."

Manuel thought about what she said. He *was* leaving everything that way. With his wife and son, leaving everything just the way it was. He couldn't do it any other way. He'd be back home soon, he hoped. Soon, and with enough money to take care of the family. Maybe even enough to buy a house. Soon. Two or three years. No, he had to leave everything just the way it was.

Ana wheeled from one stack of belongings to another, picking up a blouse and setting it back down again, overcome by the enormity of the task before her, bewildered by the complexity of its many parts. There were so many things to do, such little time. . . . Finally, a thought asserted itself: "Have you heard anything about the boys? It would be difficult leaving without knowing they are all right."

Ana bent over a small propane stove, turned on the gas and lit a match so she could boil water for coffee. She was not completely aware of the question she had asked, her mind sorting thoughts and reinventing priorities. There was so much to do! Manuel gazed out the window at the patio and wished he had a cigarette.

"I hope it is a safe time for us to leave," Ana said, struggling to hold on to one thought. "There are so many things happening. Do you think it is safe?"

"When do you think it will ever be safe, niña?" he replied bitterly. Then, realizing his mistake, he struggled to cover his footsteps. "Sure, it is safe! We will be all right! And we have got a good coyote!"

Ana noticed the abrupt change despite her confused state of mind. "What's wrong, Manuel?"

"Nothing!"

Ana searched his eyes. And she saw it. "What's wrong? What is it? Are you in trouble again? Hay Dios miyo! They didn't go looking for you again, did they? The police—they didn't... that was two years ago! You haven't been in the union for two years—not since it was dissolved! Oh, God!" Ana stumbled over to her bed.

"Ana, no! That isn't it! Really! I swear to you, they did not come looking for me! Don't worry—everything is fine."

But Ana knew better. She knew Manuel. He would never admit anything was wrong, even when it was. Ana fell back on her bed, knocking over stacks of carefully arranged clothing, staring at the ceiling with a vacant gaze.

"Okay, Ana. I'm going to tell you. There is bad news. It is very bad. But it isn't anything like that. It's los cipotes—the boys. They . . . well . . . they are dead."

Ana seemed to fall back through her bed, through the cement slab and through the earth, tumbling head over heels down a deep chasm. Her body began to quiver and spasm and she tossed her head from side to side.

Manuel reached for a bottle of rubbing alcohol. He carefully splashed liberal doses on Ana's arms and neck. Then he picked up a newspaper and gently fanned her face. Manuel had known what would happen if he told Ana about the boys. He had known. Still. It was better *he* told her than somebody else. And it was better she learned the truth today than tomorrow.

"There is nothing we can do for them. They are dead and gone. We have to take care of our families now. Soon, we will be in the United States. Maybe we'll make enough money to bring our families there. Or at least enough to get them away from all of this. Really, Ana—everything will be all right."

But for Ana, the world continued to spin. Somewhere, from far away, she could hear Manuel's voice. But his words seemed so far apart from one another that they did not make any sense. She tried to focus her eyes, but other forces were at work, stronger than her will. Suddenly she felt sleepy, as though she had been brought under a hypnotic spell; her eyes became heavy and she began to fall again. She tossed and turned, tormented by specters that raced through her brain severing arteries with sharp bloody knives as they screamed and laughed with delight.

Then Ana thought about the boys. She remembered how things were a couple of years before, back when she was still in school, back when the boys were small children running barefoot in the streets. She remembered how things were back then, before the war, before the death squads, before all the killing. Ana remembered how the boys played with the other children in the streets until well after dark. Parents and grandparents would watch them from chairs set out in front of their apartments. They would sit there in the cool night air and listen to crickets and radios while the children played. And those two little boys—ellos eran bien tremendos! What *rascals* they were!

Ana remembered a day at the marketplace. The boys wove their way through the crowd, carrying a small sack as though it was filled with treasure. "What have you got in the bag?" Ana asked them.

"Something Grandma sent us to sell."

"Well? What is it?" But they would not show her. Their grandmother had warned them against sharing such information: They might get robbed if they did.

Ana was curious. She followed them as they approached a merchant who sold handmade guitars. The boys glanced over their shoulders to see if anyone was watching, then carefully handed the merchant the sack.

"What have we here?" the merchant asked.

"Guitar picks," the boys replied. "And they are very valuable. They are homemade."

The merchant opened the sack and began to laugh. "Who sent you with this?" he asked.

"Our grandma."

"She did, did she? And what did she say would be a fair price?"

The children looked at him with wide, innocent eyes. "She didn't say."

As the merchant cackled and groaned, Ana nudged her way to the counter and peeked into the sack. It was half-filled with clipped toenails—yellow, wood-like crescents. The merchant held one between his thumb and index finger. "Guitar picks!" he snorted. As Ana tilted her head back and laughed, the boys made designs in the dirt with their toes. Oh, how their grandmother used to love to play tricks on them! How she loved to play tricks! Poor boys! They didn't know what to do.

Ana could hear Manuel's voice. But she could not understand what he said. She wanted to. She wanted to come back. But she could not. The specters were running again. And the streets downtown—they were red. A torrent of blood gushed into the streets from the concrete drains of the National Guard Armory—blood washed from the walls and tiles of the Armory's patio, blood removed by soldiers with hoses and straw brooms, diverted into the streets where they thought it might do some good. Ana wanted to come back. She did not want to dream anymore. She did not want to remember. But she heard the screams of men in the dead of night—men whose dismembered bodies lay in stacks by the city incinerator in the morning, wild dogs tearing at burnt flesh.

Manuel tried to reach her as she thrashed about. He continued to massage her scalp, to call her name—to comfort her. And, slowly, her pain did subside and she could breathe again. Her thoughts drifted to happier times.

She thought about the mountains and the tropical forests and a holiday when she was eighteen. Ana remembered traveling by bus with friends to La Costa del Sol. She and her friends had all worked very hard to save their money for the trip. When they arrived at the sea, they rented a hut made of palm leaves for five colones a day—right on the beach! How beautiful it was back then. The sea was warm and clear and parrots sang in the trees. Ana and her friends danced cumbias in the sand, told stories and jokes and felt what young people feel. Gentle waves washed the shore, palm leaves rustled in the breeze and the days were long and carefree.

"Really, Ana! Everything is going to be all right! Believe me!" Ana looked up and saw Manuel standing over her, his face lined with worry. She nodded her head yes and he helped her to sit up. "Would you get me a cup of water?" she asked, and Manuel smiled, happy she was talking again.

As Ana sipped from her cup, she glanced around the room. And it seemed she had been gone for a long time. There were the piles of clothing, arranged in stacks—clothes that had been hard to come by and were harder still to part with.

"Do you think Dolores would use some of these things?" Ana asked.

"What? Your clothes? Well, yes. She will keep them for you. For when we return."

"*If* we return."

"Don't talk like that! We are going to be fine. And listen—in just a week or so, we'll be in Los Angeles with my sister, Sonia. And they say every house has a television and people eat meat every day and still make enough money to send back home! Your mother won't have to worry anymore! And my boy—he can eat chicken—and drink milk! Maybe he will even be able to attend a good school! Ana—think about what we are trying to do. Think how good it is going to be!"

Ana smiled. She knew her cousin well. He always wanted to make things look nice, even when they were not. After all, what could possibly be better than the warm sandy beach of La Costa del Sol?

6

Antonio was at the Mersola factory gates at 6:30 in the morning, earlier than the catering truck that sold coffee, cigarettes, burritos and donuts — all essentials for those facing another day on the assembly line.

It was a chilly day for Los Angeles. Antonio turned his collar up, blew long columns of vapor into the gray morning air and sipped bitter coffee from a Styrofoam cup. He walked in place to stay warm, cupped his hands around his coffee and breathed in steam and mist. And though he had slept only four hours the night before, he felt good.

By the time people began to arrive for work, Antonio was ready — enthusiastic but not solicitous, reading people by the pace they kept, the way they held their cigarettes and moved their hips. By glancing into their eyes, he could judge which folks were open and which were not, knowing from experience that some of them wouldn't speak to grandmothers resurrected from their graves at this time of the morning.

At 6:45, the catering truck arrived, followed by two men wearing three-piece suits, organizers from the local union. In no apparent hurry, they bought coffee and donuts and examined items wrapped in aluminum foil while Antonio passed out leaflets.

The overwhelming majority of the workers at the Mersola factory were Latino and did not speak English. As they approached the gates, Antonio spoke to them in Spanish about the union drive. The two union organizers looked on with amusement as they dunked their donuts and sipped their coffee. Antonio motioned them to join in the leafleting. But they would not be rushed. After all, neither of them had eaten breakfast and they had both made what they considered to be a herculean effort to be at the factory gates on time. What more did Antonio want? Besides, they thought, just who do you think you *are*, telling us what to do? Fucking asshole. We're just as important as *you* are, dickhead.

But Antonio persisted. He wasn't there to play games. As far as he was concerned, what they were doing was not just a nine-to-five job. There was more to it than that. He thought: If you want to play office politics, get a job in a fucking office! Then you can argue over who has the best chair or the biggest desk. Man, I can't *believe* this shit!

Finally the organizers from the local gave in. They gave in under the pressure of Antonio's unrelenting glare. But not without making one final statement: They dropped what remained of their coffee into a wire trash can, gloating over the mess they made, the sidewalk stained by streaks of coffee scrawled like gang graffiti. Then, with a swagger, they joined Antonio, their movements choreographed to demonstrate contempt. But despite all their bravado, they were edgy. And when workers asked questions in a language they did not understand, they hid their anxiety behind an almost giddy laughter.

"Hey, Tony!" one of the organizers sneered. "This guy over here, he's asking me somethin'." He laughed nervously. "Want to talk to him?"

Antonio bounded over to a stocky young Mexican with dark brown skin and a thick handlebar mustache. "Javier! Qué ondas, bato? What's happening, brother?"

"Nada, hombre. Nothing. What's the matter with this guy?" Javier asked in Spanish. "Is he with you?"

Antonio smiled and nodded his head.

"Pues. . . . Well, where does he think he *is*? Canoga Park? He looks like a used car salesman."

The organizer listened as though he could understand and eyed Javier with suspicion when he broke into laughter. He knew he was being talked about and he didn't like it.

"What's he sayin', Tony?"

"Nothin', man."

"C'mon, Tony. Don't bullshit me. What's he sayin'?"

Antonio hesitated. "He just said he wasn't sure if you were from the union. He thought maybe you were a used car salesman." Antonio and Javier laughed, Javier watching the organizer's face to gauge his reaction.

"Shee-it! What does he think I'm doing here at this fucked-up time of the morning? I oughta be home in bed!"

"Qué dice?" Javier asked. "What did he say?"

"No importa, hombre. Don't worry about him. Hey, look, Javier. I'd like to bullshit with you, but I've got to pass these leaflets out."

"Give me some, man. I'll help you."

"No, I don't think it would be a good idea, brother. Check out the guard."

Javier casually turned his head toward the guard shack where two men in uniforms watched him through a sliding glass window, craning their necks so they wouldn't have to venture too far from their portable electric heater.

"Chingados. Who cares about them? Give me some of those."

"Hey, man, look. There's no point in you sticking your neck out. They'll just fire you. You'll do the union more good working inside like you have been."

Javier was frustrated. He didn't like being faced down, especially by men in uniforms.

"Okay, Antonio. All right. I'll see you tonight then."

"Right."

"Hey, hombre," Javier said, smiling and turning to the other organizer. "I bet you drive a LTD, no?" he asked, saying the words and letters in Spanish.

"What?" the organizer answered angrily.

"You . . . El Tay Day. No?"

"I'm in L.A. today? Well, where do you *think* I am, fool?"

Javier laughed at the organizer's reaction, sensing his anger, realizing he had touched a raw nerve. But he was famous for that and it didn't bother him. He was famous for saying things everybody else wanted to say, but would not. So he shook off the whole incident and headed in through the gates, glaring at the guards as he passed.

"What's wrong with that guy, anyway?" the organizer asked Antonio.

"Don't worry about him. Just pass out the leaflets, will you? It's almost seven, and everyone's going to be in a big hurry. They only have two time clocks for four hundred people."

Once inside the factory, everyone rushed to punch in, then made their way to their workstations. Women put on blue smocks and tied their hair back with bandanas. Men smoked the rest of their cigarettes and hurried to gulp down what remained of their coffee before the buzzer sounded.

It was an old factory, built during World War II. It smelled old and musty, like a garage or a basement. And though it was cold outside, inside it was already quite warm. By lunchtime it would be oppressively hot.

One by one, machines were switched on, the steady drone of metal gears growing louder and louder, soon punctuated by the pounding of levers, the belching of machines and the whirling of tools as they spun and spat.

A group of men stood around a workbench and read one of the union leaflets. Whenever someone rounded the corner, they all glanced up with apprehension; they were afraid they might be caught reading what was forbidden. And none of them could afford to lose his job.

So they were cautious. They read the leaflet despite the company and they read it out loud. But they were nervous and maintained a lookout.

"It says here the union will fight to get us a raise in pay, pay for overtime and medical benefits," one of the workers whispered for the benefit of those who could not read.

"I've been here six years, and I'm still getting the minimum," another man complained.

Javier spotted the clandestine gathering and rushed to be a part of it. " Bueno. Are you all going to come to the meeting tonight?" he asked. "The union will be there to answer your questions."

As he spoke, his foreman suddenly rounded the corner, side-stepping the lookout and instantly striking a menacing pose. All of the workers but Javier scattered instantly, racing to their assigned work areas, though the starting-time buzzer had yet to sound.

"What are you people running from?" the foreman cried in Spanish, amused by their flight. "I'm not the immigration, you know."

"You sure are *ugly* enough to be," Javier said.

The foreman was at a loss for words. He struggled to think of a retort, though such things did not come easy to him. His first thought was: Write him up! But that wouldn't be a good idea. Not at the moment, anyway, he thought. Besides, I have more important things to do. Now is not the time to set that punk straight. Later. When it's more convenient. "Look, everyone," the foreman said with the sincerity of a salesman, "there's something I want to tell you. There's gonna be a very important meeting in front of my office in ten minutes. Everyone is required to attend."

"Everyone is going to meet *here*?" Javier asked.

"No, pendejo. Just our department and department eleven."

Javier ignored the insult. And he wondered, What the hell is going on?

Soon, workers from the two departments gathered together along the corridor in front of the foreman's office, a nervous murmur replacing the pounding of machinery.

To everyone's surprise, Amerio Mersola burst through the heavy oak doors of the executive offices nearby, accompanied by an entourage of men in suits, including the plant supervisor, who pushed a shopping cart of groceries, embarrassed by the task he had been assigned.

Amerio Mersola instructed the foremen to gather the workers into a circle around the shopping cart. The three of them leaped into action, anxious to make an impression, falling over each other in their efforts to please the boss.

When everyone was in place and all eyes were on him, Mersola nudged a Chicano foreman in the ribs, indicating that he was ready to begin. "You all know that I've always been very concerned about your welfare. I see you all like part of my family." Mersola nudged the Chicano foreman again and listened as his words were translated into Spanish. And though he could have understood a lot of what the foreman said, he preferred not to. Instead, as his thoughts were translated, he examined the impact they had upon the workers gathered there.

"There are a lot of lies being circulated around here by *outsiders* who are trying to cause trouble," Mersola continued. "They are not wanted here and they won't do any of us any good. So I want all to know the truth—the plain simple truth about what it would mean if the union was able to force its way in here."

Javier rolled his eyes, unable to conceal his disgust. And while there were others who flinched, most of the people betrayed no emotion and listened politely.

"If you all are forced to join the union—and that's what they're trying to do—to *force* you all to join—you're going to have to pay union *dues* every month. Now, that's something I bet they didn't tell you about in their propaganda, did they? Well, I just thought you'd like to know that with the money you'd have to pay the union every month—*if* they won—you could buy *all* the things I have in this shopping cart."

As the foreman translated his words into Spanish, Mersola lifted a large frozen turkey into the air, then quickly passed it on to another foreman. He reached for a family-size package of T-bone steaks, a devil's food cake, two bottles of champagne and two six-packs of imported beer. Before long, all the foremen were standing in the aisle awkwardly, holding groceries as if they were at a PTA raffle.

"Now, I'm sure you would rather have food on your table than have to pay a bunch of outsiders dues—for nothing!" Mersola paused momentarily to survey the crowd and measure their response. Not happy with his findings, he made a quick adjustment. "And when this whole thing is over, we can talk about a raise. It's been a while since I could afford to give you one. Unfortunately, I can't promise you one now because the union has gone to the courts and prevented me from doing so. But—I can promise you this—if any one of you ever has a problem or something you need to talk about concerning your job, my door will be open. If you have a complaint, or if there is anything bothering you, please feel free to talk to me about it. We're all working together here, you know."

As the Chicano foreman translated the last of Mersola's words, the people stood dumbfounded. To many, what Mersola had promised sounded good—*very* good. And they wanted to hear good news. But to Javier, the whole thing was ludicrous. He cleared his throat: "Bueno. Excuse me, señor. I am just a poor, dumb Mexican," he said in Spanish. His friends laughed. As a warning to Mersola, the Chicano foreman translated what Javier said with a hint of sarcasm not detectable in Javier's voice, arching his eyebrows to underline the point. Javier continued: "Is it really true, señor? Are we really free to voice our complaints to you?"

Mersola listened as the question was translated. "Yes, it is

43

true. I meant every word I said. Is there something you want to say?"

As the foreman put the question back to Javier, Javier repressed a smile. "Señor, I am very sorry to bother you with this. I know you are a very busy man. But. Well . . . I am sorry. Son los baños."

The foreman translated what Javier said, though he was losing patience with the way he was posing his question. It was taking too much time.

"The bathrooms," Mersola repeated, after hearing the translation.

"Sí, señor!" Javier replied. "That is it! Los baños!"

Both the foreman and Mersola waited, the silence between Javier's words unnerving them. They waited for the rest of his question, and when it was not forthcoming, the foreman finally blurted out, "Que pasa con los pinche baños? What's happening with the damn bathrooms?"

The workers could no longer restrain themselves and burst out laughing.

The foremen were ready to reestablish order. But Mersola used the opportunity to play a card. " Let them speak!" he told the foremen sternly. "They are not doing anything wrong! Now, sir. What is it you want to say about *los baños*?" Mersola smiled at the workers as he pronounced the words with an Italian accent and they laughed and smiled back. The ball was back in Javier's court and he was beginning to feel the pressure.

"Bueno. Well. You know—it is like *this* . . ." Javier squatted down with his knees pulled in tight toward his chest and his elbows flush against his hips, his face contorted in agony. Again, the workers laughed.

Mersola realized he had a formidable opponent, though he didn't have the slightest idea what Javier was doing. Still, he joined in the laughter with the others, and turned to the foreman as he translated what Javier had said. But the foreman did not know what to do.

"I'm sorry," Mersola said, forcing a grin. "I don't understand your joke."

"Oh, señor! But it is no joke!" Javier explained. "It is serious! You see, it is the boxes. They are so small that you can barely sit down!"

As the workers laughed, Mersola saw that things were getting out of control. The foreman summarized: "I think what he is trying to say is that he thinks they need more room in the stalls. You know . . . so they can sit down when they—"

"I understand, I understand. Well. To tell you the truth, I wasn't aware there was anything wrong with the bathrooms. I'll have somebody check into it."

The people were encouraged by his reaction. "Thank you, Señor Mersola," a short plump woman said. "And while you are doing that, do you think you could do something so somebody will *clean* the bathrooms? They are very dirty. And there is never any soap there! We have to bring our own. Oh, Mr. Mersola, you wouldn't believe it! The bathrooms are sometimes so dirty nobody even wants to go in there! Really! It is terrible!"

"Claro!" most of the workers agreed.

"Well, we'll have to get on the janitor. He must not be doing his job," Mersola replied.

Sonia, a bright-eyed Salvadorean, spoke up. "And what about the heat? In the summertime, it gets really hot in here. There isn't any ventilation—only those windows in the roof. And they only seem to be good for letting in the rain in winter. There was a man who fainted last summer. Remember?" she asked, turning to the workers for support. "He was so sick they took him to the hospital." The people nodded in agreement and Sonia turned back to Mersola. "Can't we get some fans or something?"

Mersola listened to the translation and frowned. "That's a difficult problem. I know it gets hot in here, and I wish there was something I could do about it. But . . . well, to be honest, business isn't too good right now. I was hoping to give you all a raise sometime soon, even though I can't really afford to do that. Still, I was hoping we could cut some corners and somehow work it out. You know, what with the foreign competition, it is very difficult to compete nowadays. You know, really, we have been doing everything we can just to avoid a layoff. We really think that is the most important thing. To keep everybody working. But there is just so much that can be done."

A murmur arose among the workers. Glances were exchanged and words were whispered from one person to the next, jarred loose like dust snapped from a blanket. But soon the conversations lost their momentum; things settled down, only a few stray words floating about searching for a place to rest.

"Are there any more questions?" Mersola asked, smiling as he scanned the faces in the crowd. All right, then. Well, thank you for your time. I have to be off now, so I can visit all the other departments. But remember—my door is always open!"

The foremen and supervisors returned the groceries to the shopping cart, pausing to commend Mersola on a most effective presentation. Then, with all the fanfare of a royal procession in a medieval borough, Mersola and his entourage made their way to another corner of the factory.

"Can you believe that?" Sonia asked angrily. "We're like a family to him? Humph! They keep the bathrooms dirty because they don't want us to use them! And what about the heat? Puta! He has the money to air-condition the offices. And look over there! The air conditioners blow hot air out of the offices into the factory! Why must we be the ones to suffer?"

As the workers plodded back to their workstations, they thought about what Sonia had said. They switched on their machines and got back into their routines, hoping to lose themselves in the endless repetitive movement. Few of them wanted to fight with the company; all they wanted was to make a living—to pay their bills and take care of their families. That was all they wanted. But it was hard to raise a family on the minimum wage. It was very hard. And it *was* too hot in the factory, and the bathrooms *were* dirty. And when they got sick, or their children got sick—well, they had no insurance to pay for it. They couldn't help but think about such things. They didn't want to, but they couldn't help it. And the more they thought, the angrier they became.

As they worked and thought, time passed slowly, the hours marked off like days scratched on a prison wall.

Finally the buzzer sounded, announcing a break. People lined up and filed out of the factory gates toward the catering truck where they bought coffee, sandwiches and burritos. Antonio was outside, waiting for them. Javier made a beeline toward him, anxious to talk about the meeting with Mersola.

"Hey, Antonio! You should have been there this morning! Híjole, bato! That pinche viejo Mersola—you should have *heard* him! He said we are like his own family! Damn! These gabachos—these Anglos— they must treat each other *bad*! I bet he doesn't even feed his own *mother*!" Javier explained what had happened and demonstrated how Mersola had lifted a turkey, pretending to buckle under the weight of the imaginary bird, waddling across the sidewalk with his eyes and tongue popping out.

Two foremen spotted him in the middle of his pantomime and knew exactly what he was saying. They strolled over to the catering truck, dug through a mound of crushed ice, and examined bottles of Coca-Cola as if they were reading the ingredients. Antonio nodded his head in their direction and tugged his earlobe, signaling Javier.

"No importa!" Javier said defiantly, looking in their direction. "It doesn't matter!"

"Be cool, carnal—"

"Why? I thought this was supposed to be a free country, hombre! Isn't that what they say all the time on TV?" Javier glared at the foremen.

Antonio looked Javier straight in the eye and raised an eyebrow, as if to say, Do you feel *better* now? Javier shrugged his shoulders and smiled foolishly.

The buzzer sounded and the workers hurried back inside the factory. Those unfortunate enough to have been last in line at the catering truck gulped down the last of their breakfasts.

"I'll see you tonight, brother," Antonio told Javier. "Make sure all your friends are there."

"Andele, pues. All right, then."

Javier followed the crowd into the factory and went directly to his machine. He flipped the switch and started to work. But before he had completed one operation, his foreman approached him.

"Would you step inside my office for a few minutes?" he asked Javier in Spanish.

"Sure, no problem."

Once inside the foreman's office, Javier was asked to shut the door. "Take a seat, Javier."

He did what he was told.

"I've been meaning to talk with you for a long time."

"I am sorry, señor." Javier dropped his head in shame, a sly smile forming. "But I am already engaged. I don't love him, you know . . . but he is a *good* man."

"Cut the crap. En serio—I'm serious."

"Yo sé! Yo tambien! So am I!" Javier grinned.

"I'm not playing games, Javier," the foreman continued.

"I know. And I am so happy that you respect me."

"Mira, Javier—get serious or I am going to write you up for insubordination! I'm not bullshiting you, hombre!"

Javier swallowed hard and sat up in his chair.

"Like I was saying, I've been meaning to talk with you for a long time. About your attendance."

"Qué?"

"You've been late twice this month."

"But that was three weeks ago, hombre!" Javier protested. "And I explained to you then that the guy who gives me a ride to work had car trouble. Besides. I was only a few minutes late."

"Well, company policy is that three tardies in a month and you are suspended. You've got two. I'm warning you now."

"*What?*"

"One more tardy this month and you will be suspended for three days. After that, if you are late again, you will be terminated. Entiendes? Now, I need for you to sign this notice."

Javier looked at the paper shoved in front of him. "What? What does it say? You know I can't read English."

"It just says you've been late and that I've given you a written notice about it. That's all. It's nothing, really. Just company procedures. Here—sign here," he said, handing Javier a pen and pointing.

Javier stared at the piece of paper, exhaled and scratched his head. "Pinche. . . ."

"What did you say, hombre?"

"Nothing. Give me the damn pen." Javier took a deep breath and scribbled his name on the form.

7

Ana and Manuel followed a dirt road beside el rió Suchiate—the river that separates Guatemala from México. They and
a handful of other Salvadorean refugees had traveled there by
bus from San Salvador, arriving at the border town of Tecúm
Umán where they hired a coyote to smuggle them into the United States.

Their faces were apricot-colored, bathed by the final blazes
of the setting sun. And though they appeared to be out for an
evening stroll, their eyes were riveted on the coyote. When the
time was right, he would wave them into the thicket that grew
beside the river. There, they would wait. Then, with the cover of
darkness, they would secretly cross the river into México.

Tecúm Umán was a way station for poor Central Americans
who wanted to emigrate to the United States. If one had the
money, one could buy anything there. But the hottest commod-
ity was the smuggler—especially los coyotes. They stood on the
corners and hustled would-be immigrants like drug dealers in
a big city.

As the Salvadoreans walked the streets of Tecúm Umán,
there were many sights that were strange to them and many familiar: musicians and thieves, preachers and soldiers. Mayans
dressed in native fabrics sold handicrafts, homemade cheese
and mangos in the streets. Young lovers sat beside each other
on the roots of la ceiba, shaped like giant gnarled hands, while
parrots bickered above them in the tree's broad branches. And
in the distance, there was el puente—the bridge. Whether they

reached the United States or not, that would be what the refugees would remember best. They would remember the bridge because it was guarded by soldiers armed for battle, and because they could not cross it.

El río Suchiate rolled under the bridge that joined México and Guatemala. Upstream, hidden in the jungles, were great pyramids and pitted stone carvings, relics of the once great Mayan nation. Vines and wildflowers covered the ruins now. Monkeys and tourists climbed the ancient temples in the gaps between torrential rains and intermittent war.

It was not long before the refugees drew the attention of a patrol of National Guardsmen, who ordered them to raise their hands above their heads—which they did so obligingly one might have thought it was a greeting in that part of the world. The soldiers asked their names, birthdates and destination, poking the men with machine guns as though they were syringes that injected truth serum. They searched everyone until satisfied they weren't armed with weapons or revolutionary literature. A pamphlet even mildly critical of the government would have spelled doom for them all.

Though they found nothing, the guardsmen were still suspicious. One thought he spotted a hint of anger in Manuel's eyes—a definite sign of subversive tendencies. He launched into an interrogation, asking questions for which there were no acceptable answers: "Why are you in Guatemala? What kind of problems did you have in El Salvador?" Watching the relentless questioning, Ana's legs began to buckle. The soldiers held a conference, Manuel's eyes the subject of debate. Things did not look good for the refugees as the guardsmen's expressions hardened and their eyes flashed with accusations.

An old woman began to cough violently. She grasped her chest and fell to her knees, gasping, "My heart! My heart!"

The soldiers began to laugh. "Some guerrillas *they* would make!" one chortled. "They're just another bunch of guanacos trying to get to the United States. Let the stupid bastards go."

The refugees were handed their papers, informed that the bridge to México was closed to all but official traffic. Then they were dismissed. As they walked down the road, heads bowed, the coyote appeared to be angry.

Soon it grew dark. The coyote kept glancing about, observing with night vision the eyes of faceless men leaning against almond trees—men who worked for him. One gave the signal he awaited and the coyote motioned to the refugees. Instantly they plunged into the thicket beside the river. As they scurried for cover, a man hidden in the brush herded them into a small enclave secretly prepared for them that morning. Huddling together, the refugees watched the coyote as he cocked his head toward the road.

It was not long before they became accustomed to the dark. The clamor of day settled as the river slipped behind them toward the sea. The refugees listened to the night. An owl hooted in a ceiba tree, its shadows etching a portrait of a woman in mourning. In the distance, raccoons ate crabs and wept. Leaves of almond trees danced in the cool breeze and a gentleman bird rushed up to them crying, "Caballero! Caballero!" warning them of danger ahead.

The coyote climbed back toward the road, pausing motionless at the edge of the thicket. As the moon rose over the forest, he avoided its light.

Across the road, someone lit a cigarette. Instantly the coyote bounded back into the brush and ordered everyone to strip and tie their clothing and other belongings into tight bundles. He herded them into the river, instructing them to stay close together in a single-file line and to move directly to the bank on the opposite side. The old woman pleaded with him, explaining she could not swim, a disadvantage shared by many others who remained silent. "Don't worry!" he told her impatiently "It's low enough to wade across." Then, with a snap of his fingers, he said, *"Move!"*

Into the river they went, one by one plopping into the rushing water, their clothes held over their heads with one hand, the other groping toward the next person in line. They squinted and struggled to spot the riverbank in the moonlight. But all they could see was a luminous spray as it rose to the sky, the darkness below them, and the bare back of the person they followed.

Ana felt the current pulling her downstream, sucking at her waist. And it seemed to her the river was alive—that a spirit lived there, throbbing and breathing, driven by an insatiable hunger, its misty breath rising up to the heavens. Yes, she *knew* there was a spirit there just as surely as one can feel another's presence when being watched. And she was scared. From the beginning of time the river had conquered everything in its path, rock polished smooth as it raced past pyramids and through the jungle, bearing gold and bloated bodies, washing clothes and blood clean. As Ana crossed el río Suchiate, she felt it reach for her breasts—and she felt strange and somehow guilty. Then, in the darkness, the river laughed.

I must hurry! Ana thought. God, please, help me! I must hurry! The night belongs to the river . . . and it is alive!

Suddenly, there was a hollow splash. A young man who had lost his balance was instantly towed downstream by the current. Ana and Manuel turned toward him, interrupting the refugees' movement forward. An old woman behind them was confused by the change of pace, slipped and was swallowed by the river. Manuel quickly reached for her flailing hand and yanked her back into line. She sputtered and coughed, struggling to remain as quiet as possible, though terrified by her ordeal. The young man scooped away by the current managed to fight his way back against the onslaught of the river, using precious time to search for his belongings as he battled to rejoin the others. The delay angered the coyote boss, who waved his arms frantically until everyone was back in line and moving again. The coyote and his partners pushed and pulled and prodded the refugees until everyone reached the bank on the Mexican side of the river.

There, the refugees struggled to get dressed, though their clothes were wet and stiff. But the boss forced them to move along, regardless of how little progress they had made. They fumbled down a path in the dark, pulling up pant legs and hopping on one foot as they tried to slip on shoes. The young man who had been swept away by the current walked barefoot, having lost his shoes in the rushing water. Days later, children would discover them on the riverbank and assume they belonged to a dead man.

Into the night they marched, the forest gradually thinning, the earth no longer soft and pliant beneath their feet, their hair blown dry by a breeze now too tenuous to carry the moisture and scent of the river. In the light of the moon they marched, climbing rocky hillsides, their footsteps setting loose streams of stones that poured into the caves of iguanas and interrupted their sleep. The hours passed and still they marched, through groves of mangos and jocotes, not able to pause and quench their thirst or satisfy their hunger. They plodded ahead toward an unknown destination in a land where they had never been.

In time, they reached a battered wood-frame building—a bus depot. The coyote signaled everyone to gather around. "We're going to take a bus now. Don't talk to anyone! Nobody! If they notice your accent, they might turn you in to immigration."

"Why would they do that?" the old woman asked.

"Vieja! Don't you know nothing? You'll find out soon enough." An hour passed, during which the immigrants struggled to remain awake. Finally, a bus arrived, an hour behind schedule. It was a machine built of iron and wood back when the old woman was young. In the daytime, this contraption would be so crowded that men and boys would ride on the luggage rack on top. But the hour and location presented many empty seats to the refugees, wooden benches as comfortable as beds to the weary travelers. Following instructions from the coyote, they sat apart from one another like strangers—except Ana and Manuel. Manuel dared not leave Ana alone.

They rode the bus for two hours, the Mexican passengers holding chickens and children on their laps as they snored. Occasionally, a particularly violent jolt would awaken them as the bus bounded over a gaping hole in the road overlooked by the drowsy driver.

Soon the bus arrived at another desolate station. Responding to a signal from the coyote, the refugees jumped down from the bus to a dusty dirt road, then followed him for more than a mile until they reached the outskirts of a small town. In the moonlight they stopped and stared at what would have appeared to be a parcel of overused land were it not for a hand-painted sign that declared in Spanish: "Place of Recreation for the People—Gift of the Benevolent Government of the People of México."

Empty bottles of tequila and beer cans lay scattered about in the tall grass. Dogs prowled the park, searching through garbage and eyeing the refugees with suspicion, as if to warn them they were trespassing on their turf. Three derelicts sharing a bottle of cheap brandy attempted to focus their eyes on the refugees, then laughed bitterly, their heads drooping in exhaustion.

"We'll be spending the rest of the night here," the coyote announced. "Stay close together and try to get some sleep. We'll be leaving first thing in the morning."

Having gone without sleep for two days, the immigrants lost little time searching for plots to spend the night. Ana and Manuel camped where they stood, though the earth was parched and hard as adobe. They lay on the ground in the park and gazed at the moon. As tired as they were, they felt as though they were still moving, waiting for a signal from the coyote.

"I wonder how my mother is doing," Ana sighed.

"She is fine. I am sure she is fine. She is sound asleep, probably dreaming about you," Manuel whispered.

Ana tried to smile. She tried to take comfort in what her cousin said. But she knew him too well. He would always find something good to say, no matter how difficult things were. When the government of El Salvador unleashed The Terror, he said it was because they were at el fin de el camino—at the end of the road. He said it was just a matter of time before the people would stand up and change things. That is what he said, even back then when there were screams in the night. And the next morning, when they found the bodies burned and mutilated in the street, he would still insist: It is the beginning of the end, my cousin. Watch and see. Something better will come.

Ana wanted to believe him. She wanted to believe things would change. She smiled and shook her head. Este hombre! He is so wonderful and so foolish! How he loves to dream! Such a typical man, thinking about football games and revolutions! Going to the United States . . . that is the most practical thing he has ever done.

Ana gazed at the sky and thought about her mother and her brothers and the way they lived. Hay Dios miyo. Help us to find work so we can send money back home to our families. Please God! It has been so hard. What have we done to deserve this life? Being born a poor Latin American—is that a crime? Dios! Por favor! Help us to make it to Los Angeles where at least we can find work!

An icy ring circled the moon; crickets sang to each other, joined in song by the drunken men.

As Ana prayed, Manuel lay on his back, hands cradling his head. Soon his thoughts drifted to his wife and son. Ah, mi familia. How much you have suffered. Now your suffering has grown ten times! Are you sleeping now, my son? Did your mother kiss you goodnight for me? Did she say: Mi niño—que tenga dúlces sueños de menta y chocolate, mi amor. Did she whisper those words to you and kiss your cheek? And did you reach for your mother and hold her close to you? Did you tell her how much you love her, my son? I am sorry I cannot be there to say goodnight to you. I am sorry you were born in a country where the people have to suffer so. Oh, but things will change, my son. I promise you! Things will change. But you are just a boy, just a child. You cannot wait to eat. When I find a job in North America, I will send money to your mother so she can buy you shoes and books. And on Christmas you will have presents to open. I promise you! You have waited long enough, mi hijo. You will never go hungry again. And though I am far away from you now, do you know how much your Papá loves you? Do you know I left you and your mother so you can live a better life? Oh God! Please! Let my son know that I left because I love him!

Before long, Ana and Manuel slipped away, lulled to sleep by the songs of crickets and mumbling of drunken men. They slept side by side in the light of the moon—two cousins, far away from home.

In the distance, a dog howled. The coyote instinctively propped himself up on one arm and listened. As he lay back down, he thought: Tomorrow I am going to sleep in a hotel. This shit is for winos and wetbacks.

8

Their shoulders were brown and bare and beautiful, and when they smiled, their eyes sparkled with a modesty so sincere it was breathtaking. "Buenas noches. Welcome to Don Ramón's Restaurant," one of the hostesses said as she greeted a customer. It was Silvino, a worker from the Mersola factory, there to attend the union meeting. For a moment, he stood speechless, smiling nervously, doing his best to conceal his beer belly. And though Silvino prided himself on being a ladies' man, he was bashful and confused, totally enamored by the black-haired woman in her bleached-white peasant blouse. "Habla español?" he asked. "Do you speak Spanish?"

"Sí, como no!" she assured him. "Le puedo ayudar en algo? Can I help you?"

"Pues . . ." Silvino wanted desperately to say something clever—something he could share with his friends later. But the hostess at Don Ramón's Mexican Restaurant was simply too young and too beautiful. "I was told there is a meeting here tonight—a union meeting."

"Oh, you must be here to meet with *Antonio*," the hostess said, smiling mysteriously. "Come right this way."

The hostess led Silvino through the restaurant, past a Spanish-style fountain where a veil of phosphorescent water danced. Young couples sat close together in plush booths. As they sipped frosty margaritas and gazed into each other's eyes, they spoke enthusiastically about the future, conjuring up wonderful lies.

Meeting in the back room of the restaurant were a hundred

people from the Mersola factory. Workers sat at a conference table usually reserved for business meetings, their animated discussions rising to a fever pitch. As the hostess opened the double doors for Silvino, everyone turned to see who had arrived. Silvino was greeted warmly, as were all the workers before him. But it was Antonio they were waiting for.

They did not have to wait long. Within a few minutes he bounded into the conference room through the back door, as confident as a first-rate boxer entering the ring.

Antonio was greeted by an enthusiastic ovation, and his eyes sparkled. He nodded his head in recognition and worked the room, shaking the hands of those he knew, making a point to introduce himself to those he did not.

Antonio stepped up to the podium at the head of the long table, and all conversations came to an abrupt end. Workers twisted napkins around their fingers, sat on the edge of their chairs and smiled at each other nervously.

"It's great to see so many of you here tonight," he began, speaking in Spanish. "It's not easy to get away from the house and kids on a weeknight. This should show everyone that there is a lot of support for the union at Mersola's.

"For those of you who don't know me, my name is Antonio Rodriguez. I'm the organizer for the Shoeworkers Union, Local 305. I know you don't have much time, so I'll get right down to business. But first, I want to thank the owner of Don Ramón's Mexican Restaurant for letting us use this room tonight. He's not charging us anything. Usually, a room like this costs at least a hundred dollars to rent. So, if any of you are hungry, there will be a waitress coming in soon. The food is very good and reasonably priced—so if you can afford it, I'd encourage you to buy something so we can use this room again."

"Bueno, Antonio," Javier said from across the room, holding a beer bottle by its neck at his side. "I hope they serve beans and tortillas. That's all I can afford."

The workers laughed, and Javier enjoyed the attention.

"I can see that," Antonio replied, eyeing Javier's beer. Javier smiled impishly, attempting to hide it under the table.

"Seriously, we all know that with what Mersola pays you, it is hard to eat much more than beans and tortillas. We all grew up on that and there's nothing wrong with it. It is good food. But sometimes we want to have something more. When the weekend comes, we all want to be able to have carne asada and guacamole. And we want our children to have things we didn't have."

As Antonio spoke, he established a rhythm, his sentences tied together and punctuated by the movement of his hands. Watching him, many of the workers were mesmerized by his movements, as though they revealed more than his words.

"There is a man here who has worked at Mersola's for twelve years. For twelve years he has worked hard, never missing a day, never late. And what does he get for all his effort?" Snapping his wrist sharply, he answered, "Nada! He's *still* getting the minimum. Mersola has two time cards for him. Two cards with two names and two social security numbers. When he works overtime, he punches out on one card and in on the other. Why? So Mersola won't have to pay him overtime pay. Last year, his wife got sick and had to go to the hospital. She was there three days and had to have surgery. It cost nine thousand dollars. If he had been covered by union benefits, he would have only had to pay a few hundred dollars. But he wasn't. Mersola *has* no health plan. He *has* no retirement plan. No vacation plan, either. The only plan Mersola has is how to make himself richer. Now, the old man who has worked hard for Mersola for twelve years has to pay nine thousand dollars. Why? Because if his wife went to the county hospital, she might get deported. Because they are what the newspapers and television call 'illegal aliens.' Legally, they do not qualify for Medi-Cal. This is the thanks the old man gets for working hard, for paying taxes and trying to make a living for his family."

The workers nodded their heads. "Claro," they agreed. Javier stood back and watched Antonio in awe.

"If you form a union at Mersola—if you get organized—you won't have to suffer as you do now. You can win the dignity and self-respect you all deserve. But, again, to do that, you have only one weapon. *Only* one . . . and that is organization."

An older man stood up. "Antonio, I'm all for the union. But what about la migra?" A nervous murmur arose. "There's already been one immigration raid at Mersola's, about a year ago. It's been pretty quiet since then. You know, my brother—he goes downtown every morning at six a.m. He waits around on Mariposa Street with around sixty other guys, waiting for a contractor to come. The contractor gets there and asks, 'Who wants to work?' And everyone shouts, 'I do!' Then the contractor says, 'Well, I need someone for the whole day, and I'll pay twenty dollars.' He gets them bidding. Someone says, 'I'll work for fifteen!' and then someone else shouts, 'I'll do it for twelve!' So they end up working from six in the morning until five at night for twelve dollars. Then, some of the contractors take away four dollars for lunch! Well, it's bad at Mersola's, I know. But at least I've got a steady job. If we try to bring in the union, maybe he is going to call in the immigration. Then we'll have nothing." Several other workers agreed, turning to each other and shaking their heads. Antonio listened, then he raised his hands to quiet the crowd. "You know, the kind of thing you are talking about, with bidding and so on, used to be true for almost everyone in this country. ¿Saben qué? People came here from Europe, from all around the world. They didn't have rights, either. Neither did the workers who had families here for generations. They worked themselves to death, working twelve, fourteen, sixteen hours a day, six or seven days a week, with no overtime pay, no benefits, nothing. If they got hurt on the job, it was their tough luck. The company or the government didn't do a damn thing to help them or their families. That's when they started to organize. The first unions in this country were organized by *immigrants!* Irish, Russian, Italian, Polish, German—most of them didn't even speak English. And they didn't have papers or any rights. They were a lot like you. Miren . . . I'm not going to tell you it is going to be easy. Nothing changes without effort. It took *years* for the unions to grow strong, and even today, a lot of them are in trouble. They are still under attack. But look, the main thing to remember is that together we are strong!

"You all have rights, the same as anyone else in this country—or any other country, for that matter. These are God-given rights—human rights. Just because right now they are not on paper does not mean they are not due to you. And, as far as that goes, you should always remember—this all used to be part of México. You have the God-given *right* to be here and to work here. If you run and hide from la migra—if you let Mersola frighten you with the immigration—you are *always* going to be behind in the rent, you are *always* going to make the minimum. Or, you can stand up and *fight* for your rights!"

There was a loud, passionate ovation. Even the old man who had brought up the specter of la migra was applauding enthusiastically.

As the applause died down, another worker stood up to be heard. Young and well dressed, he glanced around the room and waited for everyone to quiet down before starting to speak. But before he said a word, Antonio wondered: Who is this guy? He knows something. It's the way he's waiting for everyone to quiet down. He knows what he's doing.

The young man began to speak to the people, though his remarks were aimed at Antonio.

"It is a beautiful idea, having a union," he began, gesturing smoothly. "Antonio—I admire you for coming here and talking to us about our problems. You're an effective speaker and you've obviously gone to college, or had some education. I, too, went to the university. In México. But almost everyone else here can't read or write that well in Spanish, much less in English. And most of us, unlike you, don't have our papers. You know, I was one of the first in the factory to talk about people getting together, to support the union. . . ."

That's who it is, Antonio thought. David. He was one of the people who came to the union about starting an organizing drive. But what is he doing?

"I lost my job because of it. I got fired for going to the union. Just a week before you filed the petition for an election. After having seen how things work, now I think differently. You *all* are taking a *big chance* of losing what little you have!"

Turning to Antonio, David asked, "Who will take care of our families if we are fired or deported? What good would the union be then?"

Many of the workers were troubled by David's question.

"What's protecting you from being fired or deported now?" Antonio said.

David glanced down at the table, smiled and shook his head as though Antonio had asked a silly question.

"Antonio, Antonio, you have papers. You were born here, have an education, speak English. You have a car and probably own your own home. I think you are well intentioned. But you don't understand the problems we face." He turned away from Antonio and faced the crowd. "We have got to do something about the way things are for us. But we have got to be realistic. We should make a petition to Mersola asking for a raise. I can take it to him since I've already been fired and have nothing to lose."

David watched the expressions of the people, prepared to shape his words to their response. When many of them nodded in agreement, he turned back to Antonio. "We have to be realistic. We all know you would look really good if you won the union election. And there is nothing wrong with wanting to move up in the world. That's what we all want. But we have to be realistic. We have to do what is best for *us*. Mersola would probably give us all fifty cents an hour more just to keep the union out. That would be a lot of money in our pockets.

"We can handle things ourselves," David said, turning again toward the workers. "Some of us have an education and know what to do. I went to the labor board when I got fired and I have an appeal there now. But we shouldn't antagonize Mersola by trying to bring in the union. It just might make him call in la migra. Like I said, we have to be realistic. We have to think about how we're going to get by *today*. Tomorrow never comes."

Many of even the staunchest supporters of the union were stunned by David's words. But Javier did not trust him. He flitted about like a bird leaping from perch to perch—he wanted to say something, but he just could not come up with the words.

As David sat down, there was a great commotion. Antonio knew he had lost control. There was nothing he could say—David had cast doubt upon his intentions. Antonio scanned the room and noticed Javier pacing about nervously. Say something! Antonio thought. Say something or all is lost!

An old man stood up and braced himself against the table. As he glanced around the room, he appeared to be weary. He shook his head in resignation as the drone of a dozen conversations continued around him.

"Let him speak!" Javier cried. "Don José has something to say!"

The room grew silent. The old man cleared his throat and took a moment to gather his thoughts. Then, slowly, he began. "I don't have any education. I went to school for three years and that is all. I'm embarrassed to admit that I cannot read or write very well. I'm not much of a speaker, either. I hope you will forgive me.

"I grew up in Chihuahua—in México—working on my father's ranch. Life was good for a while. Then my father died, and it was not long before we lost our land. I went to work when I was nine years old. My life has been difficult, just like it has for most of us in this room. Only working and working. And still, I have nothing. But I think I learned one thing after working all these years. And that is, if you don't have hope—if you don't plant the seeds for harvest—then, it is true: Tomorrow never comes.

"You must turn the soil and plant the seeds. Then you must water and nurture the seeds until they sprout, and care for them until they are tall and strong. Isn't that the way life is?

"But what happens if you don't tend the crops? What will you have for your children when it is time for the harvest? You will have nothing!" José took a deep, troubled breath. He cleared his throat and arched his eyebrows as if he were exhausted.

"There is one other thing I have learned. Don't ever beg." He shook his head slowly. "No, my friends, only then have you lost everything. And let me tell you something from my heart: I would go hungry first, and I would let my children go hungry. It sounds hard, but it is true. I would *never* get down on my knees. Why? Because I love my family, and there are some things that are more important than food. Would you want your family to see you on your knees?

"I am an old man. And I am tired. But I can tell you something. I would rather go to my grave like a man than live like a beggar. It is time for us to stand up and be *men*!" José clutched his fist and pounded it against his chest. "We have nothing to lose! We have got to think of our children! We must have our dignity!"

José paused again and gazed down at the table. "It will not be easy fighting a rich man. He has money and power and just about everything is on his side. Except one thing. And that is justice. Justice is on our side. We must fight for what is right. We must do it for our children. Otherwise, what will they learn? What hope will they have? What kind of a world will we leave for them?

"Antonio. This is a difficult thing you ask us to do. It will not be easy. But—win or lose—I can assure you—you can count me *in*!"

The meeting erupted into wild applause, workers standing on their chairs and shouting, "Viva la unión! Huelga! Long live the union! Strike!"

Javier clapped his hands, danced and carried on, savoring the moment, thrilled by the chanting. Men shook hands and slapped each other on the back, and women embraced.

David watched and took it all in. Like an actor at an audition, he slipped into character, his face undergoing a transformation as radical as any accomplished by trick photography. A sly grin took form and as the workers hooted and clapped their hands, David thrust his fist into the air and cried, "Viva la *unión*!"

9

Where the hell *are* those guys? Shit! They're even later than usual! Antonio passed out leaflets to workers as they approached the gate at the Mersola factory. He paused for a moment to take a long drag from his cigarette, the nicotine rushing through his temples, down to his fingertips already numb from the brisk morning air. Shitheads! Brady probably told them to take their time getting here. That son of a bitch! He'd do just about anything to screw up this union drive.

The more Antonio thought about Brady, the angrier he became. Bastard! You know what's gonna happen to you if we win here, don't you? You'll be finished. Then the party is over, eh, cabrón? What you gonna do when you're not president of the union anymore? You gonna lose your Cadillac, you gonna lose your expense account. Might even have to give up that big-ass boat you've got. Eso. You're gonna lose all that shit. Maybe you'll have to go back to work again! Hah!

The prospect of Brady working pleased Antonio. Brady had been the president of the Shoeworkers Union for eighteen years. For eighteen years, he had built his machine—lubricating it with the dues of union members, making deals with bosses, investing in pension funds secretly, manipulating the books. Still, he had gone unchallenged in six of the last eight union elections. But all of that was about to change.

Four hundred people worked at the Mersola factory. That translated into four hundred potential votes. Though Brady was tempted by the dues that would be generated by a factory of that size, there was simply too much at stake. Maybe the workers there would be "good, loyal union members"—meaning they would vote for him—and maybe they would not. Brady was not a gambling man, unless the cards were stacked in his favor. And he knew that at the Mersola factory, the odds were against him . . . as long as Antonio was organizing there.

The factory guards watched Antonio as he smoked his cigarette and passed out union leaflets. They nodded their heads in his direction, smiled twisted smiles and laughed with contempt. What's so funny, motherfuckers? Antonio thought. Idiots! Think you're big shots—"cops"—don't you know you're just being used by Mersola? I bet you don't even have a medical plan. Shit! Forget it, man. Forget about them. They're hopeless. Concentrate on the people going to work. There isn't much time. The two-minute buzzer is gonna sound pretty soon. Where are those guys, anyway? Damn! I spend as much time fighting the union as I do the company!

Cars pulled up to the factory gates and spouses kissed each other goodbye. Workers grabbed their lunches and newspapers and rushed inside, afraid to be even a minute late.

By the time the buzzer sounded, the street was empty. Antonio lit another cigarette and looked around. But there was no movement anywhere. Antonio blew the smoke from his lungs. Didn't show up at all today. Didn't even bother to show up.

A car whisked by, leaving a wake of tumbling leaves, dirt and soot. Antonio dropped his cigarette on the sidewalk and rubbed his eye.

The guards laughed and pointed his way. "That smart-ass is sure in for one hell of a surprise!" one of them said.

Antonio could not hear them, their words and laughter insulated by the walls and windows of the guard shack. Still, he understood. Instinct took over and he squared off to them, though they were some distance away. The guards laughed nervously, forcing up sounds from deep in their guts.

Something is going down, Antonio thought. Once again, he glanced up and down the street. But it was as quiet as a Sunday morning.

One of the guards slid open a window of the shack and shouted: "Hey, bigshot! What's the *mad*-der? All a-*lone*?"

Antonio stared at him across the driveway and as their eyes met, the guard was instantly transported from the protection of the shack to a long, dark tunnel. At the other end stood Antonio, framed by misty light, moving toward him with deliberation, a killer in a black-and-white movie. He saw a knife flash in Antonio's hand. God, please! I didn't mean nothin! Oh, shit! Please!

Then the lights came back on; he was safe in the shack again. The guard tried to laugh and dismiss everything he had imagined. But it seemed so *real*.

If Antonio had been aware of the guard's delusion, it would not have surprised him. He'd run into that kind of thinking a thousand times before. If he could have read his mind, he would have simply shrugged him off. *You fucking idiot!* he would have said. Don't you understand *anything*? Shit. No *wonder* you're a guard! You love the bossman! Unbelievable!

But Antonio had other things on his mind. Something was definitely wrong. He couldn't put his finger on it, but there was an uneasy feeling in the air. Everything seemed to be sitting on edge, midway between standing up and falling down, held in place by a breath, by a hair, by a distant star. It was like the drumbeat before a war, the silence before an earthquake. Something was going to happen—but he didn't know what.

Antonio replayed the morning in his mind—the absence of the other organizers, the stillness of the street, the cocky attitude of the guards. What did it mean? Then it dawned on him: Shit! He's done it! Brady has done it! He's called off the campaign! That's why no one showed up! And I'm probably the only one who doesn't know about it!

Quickly he headed for his car. I knew it. I *knew* Brady would pull something like this! But he isn't gonna get away with it. That bastard!

Antonio's mind was whirling as he considered twenty questions at once, foremost among them the quickest route to the union hall. He started the engine of his car, slammed it in gear, and raced off, wheels spinning, rubber burning. The guards bounded from their shack after him, their chests inflated as they shouted, "That's right, you fucking pachuco! You're history! Go write your name on a wall somewhere, motherfucker! And don't bother coming back!"

Once they had completed their primal display in the street, the guards returned to their shack, faces red, hands still trembling. Their anger vented, they appeared to calm down. They poured themselves fresh cups of coffee, leaned back in their chairs and dunked their donuts. But before they could fully enjoy their victory over Antonio, two green immigration buses with barred windows pulled up in front of the factory gates. The buses looked like giant bulls kicking up dirt with their hooves, grunting and snorting, ready to charge. Several squad cars followed close behind, tires squealing as they skidded to a stop in military formation. Everything was still, though the vehicles appeared to pulsate and breathe angrily.

In tandem all the squad car doors opened at once and scores of immigration agents descended upon the factory, swarming to block all visible exits. The guards watched with admiration, although, deep inside, they were afraid. A man in a three-piece suit approached them, followed by a phalanx of uniformed officers.

Identifying himself as a special agent for the Immigration and Naturalization Service, the man in the suit asked the guards to point out every possible exit from the plant. Excited by the display of militarism, they eagerly pointed north, south, east, and west. The special agent surveyed the plant as if he could see through it. He adjusted his sunglasses and issued his orders.

Uniformed men and women rushed to seal off exits not already blocked.

Within minutes, two more buses arrived, followed by additional backup. One of the guards marveled to the other, "Shit, they're like a fucking *army!*"

Inside the factory, after all the exits were blocked, an agent burst through the doors, flanked by a dozen others. In Spanish, he announced: "My name is Officer Gomez. I am with the United States Department of Immigration. Please remain where you are. Have your documents ready for inspection. Anyone who attempts to leave will be arrested."

Panic swept through the factory before the agent had completed his first sentence. Workers ran in all directions—toward the back exits, into the stockroom, under tables—in desperate attempts to escape the dragnet. Those who ran were chased by agents, wrestled to the ground and handcuffed. Amid the screams and confusion, Rosa watched in disbelief, stunned and frozen by terror.

Sonia dropped her work and ran toward the women's bathroom, but was quickly apprehended by a female agent who seemed to enjoy the challenge. She grabbed Sonia's arms and twisted them behind her back until she grimaced in pain. "Okay, okay, you've got me," Sonia cried in Spanish. "Don't hurt me! I won't run!"

The agent smiled a sardonic grin like a defensive guard who had made a good tackle. "Don't give me that mumo-jumbo," she said, glancing from side to side, her victim pinned in a half nelson as she waited for a high-five from a teammate.

Within minutes, the last of those who had attempted escape were rounded up and handcuffed.

The agents laughed among themselves at some of the hiding places chosen by the terrified workers.

"Hey, Ben! C'mere! Take a look at this!" one agent called out. "You gotta see this guy!"

A worker had tunneled into a canvas hopper filled with shoes. He was well hidden—except for his rear end. The agents pointed at him and laughed. One of them reached over and yanked a hair from the worker's lower back, causing him to leap out of the pile with a yelp, shoes flying in all directions.

"Stupid fucking wetback!" they laughed. "He might have made it if his ass wasn't so big!"

Soon the occupying force had everything under control. Those who had attempted to flee stood in line, their hands cuffed. Immigration agents went through the motions of checking the papers of those who had remained at their stations as ordered, but most of the others were simply rounded up and taken into custody. Rosa was among those arrested with no questions asked. She was Mexican, meek, and, in the mind of an immigration officer, an illegal alien. That was all there was to it.

The prisoners were marched outdoors where the buses waited, engines roaring, exhaust fouling the already polluted air. Agents pressured the prisoners to sign forms euphemistically called "voluntary departures" —papers that surrendered their rights to a deportation hearing. The captives were asked where they lived and where they were born. Those with the presence of mind lied or refused to give the agents the information they demanded. They knew if they told the truth, their families would be arrested and deported.

Javier was one of those who refused to cooperate. He was indignant at the way he and the other workers were being treated and stared defiantly at the agents as they prodded him and tried to extract information.

"No soy un criminal!" he told them. "I'm not a criminal! And I've done nothing wrong!"

"Tú eres un mojado!" an agent declared. "You're a *wetback*!"

"And you? What are you, cabrón? You don't look like an Indian to me."

"Don't talk back to me, shithead!" the agent warned him in

English. "You got *no* rights here, motherfucker. Huh. A *dog* has more rights here than you do. Shit."

Javier spat on the ground beside the agent and promptly received a forearm to his stomach. He doubled over and fell to his knees, struggling against handcuffs that sliced into his wrists.

"Mira, puto. Don't fuck with me. I'll put your ass in the joint in a minute! Then, after you've been reamed inside-out, I'll have your wet ass deported so far south you won't know if you're coming or going!"

Javier looked up at the guard, who stood over him with his arms folded across his chest. Javier could do little but glare at him as he lay bent over on the blacktop, his face contorted with rage.

The workers were separated into two lines, the larger one composed of Mexicans, the other Central Americans. Sonia managed to convince the agents she was from México, knowing that to do otherwise meant a one-way ticket back to El Salvador.

But Rosa was not aware of what was happening. The shock of being arrested had left her nearly catatonic. This can't be happening to me! she said to herself as the line of workers marched toward a bus. No! This can't be happening! I've done nothing wrong! I've done nothing!

As Rosa boarded the bus with the others, a thought cut through the numbness of her shock: Mis hijos! My children! Who will take care of my children?

She looked into the faces of other workers for help. But they turned away, overcome by the same thoughts. Women sobbed and men cradled their heads in their hands.

Who will take care of my children? The question tormented Rosa. I have no one! What will happen to them? A thought occurred. Desperately she searched through her purse, combs and photographs and papers, all randomly stuffed there after a search by an immigration agent. When she found what she was looking for, she took a deep breath and closed her eyes in relief.

In her hand she clutched a business card, which said: "Antonio Rodriguez—Organizer—Shoeworkers Union, Local 305."

The doors of the bus slammed shut. Air brakes hissed and the bus roared away, leaving behind a blue cloud, a dozen agents, and the security guards, still shaking their heads in awe. And as the bus raced down the street past the Mersola factory, Rosa clutched the business card in her hands and wept.

10

Ana peered through the window of a ramshackle bus. Smoke rose skyward like a black ribbon, curling and twisting in the blue sky. A Mexican woman grilled tortillas over a fire, three barefoot children clinging to her legs as she prepared breakfast just outside their home—a tiny dwelling built of discarded lumber, cardboard and pieces of corrugated tin. Ana watched as the woman fanned the coals, then flipped the tortillas on the grill with bare hands well accustomed to heat, smoke and poverty.

Ana rubbed her eyes as the family drifted past her window, disappearing in the distance. Only the Sierra, far away on the horizon, seemed to stand still. Fence posts and fields slipped past as if the earth's surface was being sucked into a giant sinkhole down the road behind the bus.

Soon another family appeared through the window, women busy tending to their fire, slapping masa into tortillas, wiping sweat from their brows.

Just like in my country, she thought. People living in casas de carton—houses of cardboard.

Ana thought about her barrio, her friends, and most of all, her lover. She remembered a day not long before. They strolled down the dusty streets of their hometown, passing shacks built by people even poorer than they. But all Ana could see was her lover, his unruly hair in revolt. "Don't you see, Ana? I have to do it!" he explained, a revolutionary fire burning in his eyes. "People cannot go on living like this!" He nodded his head at the shantytown. "It isn't right."

Until that moment, Ana had not really taken notice of where

they were. She had been unaware of the squatters cooking over open fires; she had not seen the children running about half-naked, their raven-black hair speckled with the eggs of lice. It was as if they had been at the park, strolling around the pathways beneath almond trees, past the blooming manzana rosa, inhaling the sweet scent of jasmine. But her lover's remarks brought her back.

"Pero Carlos—tengo miedo. I'm scared. What if something happens to you?"

Carlos was pleased by the opportunity to be a man. He cocked his head back with confidence: "Nothing will happen, mi amor. I'll be all right. Really. Besides, the junta is ready to fall! It can't last. Since they killed the archbishop, the people are ready to act. The only thing keeping the fourteen families in power is the guns they get from the Yankees."

"But Carlos! Please! Think about what you are doing! What if something should happen to you? What would I do?"

"Oh, Ana, you worry too much. Really! Believe me! Los muchachos are very strong! And now that the guerrillas have united—really! It's just a matter of time! This is the final offensive, you know."

Ana was frightened by his confidence. "But you're not going to leave me, are you? You're not going to run off to the mountains?"

"No, Ana," he smiled, gazing deep into her eyes. "I couldn't do that. I thought about it. It was hard. But I can't leave you, you know. So I'm going to help them here in the city. It's not very much what I am going to do. I'm just going to pass out some leaflets—in secret. That's all. But I have to do *something*. Please understand, Ana. I have to do something."

Ana gazed out the bus window at fields of corn and beans glistening with morning dew. She wanted to be where she was—far away from her barrio, far away from the things she knew and loved. But her memories kept calling to her. They would not let her go.

She remembered a morning trip to the market in the not-too-distant past. Ana and her mother had run from thunderclouds as they slid across the heavens chasing them, raindrops slapping in the dirt behind them as they ran. Then the clouds rolled away, leaving behind a blue sky and the scent of wet grass and fresh mud.

Ana remembered the walk home from the market, laughing with her mother as they struggled to carry a large bag of platanos and crema, yuca and black beans. On the corner, a crowd had gathered, standing solemnly in a circle, covering their mouths in disbelief. Ana's best friend was there. Ana saw her as she hastily turned away from the others and vomited, spitting her guts on the dirt road. Then she spotted Ana. She tried to warn her, fighting the demon that was throwing her body into convulsions, wiping her mouth and chin with the back of her hand. But she was only able to utter one word and no more: "Ana!"

It was then Ana saw the outstretched hand, fingers contorted and stiff. And she knew.

Neighbors reluctantly gave way as she approached.

He lay on a mat of blood, a wooden stake hammered through his throat. His forehead had been sliced open, dried blood forming a crusty cross. Flies circled his body, searching vainly for moisture in his eyes and mouth.

Ana fell to his side and screamed, "Carlos!" And the shock that had numbed her neighbors gave way to grief. Grown men sobbed at the sight of Ana holding her lover, pressing her face against his chest.

The bus jarred to a sudden stop. Doors flew open and Mexican immigration agents climbed aboard. They strutted down the aisle of the bus, cocksure and arrogant as they examined the faces of the passengers. The refugees did their best to blend in with the others. But the agents knew what they were looking for. In a ritual common in most of the Americas, the agents demanded their papers, knowing from experience the travelers were not Mexicans—knowing from experience that they were illegally in México. They ordered the refugees off the bus, herding them into an easily manageable group. The coyote waited a few minutes, then stepped outside, watching from a distance as the agents conducted an interrogation.

Ana and Manuel looked into each other's eyes, silently asking: Should we run? Should we? They surveyed the open fields of the countryside where corn grew—not in rows, but in scattered patches and at different heights. The cornfield was the only possible escape. But an escape to what? Where would they go? They didn't even know where they were. Again, they turned to each other, communicating secretly. Wait and see. Let the coyote handle this. Wait and see.

The coyote approached the immigration agents, presenting his passport like a business card. He cupped his hand near his mouth and whispered to the agents. There was a nodding of heads and other efforts to disguise what was obvious. The coyote strolled to the front of the bus, out of sight of the refugees, soon joined by the two immigration agents. After some bartering, he reluctantly handed the agents one hundred dollars in North American bills. The coyote would later add the expense to the refugees' bill, charging substantial interest.

The coyote boarded the bus, and the agents tucked the money into their pockets, arguing over percentages. Finally, they appeared to reach an agreement. One of the agents slapped the passports in his palm. "Okay, you can get back on the bus," he said.

Manuel thrust his hand forward, gesturing for the return of his papers. The agent took a step backward. "No, hombre! I said you can get back on the *bus*! But I'm going to have to *keep* these."

In mock disagreement, the other agent said, "Maybe you had

better give them back. What if they turn up dead? No one will know what to do with the bodies." The agents smiled ghoulishly.

"Well I suppose they can have them back. But—well, *you* know the rules. We'll have to collect a processing tax. A tax to feed the poor, you know." He turned toward the immigrants. "You can have them back for five hundred pesos. I'm authorized to charge you more, you know. But five hundred pesos is fair enough."

The refugees were dumbstruck. Manuel was so angry he could barely move. His hands shook and all color drained from his face. Still, he reached into his pocket and handed the agents ten American dollars, money sent to him by his sister Sonia, money he had put aside for just such an encounter.

"What's *this*? Dollars?" an agent smiled. "Don't you have pesos?" Manuel shook his head. "Well, then, this will have to do!"

One by one, the refugees reached into their pockets, paid for their identification, and climbed back onto the bus. When everyone was safely aboard, the bus coughed and sputtered and bounded away. The agents stood on the roadway, heads bowed, as they counted their loot.

"What time does the next bus pass this way?" one asked the other. "No sé, hombre! Anyway, what does it matter? If we hurry, we can stop *that* one again!"

11

The Shoeworkers Union had changed a great deal under the twelve year reign of its president, Don Brady. He had insisted: "A union must be run like a business." And operate like a business it did, with secret slush funds, dubious investments, and two separate sets of books.

One of the first things Brady did as president of the union was to construct a new building for the local, arguing it was a "good investment"—which, of course, it was. The construction also provided many people with jobs, the most lucrative contracts awarded to those with a "special relationship" to the union—meaning, of course, personal ties to the president.

The new offices were spacious and well lit, with wall-to-wall carpeting and rented plants, watered and treated weekly by a business owned and operated by Brady's nephew. Those who worked there had the most modern equipment available, from correcting typewriters to electronic beepers. And just like any other modern-day operation, workers who called were put on hold and treated to recordings of Muzak while they waited to speak to the men whose salaries they paid.

Representatives for firms with union contracts were made to feel right at home at Local 305. Upon arrival, they were immediately escorted past the large overstuffed couch in the lobby where union members sat, smoked, and read magazines while they waited. There they sat as men in twelve-hundred-dollar suits sauntered by, admiring the building union dues had built. And before the workers could turn a page, the very same men were whisked by again, this time escorted by union officials.

If it had not been for the officers' stilted display of cordiality, it would have been difficult to distinguish which of the party were union officials and which represented business. After all, both were tailor-dressed and both wore Italian-made shoes and carried leather briefcases. The only distinction that separated the men on their way to lunch was that some of them wore their hair in a pompadour, blow-dried and carefully combed, while others wore theirs parted, with the "natural" look.

Antonio sat outside Brady's office, smoking and thumping his fingers impatiently on a leather chair that faced Brady's personal secretary.

Interrupting the secretary's typing, Antonio asked, "How much longer do you think he's going to be? I've been here over an hour."

"He should be finished any moment now, " she answered curtly, examining a crack in her nails, glaring at Antonio as if he had been the cause of it.

Antonio took a drag from his cigarette and blew a long column of smoke from deep in his lungs as was his custom when angry. As the secretary fanned the air around her face, her phone rang.

"Don Brady's office," she answered with a little girl's voice. Antonio rolled his eyes.

Grimacing, she said, "It's for you," and handed him the receiver as if it were a dirty undergarment.

"Hello? Yeah, Bill," he answered, smashing his cigarette out in an ashtray. "What! *When?*"

As Antonio concentrated on the call, the door to Brady's office swung open. Brady emerged, puffing on a pipe and joking with another man in a tailored silk business suit.

"Jesus Christ!" Antonio shouted in disbelief, interrupting the businessmen's jocular laughter. "Those chingados! Son of a *bitch*! Okay. I'll get right back to you. Thanks, bro'!" Antonio slammed the receiver down on its bracket. Brady and the other man stared at Antonio in disbelief, unable to disguise their surprise, or their animosity.

"Immigration just raided Mersola's and picked up over three hundred people!"

Brady was astonished, though not by Antonio's announcement; it was his impertinence that stunned him.

"I said the immigration—"

"I heard you!" Brady snapped. He turned his back to Antonio, puffed calmly on his pipe and arched his eyebrows, as if to say to the man he'd been negotiating with for the past hour, "See what kind of bullshit I have to put up with?"

Antonio could not stand still. He paced the floor, pausing only to light another cigarette while the two men resumed their conversation. Brady apologized for the interruption and suggested to the businessman that they continue their talk over lunch on Tuesday. He agreed graciously, and they shook hands. "I'm sorry I can't show you the way out," Brady said, "but, as you can see, we have a minor emergency to resolve."

"I understand completely," the businessman acknowledged, tilting his head toward Antonio and otherwise extending his sympathy. "I'll see you Tuesday, then. At the regular place?"

"Of course! And don't forget to bring along your . . . friend." They nodded in agreement and the businessman started down the stairs. Brady smiled and waved goodbye, adjusted his tie, then turned back to Antonio, his expression completely changed.

"Well? What are we going to do?" Antonio asked.

Brady struggled to maintain his composure. "I told you, Tony. I warned you before this thing ever got started. Now— there's nothing we can do."

The union president fiddled with his pipe, biding his time. "Now, Tony," he continued without looking up. "I've told you from the beginning that you can't organize these people. We've spent a lot of time and money for *nothing*. Now, the Federation's got a position. You've pushed everyone this far, and they went along with you, against my recommendation. But now it's gone far enough." Brady studied the tobacco in the bowl of his pipe, lit his lighter and watched the flame leap as he bellowed the smoke, reveling in the light.

Antonio didn't take his eyes off Brady for a moment. His shoulders were hunched and his pupils dilated—sure signs to anyone street-wise to move out of the way or get popped. When Brady finally glanced up at Antonio, he seemed to take a restrained delight in his expression, smiling wryly as if to say, "Go ahead and *hit* me, motherfucker! That would be *perfect!*" Antonio measured his response, understood it, and regained his composure.

"Look, Don. I know you've never been behind this drive. But you can't just sit back and let the immigration raid Mersola's and do nothing. It's a union-busting tactic, pure and simple. Are you gonna let them do that to you?"

Brady continued to puff on his pipe. They knew each other too well. Antonio waited for a response. Getting none, he turned to walk away, telling Brady over his shoulder, "Well, if you're not going to do nothin', then I will."

"Look, dammit! Don't you turn your back on me!" Brady warned. Antonio froze. One could almost see the muscles in his back and neck swell. Then he rotated his torso and slowly pivoted around until he faced the union president.

"Listen to me," Brady said. "Suzanne. You listen up, too. I want you to hear this." Brady's secretary glanced up, still fidgeting with her nails. "Look," Brady continued. "That's it! Not one more penny is going to be spent on that goddamned place. Do you hear me? It's over." Antonio repressed a laugh, shook his head and walked away.

Brady watched him leave, squinting his eyes. "That shithead. He's going to try something. I *know* it. Fucking punk. Tryin' to build his wetback empire with him king. He's had it this time.

I'm not going to take his crap anymore. It's bye-bye Tony."

Antonio marched out of the union hall, oblivious to the others in the building. Striding down the street, he headed toward a bar-and-grill he frequented, folks on the sidewalk clearing out of his way. Pinche cabrón, he thought. To hell with him! I'll call up Mike Logan at the coalition. They're ready. They've been wanting to do something like this for the longest time. We'll have a dozen priests and nuns at the federal building in an hour.

Antonio considered strategies and tactics, moving the pieces of the three-dimensional chess game in his head. He entered the bar at full stride and headed directly to the pay phone. How long will it take the bus to get to the detention center? A class action suit, maybe. Well, Logan will know about that. Call the *Examiner* and the *Times*—that labor writer—he's not too bad. And the church—Sister Kate. And that Lutheran pastor, Pastor Bill Ruth. He's a good man. Ten cents! I *know* I've got a dime, dammit! I'll get over to Mersola's before they let out. Got to get the press there. Got to stop the bus before they cross the border. Shit! I know I've got a goddamn dime! Son of a bitch!

Antonio finally dropped ten cents into the pay phone and dialed, thumping his fingers against the wall as it rang. Two rings, three . . . oh, and the Lawyer's Guild . . . the Longshoremen's Union. There's that chick who's president there now. She'll help . . . five, six . . . better call KMEX right away. We'll tend to the others later.

Suddenly Antonio froze, overcome by one thought that overpowered all the others. Oh, man, what if. . . . He caught his breath, staggering under the weight of a thought, bracing himself against the wall. As the phone rang for the tenth time, he whispered: "Rosa's kids."

12

The Pacific Ocean is gentle to San Diego, a bay painted in watercolor and Mediterranean pastels. A steady breeze fills the sails of boats piloted by the wealthy, while the less affluent watch from shore.

In the arms of the bay, ships are built. Sailors on leave anxiously walk the piers and stroll through arcades and tourist traps, buying magazines, hot dogs and pitchers of cold beer. Old folks fish with the poor, and nearby, at sandy beaches, the young drink wine, bake in the sun and tantalize each other with bodies lusty and firm.

Just south of San Diego is Chula Vista, an area the Spanish and Mexican settlers named "Beautiful View." Rosa and the other Mexican workers arrested at the Mersola factory were going to spend a night there as guests of the United States government, in a prison for undocumented workers.

Rosa sat perched on the edge of her bunk, exhausted by her ordeal. The mattress reeked of stale urine—an odor that permeated the prison, sealing its walls—along with the more subtle stench of sweat and fear. Previous guests had scrawled messages on those walls in Spanish, slogans such as "Down with la migra!" and other less glorious proclamations. As Rosa gazed through the barred windows at a small square of blue sky, she worked Antonio's now battered business card between her fingers, all of her other possessions having been confiscated by immigration agents. As the government-green walls glowed with fluorescent light, Rosa closed her eyes for a moment and thought about her children.

The prison lobby had chairs for visitors and family members of the "detained," a place where folks could deliver clean clothes to their loved ones—if they dared. Agents scrutinized the eyes of those who waited, grudgingly admitting those who passed the visual test. Tubes of toothpaste, combs and brushes were removed from packages before delivery, the agents explaining with firmness that such things could be "fashioned into weapons." If anyone doubted them, they pointed to a glass display case set up near the desk. There, under a label that read "Weapons Made by Illegals," the unbelieving could view spoons filed to a sharp point. Plastic baggies filled with white powder had tags that said, "Drugs Smuggled into America by Illegals." The agents smirked with satisfaction: They were doing their jobs.

Inside the jail, workers from the Mersola factory sat on their bunks and waited. They waited to be called by agents who would repeat the same questions the prisoners had been asked when arrested: "What is your *real* name? Where were you born? What is your address in America?"

Rosa was called to be interviewed. She sat quietly as a woman asked her in broken Spanish all the pertinent questions. She answered carefully, declining to give the location of her children, despite several heavy-handed attempts by the young Chicana agent to wrestle that information from her. The agent seemed to speak poor Spanish intentionally, making it difficult for Rosa to understand her.

Finally the agent threw up her hands in frustration and told Rosa she was finished.

"Finish?" Rosa asked meekly. "Yeah, you're finished all right."

"Can . . . can I telephono?" Rosa asked. The agent ignored her.

"Pleeze? Telephono?" Rosa asked carefully, doing her best to speak clearly. The young woman tossed a form to one side in disgust. "Yeah, all right. One call." She signaled to an office worker who carried a gun. "Take her to a pay phone and let her make one call," she told the clerk, who rolled her eyes and led Rosa down a corridor.

Rosa glanced from side to side, not knowing where she would get the money to pay for the call. "Just dial," the hefty Angla told her. "You don't need money. Just call collect." Rosa didn't understand, so the clerk picked up the phone, raised it to her ear, and with controlled condescension, said, "See? It works. No money. No dinero. Comprende? You got two minutes. Got it?"

Rosa's eyes lit up. She held on to the receiver awkwardly and struggled to dial the numbers on Antonio's card.

A voice answered. "Operator. May I help you?" Rosa panicked.

"Just tell her you're calling collect," the clerk said as she picked her face.

"Collect, pleeze."

"Your name?"

"Rosa Orosco."

"Thank you," replied the operator, much to Rosa's relief. The phone rang several times before someone answered.

"Shoeworkers Union, Local 305—please hold." Before Rosa could speak a word, and before the operator could ask if they would accept the charge, a Muzak version of *Yesterday* played. Rosa pulled the phone away from her ear and examined it, wondering if she had dialed correctly. Frightened, she spoke into the receiver. "Hallo? Está Antonio Rodriguez? Hallo?"

"I'm sorry, ma'am, but they seemed to have put you on hold. Please hang up and try again."

"Está Antonio Rodriguez?" Rosa asked, not understanding the operator.

"Please hang up and dial again."

The phone clicked, and in a moment, a dial tone returned.

Rosa was stunned. She gazed into the receiver, then at the clerk. But the clerk was preoccupied with removing a scab from her chin. Rosa reluctantly hung up, then turned to the woman for help. "No work," she explained.

"Sorry. Just one call per person. You can call again tomorrow morning before you leave."

"Por favor! Pleeze! No call. No talk!"

"That's the rules. One call, no more."

Rosa reached for the clerk's arm, imploring her to give her another chance. "Pleeze! Mis hijos! Como van a comer mis hijos? How will my children eat?"

"Look. That's it!" the clerk said, angrily shaking her arm free. "Now come with me. Let's go!"

"Plee—"

"Go! Now!" shouted the clerk, drawing the attention of another agent.

"What's the matter?" he asked.

"This bitch wants to make another call. And she doesn't want to go back to the compound."

The agent examined Rosa's face. Awkwardly speaking what little Spanish he knew, he said, "Señora. Vamos! Sorry, but you've got to go! Vamos! Yá!"

Rosa bit her lip with such intensity it made the agents squirm. She gazed into their eyes, pleading for another chance, pleading for her children. But God Almighty Himself could not have moved them. And so Rosa was led down the corridor, back to the compound and back to her bunk, where she would wait until morning to be deported.

13

It was late afternoon and the refugees sat on a cool sandy beach in Mazatlán. They rubbed their aching feet and watched the waters of the Pacific Ocean rock in the wind and the sun. The beach was a welcome luxury, soft and giving, the cries of gulls overhead and the sound of waves washing the shore the first true pleasures experienced by the Salvadoreans since their journey began.

As the refugees rested in the sand, the coyotes huddled together nearby. Sharing a fifth of El Presidente brandy, they gulped the liquor down, wiped their mouths and burst into spasms of laughter that made Ana shudder. The more the coyotes drank, the harder they looked at the young women in the group, their eyes burning with a lust only sex or violence could satisfy. Ana and the other women knew what was coming — they had all heard that laughter and felt those stares before. But there was nothing they could do. So they dug their fingers into the sand, said prayers to the saints and waited.

"Okay," the coyote boss said. "Go for it! Consider it my little gift to you. You can have the bitches. I'll take care of the tough guy."

"What are you going to do, Peligro?" a Salvadorean coyote asked, calling the boss by his nickname. "I don't know if you can handle him, you know. I heard someone say he was a guerrillero! Better watch out! He might blow you up with a *bomb*!"

The other coyotes snickered.

"Don't worry about him. Maybe he'll just get lost. Anyway, I've got my secret weapon," he said, patting a pint of brandy tucked in his pants. "But, if he does come back, he's gonna be pissed off. And it's not me he's going to be mad at."

"Oh, I'm *scared*," the Salvadorean said, pretending to tremble. "A real live guerrillero! Running like a dog with his tail between his legs. He probably saw my cousin, Ramón. He's in la guardia, you know. He's a big, fat, *ugly* motherfucker."

"I guess it runs in the family," Peligro said.

"I'll tell him that next time you're in Santa Ana."

"I was just kidding, cabrón," Peligro said. "Anyway. Why in the hell would I ever go to Santa Ana again? I make more money doing this shit than I ever could in that stinking little town."

"Ah, sí, Peligro. Now you're a big shot. But just remember how you got started. And also, remember this—if you want to make some *good* money, you've got to know somebody in the guardia nacional. At least in *my* country, cabrón!"

"Who are you calling cabrón, cabrón?" one of the Mexican coyotes said, pointing his finger at the Salvadorean's throat. Tempers rose and fists were bared. But Peligro quickly stepped in before punches could be thrown.

"Okay, okay. Yá! This is all stupid. You're arguing over stupid shit. The guanaco is entitled to his opinions. Just don't let him have any pussy tonight."

"No panocha for you!" one of the Mexicans cried. The other coyotes laughed raspy laughs and stuck their tongues out, pointing at the Salvadorean and grabbing their groins. Peligro knew how to bring them back together: all he had to do was appeal to the Devil in them. Only the Salvadorean remained upset, though his anger was quickly abated by a couple of slaps on the back and a long gulp of brandy.

"All right, now. No more fighting. It's bad for morale," Peligro said with sarcasm. "I'll be back in an hour or so. And don't get too drunk. We don't need any problems."

Peligro left his companions and approached the refugees as they sat peacefully on the sand. He made an announcement:

"I'm going to town to buy some food. You all give me ten colones, or, if you've got it, one hundred and thirty pesos, and I'll buy you something to eat."

The refugees searched furtively for money hidden in socks and brassieres and shoes. As Peligro stood over them with his hands on his hips, Ana felt somewhat relieved. And as she combined her money with Manuel's, she thought: Maybe I'm overreacting. Maybe it's just me. Nothing bad is going to happen. She glanced at her cousin for a sign. Manuel smiled. "I have the hunger of a dog!" he said, unaware of any problems.

There's nothing to worry about, Ana thought. It's just me. I guess I'm just tired. That's all. Tired and hungry.

As Peligro collected the currency of two nations, he pointed at Manuel. "I need you to go with me. We won't be long."

"Who, me?" Manuel asked.

"Sí, pendejo! You!"

Manuel did not like to be disrespected. But he was in a bind. Grumbling, he stood up and brushed the sand from his trousers. He turned toward Ana, knowing she would understand. But she was withdrawn and idly dug her fingers into the sand. "It's all right, mujer," Manuel said. "I'm not going to let him get to me. I'll be fine."

Ana drew circles in the sand. She moved her lips, but said nothing. "Ana! Don't worry! I'll be all right!" Manuel assured her.

From their spot on the beach the other coyotes watched and laughed. Manuel's muscles tightened. He squared off to them, certain he was the object of ridicule.

An old woman who had been observing close by left her spot on the sand and plopped herself down beside Ana. "I've never had the opportunity to introduce myself. My name is Irma Chavez."

"Let's go, hombre!" Peligro told Manuel. But Manuel did not move. "Don't worry," the old woman said. "She'll be all right.

95

I'm not going to let her out of my sight."

"Apurate, hombre! There's not much time! Do you expect me to carry all that food back by myself?" Peligro cried as he approached the road.

"It's all right, Manuel," Ana said softly. "I'll be fine."

"Are you *sure*?"

Ana nodded as she poked holes in the sand with her fingers. "Okay . . . if you are sure."

Ana nodded again and Manuel plodded off after Peligro, who gestured for him to hurry. Manuel did not see the coyotes who remained on the beach as they nudged each other in the ribs and laughed.

When Manuel was well out of sight, the coyotes made their move, approaching the three women as they sat together in a circle.

"Well, what have we *here*?" one of them sneered. "An old hen and her two chicks!"

The old woman moved closer to Ana and reached for a pretty young peasant from Metapán who wore her innocence like a crucifix. "I may be an old hen, but if you bother either of these girls, you're going to wake up one morning and wonder why your pajarito flew away."

The coyotes laughed. Yet their eyes betrayed a certain anxiety. "Say, hombre. I think she is *threatening* us," one said. "Imagine that!"

Ana and the old woman huddled close together, but the young peasant stared at the coyotes as if star-struck. The old woman continued to glare at them with defiance. "My husband was a butcher, you know. I can cut through a joint that fast," she said, snapping her fingers.

The coyotes took a step backward. "Pinche vieja! We were only being hospitable! We just wanted to invite you to have a little drink. That is all. It gets cold here when the sun goes down. Híjole!"

As the coyotes retreated, they noticed the young peasant's glazed eyes and smiled. "But if one of you gets a *chill* and changes your mind," one called out, "the invitation is still open. We are men of honor, and *respect* our women. Even you, vieja!"

The old woman continued to glare at them until they were back at their campsite down the beach. "Los hombres!" she said. "They're all the same. But don't worry, niña. Your husband will be back soon."

Ana took a deep breath and managed a smile. "Thank you, señora. But Manuel—he is not my husband. He is my cousin."

The old woman smiled mischievously. "Oh, really? Then you won't mind if I use my charms on him?"

Ana laughed. "No, I wouldn't mind. But his wife—she has a temper, you know. Como la jodida!"

The old woman coughed up a laugh. "Oh, well. It doesn't matter. It's been such a long time since I was with a man it would probably kill me anyway." The three women burst into laughter, an experience that in itself appeared to be life-threatening to the old woman.

The women watched as the sun melted where the Gulf of California meets the Pacific. Clouds burned in the distance, set aflame by the sinking sun. Ana and the old woman were mesmerized by what they saw. But the young peasant from Metapán was not impressed; she was distracted by the distant presence of three men.

"The sunset reminds me of when I was a small girl growing up in Sonsonate. There is a volcano there, you know. When I was a child, it used to make fireworks."

"Really? Weren't you frightened?"

"No," the old woman smiled. "My grandmother used to say there was no need to worry as long as it was erupting every day. It was when it stopped—that was when the old people used to get nervous. In the evening, we would all go outside and watch it. It was beautiful at night! Just like fire in the sky!

Oh, I remember that. We would drink horchata and watch the fireworks. Then one day, a bunch of gringos in white jackets came. They started visiting the volcano. They climbed right up to the top. People said they were *scientists*. And they made the volcano stop. It just stopped erupting as if they had turned it off. It's been quiet ever since.

"Oh, how the old people used to worry! And my grandmother used to say, 'Someday the whole thing is going to blow up!' And I think so. I believe her. She was a very wise woman. A Pipíl, you know. A Mayan. Yes, she used to say the gringos, they stopped it. But some day, the whole *country* is going to explode!"

******

Manuel and the coyote made their way back toward the beach carrying soda and bags of tortas—Mexican sandwiches. A pickup truck with three rifle-bearing sheriffs pulled up behind them.

"Alto!" they shouted, two of the men leaping from the pickup and pointing their rifles like accusing fingers. They demanded to see identification.

Peligro calmly showed them his Mexican passport, watching Manuel out of the corner of his eye.

"And yours?" they asked Manuel.

"I don't have mine with me."

"Where are you from?"

"Veracruz."

Not easily dissuaded from a quick profit, the sheriffs scratched their chins and eyed Manuel suspiciously, knowing Salvadoreans have accents much like the people of Veracruz.

"What's in the bag?" one demanded. The coyote shrugged his shoulders.

"Tortas," Manuel volunteered.

Probing his eyes, the sheriff scratched his chin one last time. "All right. Get moving. And don't cause any more trouble!" The men climbed back into their truck and raced away.

"You're a smart one," Peligro said. "How did you know the slang for tortas? They don't call them like that in El Salvador."

Manuel shrugged his shoulders, mimicking the coyote.

"Yes, you are a smart one," he went on as they continued down the road. "You know about Veracruz, too. Have you been to México before?" Manuel shook his head no. The coyote reached into his trousers for a pint of brandy. "Want some?"

"No, gracias."

Taking a swig, Peligro exhaled contentedly and belched. "Yes, you are really a smart one. And you have good taste in women, also. I bet your wife is as good in bed as she looks, no?"

Manuel stopped abruptly and faced the coyote. "Why are you talking that way? She's not my wife. But anyway, you shouldn't talk like that! You're not just talking to anybody, you know! Understand, you might be the boss here, but if you know what's good for you, you won't touch my cousin."

The coyote laughed. "Take it easy, hombre! You are getting upset for nothing! I was just talking to you man to man! Híjole! I didn't mean anything! Son of a bitch!"

Manuel thought about Ana: I shouldn't have left her alone. I won't do it again. These coyotes, they have people by the balls! All they want to do is make money, get drunk, and take advantage of people. Cabrones! But I have to be careful. I can't just do anything. I have to think what is best. It's a long way to the border.

"Okay," Manuel said. "Forget about it. Maybe I didn't understand you too good."

"That's right! Let's forget the whole thing, eh? And let's celebrate our new understanding with a little toast? What do you say?"

"No, thank you. I don't drink liquor."

"You don't drink liquor, eh? Too bad. This is good brandy. The best! Está seguro?"

"Sí, hombre. I am sure."

It wasn't long before Manuel and the coyote were back at the beach. The refugees were huddled together, what little clothing they had wrapped tightly around their shoulders to protect them from the cool breeze rising from the sea. Down the shore they could see Mazatlán, lights twinkling where tourists and wealthy Mexicans laughed, drank margaritas de oro, ate lobster and crab and danced.

Manuel raced toward Ana. "Is everything okay?" he asked.

The old woman answered, "She's all right. It's the other one who is in trouble."

Manuel spotted the young woman from Metapán down the beach, surrounded by coyotes, laughing like a child, and, with strong encouragement, drinking from a bottle of brandy, taking it like medicine. "She's traveling alone," the old woman explained. "She thinks the coyotes are going to help her once she's across the border. Pobrecita!" Manuel watched the young woman, wondering whether he should intervene, knowing from a glance there was nothing he could do. He sat down with Ana and the old woman. In the light of the moon, they counted what remained of their money—all of it sent to them by relatives living in the United States.

"Only fifty dollars more," Ana sighed. "I hope we don't get stopped by the immigration again. We might not have enough for a bribe."

"Don't worry, Ana. When we get to Tijuana, we can call Sonia. She can send us more money. She said to call if we ran short."

The refugees ate their dinner, savoring every morsel. They watched the moon as it gazed at its reflection in the gulf. While gentle waves lapped the shore, they prepared their beds, wrapping sweaters into balls for pillows, spreading thin blankets over flattened sand. As Ana and Manuel lay down to sleep, the young peasant from Metapán returned, staggering about, searching for her belongings. Tripping over the old woman, she apologized, then asked: "Have you seen my comb and jacket?" The old woman handed her all her things, which she had kept in the hope the young woman would return to bed down with them.

"Are you all right?" the old woman asked.

"Oh, yes," she replied, nodding her head too many times.

"Where are you going? Why don't you stay with us?"

"No, no, it's okay."

"Are you going to stay with the coyotes?" the old woman asked.

"It's all right," the young woman assured her, nodding her head fervently. "He loves me and wants to marry me. And he has a big house in Los Angeles where I can stay until we're married. He really loves me, you know."

The old woman dropped her head in disappointment as the young peasant staggered back toward the laughter of the coyotes, still nodding her head and assuring everyone everything was fine. "He's going to take care of me," she muttered as she stumbled in the dark.

Slowly, and with regret, Ana, Manuel and the old woman lay down, digging their shoulders into the soft sand, restless and uneasy. Stars glittered around the moon and strains of salsa floated down the beach from nearby clubs like jasmine in the wind. In time, the refugees fell asleep, the old woman troubled by nightmares, her cries drowned out by the sea.

Near midnight, a sharp scream jolted the immigrants awake. They sat up, leaning their weight upon their arms, not certain where they were. They focused their eyes in the direction of the disturbance. A woman jumped up and down madly as something darted across the sand in the dark, joining a faint tide ebbing away from the mound of refugees. "Ratas!" she screamed.

"Rats! They bit my finger!"

The refugees leaped to their feet and quickly threw sand at the rats until they all retreated. They gathered up what remained of their dinner—sandwiches wrapped in wax paper put aside for breakfast—and buried it in the sand. As they settled down, they covered their faces and arms with sweaters, afraid the rats might return.

"I thought it was la cipota from Metapán," Manuel said.

"She's sleeping with something worse than rats," the old woman said.

The refugees lowered their heads to the sand, closed their eyes and waited, listening to the surf and the sound of sifting sand. And with every movement, with every rustling, they sat up, prepared to defend themselves against the rats, the coyotes and things unknown in the night.

14

"BROTH-ERS AND-A SISters! The TIE-MAH is GROW-ING KNEEyer... Are you all RED-DEE ? ARE YOU ALL RED-dee? I'M red- dee! I'm RED-DEE for the COM-ING of *SWEET* JE-sus!"

The child-faced evangelist licked his lips and beamed from the black-and-white television set. Four young children sat and watched, mesmerized, not understanding a word, but enthralled by the preacher's strange eyes and jerking gestures.

"I want you ALL NOW to place your HAN-zah upon your television sets . . . put your HAN-zah up against MINE-ah for the bapTIS-MMM of the HO-LY SPIR-it!" The preacher squeezed his eyes together and reached his hand out toward the screen, his fingers moving apart uncontrollably as he spoke. His body shook violently as he shouted, "In the NAME of GOD, I COM-MAND! HEE-yal! HEE-yal! HEE-yal!" The children glanced at each other in astonishment, their eyes wide open, their mouths agape.

"*SWEET* JE-sus! Ber-RING our FAM-AH-lees BACK to-GE-ther! The DEV-il has SEP-ar-ate-ed usss. He has broken up ow-wer FAM-AH- lees with de-VOR-sez. He has brought SHAME upon usss, KILL-ing our UN-BORN IN-FANTzah."

Antonio took a long drag from his cigarette, grimacing. The old woman sitting across from him dabbed the corners of her eyes with a handkerchief.

"Mire, señora. José will be back soon! We've filed an injunction to stop the bus. It will never get to the border. And—if everything goes well—everyone should be on their way back home tomorrow."

The old woman blew her nose and gazed at her grandchildren as they watched the program they did not understand.

On the wall behind her was a gallery of family portraits— photos of weddings, birthday parties and baptisms. In the spaces between the photos were crayon drawings and finger paintings taped over cracks in the wall, cock-eyed and frayed at the edges. The old woman was drawn for a moment to the evangelist as he preached, but her eyebrows were knitted with concern, her fingers tapping her lips. Above the television was a traditional portrait of the Virgin of Guadalupe in a gaudy frame. Nearby, a corner table stood like an altar; upon it sat a fading zinc portrait of a couple on their wedding day—husband and wife, stiff and formal and proud. A candle burned endlessly in their memory, their bodies long since part of the earth they had worked and called their own.

The old woman began to cry again, wiping away her tears with a handkerchief. Her daughter moved close beside her and offered comfort.

Three generations lived in the tiny apartment, where the couch became a bed at night, where every blanket, every meal, every problem was shared. Yet only the young children lived there "legally." The others were all criminals in the eyes of the law. They were "illegal aliens."

"Señora," Antonio said to the old woman, "we've formed a coalition of priests, lawyers, and community activists. A reverend from the Lutheran Church, several priests and nuns, and a team of lawyers are at the federal courthouse at this very moment trying to stop the bus your husband is on—and they assure me they have a very good chance of succeeding! José should be home soon. You see, la migra violated the rights of José and the others when they deported them without having a hearing. I know how you must feel. But try to be strong. If José calls, tell him not to sign *anything*. And if the immigration asks him if he wants a deportation hearing, tell him to say yes. We've got the lawyers all ready for him and the others. And he doesn't have to worry about the money. The attorneys have all volunteered."

The old woman coughed, blinked her eyes and sat up straight. Two teenage girls struggled to find room between her and their mother on an overstuffed love seat; they stroked their grandmother's hair and caressed her face.

Antonio sat back in a sagging sofa, shaped by the impression of José's grandson who slept there every night. "Yo sé está bien difícil. I know it is hard for you. But there are other families who are in even more serious trouble than you are. One young mother who was deported has four young children. Her name is Rosa. She has no husband and no family here. Her oldest child is ten years old."

Before Antonio could say another word, the old woman said, "Bring them here! They can all stay here! Pobrecitos."

Antonio smiled and took another drag from his cigarette. "That's very kind of you, señora. That's beautiful. But what would you do with four more children here? Where would they sleep?"

"Vamos hacer todo lo posible. We would manage," the old woman replied confidently, somehow gaining courage from the knowledge there were children in need.

"I admire your generosity, señora. But would it be possible for someone to stay with them at their home? It's over in Echo Park. That way, they could go to school in the morning and you wouldn't be burdened with the responsibility of four more niños in the house."

The old woman and her daughter considered the question, a host of terrible scenarios flashing across their minds. Cecilia, the oldest of the teenagers, perked up. "I'll go, Abuelita!" she volunteered. The old woman frowned and turned to her daughter, the girl's mother, to see what she would say.

"Cecilia's very young," her mother said, glancing at her daughter as if measuring her maturity.

"Yo puedo, Mamá!" Cecilia said. "I can do it!"

Antonio glanced at the two women and gauged their response. "I'd keep a close eye on her," he assured them. "I'd bring them food and check up on them every day. And I think either the union or the coalition would pay for babysitting."

"Nooo!" the women replied adamantly, frowning as they shook their heads.

"You don't have to pay her!" her mother said. "We won't do that!"

"I didn't mean to offend you," Antonio said. "I know you don't want money. I just want you to know that Cecilia wouldn't be left on her own. We'll be responsible for making certain everything is as it should be and that everyone is safe."

"There won't be any men in the house, will there?" Cecilia's mother asked.

"No, señora. Don't worry. And I'll see if the neighbors can help keep an eye out also. I would have asked them, but I don't know them, you know."

Cecilia's mother hesitated. She turned toward the old woman for guidance. The old woman nodded her head yes.

"How long would she need to stay with the children?" Cecilia's mother asked.

"Probably only for one night. Possibly two. I don't know for sure. I'll know exactly once I've spoken to the attorneys."

"Well . . . I guess it will be all right."

"Gracias, Mamá!" Cecilia cried, embracing her mother. "I'll take good care of the children!" She kissed her mother and grandmother on the cheek.

"I know you will, mija. You're a good girl."

Antonio smiled and his eyes sparkled.

"You see? You already *have* a union!" Cecilia's mother beamed with pride, and the old woman touched her handkerchief to her eyes.

And in the corner, on the black-and-white television set, the evangelist preacher raised his arms above his head and shouted, "Praise the Lord!"

15

It was afternoon and the traffic on Macy Street was maddening. Cars edged forward a yard at a time; commuters honked their horns, lost their tempers and nearly lost their minds as drivers blocked intersections in impulsive attempts to sneak through a traffic light, cut off another commuter and advance a car length.

On his way to Rosa's flat, Antonio sat in his Chevy and smoked, his window rolled down to circulate the air—though he probably would have been better off with the windows up. Cecilia, impervious to the obstacles facing adults, peered out at children still on their way home from school.

As Antonio waited for the streetlight to change, he gazed across the street. They were passing La Plaza del Centro—or, as the Anglos called it, Olvera Street. Tourists roamed the plaza, shopping for souvenirs amid concession stands hawking handmade leather belts and purses, embroidered cotton shirts and framed felt paintings.

Antonio turned to Cecilia. "Did you know this was the first settlement in Los Angeles?" he asked. She nodded shyly, then turned back to watch the schoolchildren.

Antonio gazed at La Placita, his eyes tracing the classical Spanish architecture of the buildings: the high archways, red tile roofs, thick whitewashed adobe walls and wrought-iron gates. Tourists lounged at tables set in patios, sipping margaritas and Mexican beer; they listened to mariachis playing in the courtyard, unable to decide whether to order chile rellenos, carne asada, or tostadas, their mouths watering as waiters whirled about from table to table with hot steaming plates, each one looking more appetizing than the last.

Antonio smiled as he remembered strolling down the same brick walkway with a lovely Chicana—a woman with almond-shaped eyes the color of honey. He remembered her hair; it was so black light could not escape it. In truth, there was nothing about her he could forget. Nothing.

Her skin was soft and brown and smooth, as though she had been created just moments before by a sculptor. And her lips— when she spoke, he could not help but watch her lips. And she would tease him, each word a dance, every breath black magic.

Zenaida. Antonio watched helplessly as she played with the string puppets that dangled from the low roofs of concession stands, their nailed-on eyes ogling like foolish old lechers. Then she led him along toward the next booth, a glass display case brimming with fresh Mexican bread, sugar and cinnamon sparkling beneath red and white heat lamps. She squeezed his hand and licked her lips and his body ached, overcome with hunger and thirst. And his loins felt the pull of the sun and the moon as they drew the tides.

Just beyond the concession stands, Antonio noticed an open door. Latinos were rushing about in a steamy kitchen, sweating and preparing dishes of Mexican food as though their lives depended upon it. As he watched them work, Zenaida turned to him and followed his eyes. Sighing, she asked, "Don't you ever think about *anything* but organizing?"

Antonio's eyes dropped from the kitchen to a row of tiny Mexican flags on sale beside the puppets. And as he considered her question, his thoughts drifted.

He imagined a place, a millennium before. In the dust of a thousand bare feet, dry and callused from an endless journey, a man dressed like the sun raised his hand and his people stopped in their tracks. The Aztec chief watched as a great eagle clutched a serpent in its talons. Extending its massive wings, with one movement the great eagle flew to the top of a giant cactus, one bearing nopal, a blood-red fruit that throbbed like a beating heart. As it ripped into the snake the eagle issued a triumphant cry. Moved by the sight, the prophet said, "Here. We stop here. This is where our journey ends."

Mexican flags flapped in the dusty light of Los Angeles, where everything looks like an overexposed photograph. Horns blasted and motorists shouted at Antonio as he sat spellbound where Macy Street becomes Sunset Boulevard. Reaching for another cigarette, Antonio turned to Cecilia: "Did you know this all used to be a part of México?"

"Oh, yes," she replied, nodding her head. "Once in school, they took us on a tour of La Placita. It was really fun! I have a picture at home of my classmates taken where they have the cart and the donkey. We were all wearing sombreros and ponchos—just like Mexicans."

Antonio was stunned. He stared at her for a moment in disbelief. Cecilia fiddled with her fingers and smiled, embarrassed by his gaze. And it dawned on him—she was only a child.

The traffic moved a few feet then came to an abrupt halt. Antonio watched a young woman help her peasant grandmother across the busy intersection, the old woman wrapping her shawl around her shoulders, bewildered by the constant movement, frightened by idling automobiles poised and ready to attack. Her granddaughter hurried her along, looking out for her safety, still not certain they belonged there.

Tar dripped from telephone poles and the afternoon smog settled against the earth. Antonio looked around and what he saw distressed him. There were gas stations and taco stands, paper wrappers and broken bottles, graffiti scribbled over graffiti. Gaunt old men in fishing caps collected trash, Vietnamese girls wore designer jeans and sneers, while cops moved about cautiously like soldiers after a military coup. And in the light and in the shadows were the others—winos sleeping at bus stops, cholos with eyes flashing, prostitutes callused by abuse, and nameless people begging for spare change. As Antonio watched from his vantage point where Macy Street becomes Sunset Boulevard, he witnessed what appeared to be an endless battle among a thousand warring factions. He paused for a moment and took a drag from his cigarette; his lungs felt as cold as ice. And Antonio hated the taste of his cigarette—it tasted like the city.

16

Rosa's oldest child, María, fried two eggs in a large cast-iron pan, while two eggs still in their shells sat upright nearby, waiting their turn. Standing on her toes to check the progress of the meal, María struggled to tilt the pan from side to side so hot grease would spill over the whites and cook them. On a burner nearby, she heated tortillas over an open flame.

While María made dinner, her brothers and sister sat on the wood floor in the living room and watched *Chapulin Colorado*, "The Red Grasshopper," starring a Mexican actor with a sad hobo-face.

El Chapulin declared, "Que no cunda el pánico! Don't panic!" He turned toward his audience, which at Rosa's flat was a little girl and two little boys playing with their feet. The children looked at each other, eyes sparkling, and they laughed at El Chapulin—they laughed until they forgot what they were laughing at. They attempted to focus their thoughts for a moment and set about to untangle their fingers from their toes. By the time they accomplished the task, the grasshopper was gazing at them again with his pitiful eyes.

"Me gusta mucho El Chapulin," Ramón said. "I love the grasshopper."

Smelling dinner, the children's expressions instantly changed. When they were hungry, the aroma of food made them sad, unless it came from a plate sitting directly in front of them. "Tenemos hambre!" they cried. "We are hungry!"

Antonio knocked on the door, but there was no answer. He could hear the television blaring and an audience laughing, and he heard the children as they cried "Tenemos hambre! Cuando vamos a comer?"

Despite all the distractions, María thought she heard something; she cocked her head and listened to the two eggs sitting upright on the stove to see if they were responsible for the faint knocking sound she heard.

After pounding on the door a second time without result, Antonio let himself into Rosa's flat. Cecilia paused politely at the doorstep.

"Buenas noches," Antonio called out as he held the door open for Cecilia.

María squinted her eyes as the grease in the pan popped, glancing up just long enough to return the greeting. "Hola, Señor Rodriguez. Oh, so it was *you*! Pues, mi Mamá no está. My mother isn't here." María quickly turned her attention back to the frying eggs.

"Yo sé," Antonio replied. "I know. Have you heard from her?"

"No." María answered matter-of-factly, as though there was nothing unusual about her mother's absence. With a large spatula, she lifted the eggs from the frying pan, taking great care not to break the yokes; her brothers complained when the yokes were not whole. "Usually she is home by five. I think maybe she had to work overtime tonight."

Antonio examined her eyes, trying to find the best way to explain what had happened. "María—this is Cecilia. She is a friend of your mother's and mine. She is going to stay here with you tonight."

María glanced up, still squinting, grasping the panhandle with both hands, trying to think about two things at once. The metamorphosis in her eyes was agonizing for Antonio, as her puzzlement faded and it dawned on her what Antonio was saying. Gripped by panic, María let go of the pan, which clanged on the burner, and cried, "Where's my Mamá?"

17

Workers from the Mersola Shoe Factory—prisoners of the Immigration and Naturalization Service were awakened early in the morning by government agents. They were ordered to use the toilets and to prepare to leave.

They arose slowly, their clothing musty and heavy from a night spent on the reeking mattresses. Their lack of urgency seemed to agitate the agents, who constantly glanced at their watches, working against a deadline.

The prisoners were given a hurried breakfast—a bitter cup of coffee and a "snak pak" of sugar-sweet cereal with milk. Then they were herded onto a bus and whisked away toward the Mexican border.

Once on the bus, the workers lost all hope of a miracle. They knew it was just a matter of time before they would be in Méxi-co, far from their families—dumped in Tijuana like refuse, with only the money they had in their pockets, forced to contact relatives still living in México, most of whom were poor and lived far away.

The majority of the workers could not afford to call their families in Los Angeles; to do so would mean spending money they would need to survive, or burdening their families with a collect call. And so they chose not to think about what awaited them in Tijuana. Instead, they leaned their heads on the seats directly in front of them, or on the shoulder of a neighbor. As they lay their heads down to sleep, they thought how much better a bad dream would be compared to what they were experiencing. What could be worse than being forcibly separated from one's family? What could be worse than to be led away in handcuffs, interrogated and imprisoned? There would be plenty of time to try to pick up the pieces of their lives in México, they thought. For now, it was better to sleep and to forget.

Javier was one of the few who did not leave a family behind in the United States. He was one of the few who was spared the thought of children going hungry. No one would need explain to anyone why *he* had not come home after work. And as he glanced around the bus at men and women separated from their loved ones, for the first time in many years he felt there was an advantage to being alone.

Javier watched the surf through the barred window of the bus and followed the flight of a pelican as it tucked in its wings and dove into the sea after a fish. He tensed all the muscles of his body and gritted his teeth until he forced out all the sadness from his heart. Then, in an effort to feel whole again, he playfully nudged the man beside him: "Hey, hombre! We'll be at the border before you can finish your dream!" But his neighbor ignored him and pushed his face back into the fold of his arm.

The air in the bus was warm and thick, an invisible pool of gases which lulled its victims to sleep. It was not long before the prisoners slipped beneath the surface and drowned. Soon, Javier also fell victim to the air. He leaned back in his seat and dozed off, seeking oblivion with the others. And as the prisoners slept, the bus driver received a call on his two-way radio.

"What? Do *what*? You've got to be kidding! What kind of shit is that? Jesus Christ! All right, if you say so. I just work here, for godsakes." At the next off-ramp, the bus exited, circled around beneath the highway and roared back up an on-ramp heading north.

The motion of the turn awakened Javier. He shook his head, blinked his eyes and gazed through the window. There were hills where the sea had been. For a moment, he was disoriented. He peered across the aisle through the window on the opposite side of the bus and saw the same stretch of beach they had passed just minutes before, where a pelican had plunged into the sea. Nudging the man beside him in the ribs, he said, "Hey! They must think this is a tour bus! They're giving us a *tour*, hombre!" Again, the man ignored him, agitated by the interruption. Javier laughed out loud; he knew something important was happening. "Oigan gente! Wake *up*! You're missing the sights!" he cried. "You paid good *money* for this tour, so you had better wake up!"

A few of the workers lifted their heads and glanced about, squinting their eyes in the sunlight, which splintered through the windows like long, sharp crystals.

Javier craned his neck and gripped the seat in front of him with both hands. Soon the bus passed Chula Vista, the location of the detention center. And it kept on going. Javier called to the driver, "Hey, mister! How come you gringos always say *Mexicans* are stupid? At least we know north from south! Don't you know Tijuana is in México?"

José and Rosa lifted their heads, awakened from a deep sleep. Many of the younger workers laughed as Javier's jokes began to make sense. "These guys from la migra—maybe they think we're a bunch of Canadians!" Javier cried. "They're taking us back to the Canadian border!"

The bus driver glared at Javier in his mirror, though he did not understand what he was saying.

Soon all the workers were awake and jabbering, wondering why they were going north. Maybe the union was able to do something! Maybe Antonio made good on his pledge! When the bus whisked past a sign that said "Oceanside," everyone broke into wild applause. Javier shouted to José, "Look! They're sending us back!"

José stood up and began a chant: "Gente sí! Migra no! Gente sí! Migra no!" Others joined in: "The people yes! La migra no!"

The bus rolled to a slow stop at the immigration checkpoint

in Oceanside, and the chanting died down. Two agents approached the bus, bewildered by what they saw.

Javier could not contain his joy. "Hey, migra! You had better arrest that driver! He's a coyote and we are all wetbacks!"

The workers laughed raucously, pointing their fingers at the agents with unfettered joy, issuing catcalls and Bronx cheers, venting emotions that had been restrained for years. The driver opened the door of the bus and climbed down to talk with the agents, who were gaping in disbelief. The officer in charge of the roadblock raced over to see what was happening, mortified by the sight of a busload of Mexicans going north.

"What the hell is going on?" he demanded of the driver.

"I've got orders to bring them back to L.A. Something about a court injunction."

"What!" the agent said.

Javier waved his arms over his head. "I surrender!" he cried. "Take me back to México!"

Flabbergasted, the officer rested his hands limply on his hips. "Hey, migra!" Javier shouted. "Don't believe what that bus driver says! He's a *coyote* and we're all *wetbacks*! We want to go back to México! It's too *cold* up here!"

There were gales of laughter from the workers, who quickly began chanting again, "Gente sí! Migra no!"

The officer in charge turned to the bus driver and asked, "What the hell is going *on*?"

18

The Los Angeles Press Club sat oddly out of place on Vermont Avenue, a busy thoroughfare that slices through the city like a concrete aqueduct. In the decades after the Club was built, mini-malls, liquor stores and fast-food restaurants grew up around it. Laundromats, gas stations and porn shops also found fertile ground there, much like the imported palm trees planted across L.A. by developers and the Chamber of Commerce.

Despite the decay that surrounded it, the Press Club managed to maintain the feel of a forgotten shrine. The building and its grounds exuded a near-stately grandeur, ivy-covered walls providing a sense of seclusion and respectability. Yet like many of the most hallowed institutions in Los Angeles, the Press Club's glamour was larger than life but also tawdry and nearly a complete farce; it was an icon to free speech and diversity in a city that historically had little tolerance for either.

Anyone could hold a press conference at the "Club," for a nominal fee. And everyone did, at one time or another. The trick was to get the press to attend. But that was the magic of Hollywood: Those who knew the secrets of publicity became famous, though their fame might be short-lived; those who did not wrote screenplays and worked part-time in bookstores and video shops.

Antonio arrived at the Press Club an hour before he was due. He knew the media would be there: the notion of undocumented workers petitioning the court for an injunction against the Immigration and Naturalization Service was something they simply could not ignore. But he was not so sure the story would make the evening news. If the injunction worked, then, well that *would* be a story. But it was all out of his hands now; it was all up to the attorneys. For the time being all he could do was wait.

The auditorium had the musty scent of fading drapes and aging movie stars. One could almost imagine Gloria Swanson parading down a wide staircase: *"All right, Mr. DeMille, I'm ready for my close-up."*

Yet that morning, an aluminum coffee urn drew the spotlight in the shadows of the otherwise empty building. Styrofoam cups were stacked neatly beside it, offerings for those who had attained celebrity and others determined to gain it.

Antonio helped himself to a cup of coffee and wandered outside, ambling through a solid oak portal that led to a patio, flower garden, and surrounding grounds, all as trim and well kept as a cemetery. As he wandered about, Antonio half-expected to see the gravestones of celebrities from another era, buried when Los Angeles still had streetcars and blue skies.

He gulped his coffee down, as was his custom, breathing in deeply then exhaling slowly, waiting with anticipation for an adrenaline-like rush to take hold. Antonio could feel his heart madly pump a torrent of blood throughout his body—millions of cells swarming up the back of his neck through arteries and capillaries, probing deep into his brain. But it was not a caffeine-high: there was no sense of elation or well-being; Antonio was overcome by what felt like a massive swarm of insects invading mind and body, mandibles gorging on everything in their path, a microscopic yet rapacious army on a frenzied march.

Antonio stumbled back, collapsing into a wooden lounge chair perched on the edge of the flower garden. Jesus, am I having a *stroke*? he thought. What the *hell*!

His mind fell back through a trail of memories all running together in a crazy blur: Endless meetings, night and day, linked by the frenzied consumption of coffee and fast-food, cigarettes and diet coke; mornings and evenings distributing flyers at factory gates, in parking lots, at store fronts, on street corners; the fast pitch on the telephone, the salesman-like knock on the doors of strangers; more meetings laced with struggle, tedium, hairsplitting, personal egos run amok, militant workers gone cold. He grit his teeth as he recollected personal insults, blustering debates, the blind-sided punch, the occasional brawl: There were victories, there were defeats, there were warm embraces, there were deranged threats. One thing was consistent through it all: As Antonio recollected the past few years of his life, he was always on the run, always in a mad rush to be somewhere other than where he was—fighting traffic, fighting time, pushing his body to the limits of endurance, working from crisis-to-crisis, from minute-to-minute, endless days and nights spent mimeographing leaflets, filing petitions, giving speeches and pep talks, all without a moment's rest, pushing and fighting with such intensity that even sleep was a chore.

Slowly he opened his eyes. A shadow slipped into the shade of an Evergreen Ash and a gentle breeze carried the soft lilting voice of a woman who asked, "¿Te recuerdas? Do you remember?" But there was nobody there.

Startled, Antonio reacted like a warrior, jumping to his feet, planting them firmly into the earth as he surveyed the grounds and the flower garden. But other than a dozen poinsettias bobbing in the breeze, all was still.

Just above the horizon an opaque morning moon rose silently, growing larger and larger in the nearly colorless sky. As Antonio watched the quivering moonscape, a rabbit took shape, panting and anxious, glancing at him for an instant with its timorous red eyes. Antonio could not believe what he saw. He rubbed his face with his fists and shook his head sharply before looking skyward again. A shrieking green cloud burst across the heavens, reaching out north and south, withdrawing into itself, stretching then contracting again like an enormous school of fish as ten thousand parrots babbled madly across the sky. Screaming bloody murder, the parrots then vanished as quickly as they appeared, swallowed by a red aura around the sun.

Again a woman's soft voice called to him, again in a whisper. This time she asked: "Antonio . . . *¿No me quieres? Do you not want me?*"

He stumbled like a punch-drunk boxer, collapsing again into the wooden lounge chair perched on the edge of the flower garden. Antonio released all the air in his lungs and for one moment he felt as though he was dead.

When he opened his eyes, a parade of hummingbirds darted across the sky. One of them, seeing Antonio, abruptly changed course, pausing directly in front of him, hovering in place, diaphanous wings like a halo of ten thousand swords whirling in the sun, a red heart throbbing on its chest. The hummingbird gazed deeply into his eyes, not moving its head as it danced and bathed in the full spectrum of the light, then vanishing, slipping away in the fractal space between one moment and the next.

A gigantic cloud appeared, emerging from a point of light, orange and black and white and orange, roiling, tumbling, as a rabble of Monarch butterflies dipped toward the earth then raced skyward, the cloud of butterflies rolling north, falling south, orange and black and white and orange, before they, too, vanished into the ether.

Then she appeared. Xochiquetzal, her raven hair braided with flowers and spices and stars, her body adorned with a thin cloak of feathers so light that she floated above the garden. Drums pounded and flutes played and the air grew hot and sultry. Xochiquetzal licked the tip of her finger and softly drew a line upon her thigh, her almond-shaped eyes and soft brown skin the color of honey. And as she gazed at Antonio, he could feel the pull of the sun and the moon and the stars on his loins.

"Pide, y recibirás," she sang to him. "Ask and you will receive." There was a crash like a fallen set of cymbals, and Antonio awoke. A television technician lumbered through the portal from the Press Club with his arms full of equipment. Unshaven and hung-over, the technician cursed as he struggled to pick up the camera light he had accidentally kicked. Straightening his baseball cap, long brown hair curled around ears pink with sunburn, he unceremoniously dumped an armful of cables he had wrapped around his shoulders as he struggled to pick the light up off the ground.

The anchorman for Channel 2 News swaggered toward an outdoor lectern like a movie star cowboy. In a booming baritone, he tilted his head back and laughed at the worker's efforts to straighten the lamp that would later highlight the cake makeup coating his face. Stepping around the worker, grasping a small clipboard like a lasso, he jutted his chin forward and asked, "Where in the hell *is* everyone?" The technician, standing behind the well-coiffed newsman, spotted Antonio. He pointed at the anchorman and, without a sound, mouthed the words "fucking asshole!" Antonio nodded his head in agreement. Suddenly aware of Antonio's presence, the newsman stretched his right arm out firmly, to bare his Rolex, then pretended to check the time; he made a notation on his clipboard and smiled smugly, confident Antonio would recognize him as a major celebrity from the Television Evening News.

Dumb ass, Antonio thought. And that instant he was back. *Who does he think he is?* The reporter turned toward him again, anxious to bathe in the glow of adulation. Instead he was met by Antonio's cold glare. The anchorman straightened up, did a little acting by pretending to check notes that were not there.

Be cool, Antonio thought: he might be the one doing the story—the fucking punk. Turning his attention to a gate where other technicians dragged in cameras and equipment for the press conference, Antonio spotted a familiar face in the crowd.

"Hey, Bato!" cried a young bearded Anglo in a three-piece

suit. It was Mike Logan, a lawyer.

"What's happening, Mike?"

"How ya been, bro'?" the attorney asked as he reached to shake Antonio's hand, his arm cocked at a right angle in a power-to-the-people handshake.

"Hey, man! We got the injunction!" the attorney said. "They stopped the bus at the border and it's on its way back as we speak!"

Antonio's face lit up and his eyes sparkled. "All *right*!" he said, shaking the attorney's hand with a little more force than the man was accustomed to.

Logan beamed as he glanced around the garden and the patio, proud of his announcement. "Yeah, I tried to reach you at the union office an hour ago." The smile faded from his face. "Hey, I'm sorry about the bad news. I guess you weren't surprised."

"What news?" Antonio asked.

"Have you been to the union hall today?"

"No, I haven't gone in yet. *What* bad news, man?"

Adjusting his tie, the lawyer explained: "Man, I tried to call you at the office this morning, but some secretary told me you don't work there anymore. I asked her, 'as of when?' and she said, 'as of this morning.' "

Antonio took a step back. "Jesus Christ. I *knew* he was going to do something. But I didn't realize he was going to act so fast."

The two of them watched as the TV crew set up their equipment. The attorney thrust his chest forward: "Look, man, don't take this shit lying down! This is your chance to expose that bastard for what he really is! You're gonna have all the media here, and, with this injunction, for sure you're gonna be on TV. Tell them what that sell-out Brady has done!"

Antonio squinted his eyes and stared at the attorney. "Did you mention anything about the press conference to the secretary at the union?"

"No, man. Why?"

"Are you sure?"

"Yeah, man, I'm sure. Why?"

Antonio stared off into the distance. "I've got a better idea. Brady doesn't know about the press conference, see, because I never told him about it. Anyway, it was called by the coalition, not by the union, so technically, I didn't need his approval. I'm just going to go ahead as if I didn't know I was fired and I'm still the organizer for the campaign. I'll commit the union to an all-out effort to win the election, and I'll give the union credit for the lawsuit. Yeah, that's it! The cabrón! He just wants to *kill* the campaign. Man is *he* in for a surprise."

Logan did not understand. "Hey, man, are you crazy? That asshole just fired you! And you're gonna give him credit for the lawsuit? What about us? Shit, Antonio. Don't you understand? He's not going to continue with the campaign!"

"Do you want to bet?" Antonio asked, grinning.

Logan shook his head in disbelief. "Man, you should *expose* that fucker!"

"Look, Mike. Check this out. I'll go on TV as the union organizer. No one has told me I'm fired, right? I'll talk about the tradition of the trade union movement organizing immigrant workers, then I'll fully commit the union to the drive. The election is just a couple of weeks away. No other union can come in now, and there's no *way* Brady can pull out after we've gone on TV like that."

The attorney still did not understand. He shook his head in disbelief. "Why do you think Brady wants to stop the drive and fire me?" Antonio asked. "If the union is voted in, there's four hundred votes against Brady in the next election. Combined with others in the Local, the workers can vote him out!" Antonio smiled as he watched Logan slowly come to understand his tactics.

"I just don't think it will work," the lawyer said, though with less confidence than before.

"It will work," Antonio winked.

The attorney could not hide his disappointment. As Logan shook his head and stroked his beard, Antonio noticed a beautiful young Asian reporter strolling through the gate. He *did* know her from the evening news. As she paused to check her notes, Antonio smiled. Without taking his eyes off her, he said, "You know, this might not be *all* bad."

19

Somewhere in México, Manuel and several other young refugees played a game of football soccer, hidden from the rest of the world by a grassy knoll and a line of shrubs that ran across the hillside forming a natural barricade. Down below their makeshift playing field sat a small train station, like an old broken toy, tossed aside and forgotten.

It was a very uncharacteristic game the young men played. Their ball was fashioned from socks, tied and bundled together. When a goal was scored, there were no hurrahs or victory shouts—only tired smiles and soft pats on the back.

The older refugees sat back and rested on the cool grass, watching the game with apprehension. They wanted to enjoy the afternoon sun, the cool grass, and the spectacle of sport—but they could not.

Peligro—the coyote boss—scowled, checked his watch, and peered over the shrubs that hid the refugees from the station below. He had grudgingly given his approval to the game while issuing strict conditions. But his reasons for permitting the contest were far from benevolent: the coyote wanted to know which men had the most stamina. Such knowledge would figure prominently in his plans.

Señora Chavez sat beside Ana and watched the young men as they played, unaware of the coyote's preoccupation. As far as she was concerned, any opportunity to rest was welcome.

"Do you have a family in the United States?" she asked Ana.

"My cousin lives there," Ana replied as she watched the coyote pace back and forth anxiously.

"Oh, that's good. Is she working?"

"Yes, she is."

The old woman rubbed her tired feet. "Can she get you a job?"

"Well, I hope so." Ana began to poke at the grass, uncomfortable with the old woman's questions. *Something is going to happen,* she thought. Something is going to happen *soon.* I can tell by the way he's pacing back and forth.

"How long are you going to stay?" the old woman asked.

"Oh, I don't know. Maybe just two years—I don't know."

"Ah, that's good," the old woman said. "My son sent for me. He's been there for two years, working and sending me money. When my man died, he decided to bring me up to live with him and his wife, to help take care of his little girl." She smiled at the thought. "He's a good boy."

Ana glanced at the old woman whose obvious affection for her son made Ana forget about the coyote for a moment. It touched her to see Señora Chavez smile with a mother's love, and it made her realize how far away from home she was.

"Does your husband work in the United States?" the old woman asked.

"I'm not married," Ana said, her eyes dropping to the ground. "We never got married. We were *going* to, but . . ."

"Ah, niña. I know. The men in El Salvador—they don't like to get married. We're a nation of bastards."

Ana dug her fingers into the grass, and the old woman coughed violently, a spasm that shook her entire body. As the old woman gasped and clutched her chest, Ana's expression began to change; the color washed from her face and her features began to melt.

Finally, the old woman brought her coughing spasms under control. "I'm sorry, niña. I was only joking. I didn't mean to upset you."

But Ana had already slipped away. She wiped the tears from

her eyes, inadvertently smearing dirt on her cheek, which the old woman quickly wiped clean with a bandana.

"I'm sorry, niña. Truly."

Ana shook her head, unable to speak. Her breathing became labored, and she began to rock forward and backward rhythmically, covering her eyes with her hands.

"Qué pasa?" the old woman asked. "What's wrong?"

Ana gasped for air and waved her arms about to signal she needed space; then she collapsed, sobbing uncontrollably as she lay on her back in the cool grass. Fearing she was suffering from convulsions, the old woman cried for help. "Manuel! Venga aquí! Apurese! Hurry!"

Peligro raced to the old woman's side. "Shut up, woman! Do you want to get us all caught?" he said between his teeth, eyes and cheeks twitching.

Manuel ran to Ana and crouched at her side.

"She's sick!" the old woman cried. "There's something terribly wrong with her! Oh, God! I think she is going to die!"

"I said shut up, woman!" the coyote ordered, pausing to peer over the bushes, making certain there was no one nearby who might have heard the old woman's cries.

"What happened?" Manuel whispered, gently stroking Ana's forehead.

"I don't know. We were talking, and then suddenly she started to cry and get like this. Hay Dios miyo! This is all my fault!"

"No, señora. Don't worry," Manuel said. "You are not to blame. This happens sometimes when she is upset. We just need to rub some water on her forehead and let her rest for a while. She'll be better soon."

Glancing at his watch, Peligro warned, "We'll be leaving very soon. If she is not better when it is time, she will be left behind."

Manuel glared at the coyote with an intensity that startled the old woman. She had not seen that side of him before, and hoped secretly she would never witness it again. Things were difficult enough without Manuel and the coyote fighting it out to the death. And that is what would happen—someone would die.

But Manuel let it go, and focused his attention on Ana, stroking her scalp and sponging her forehead with water.

"I'm sorry, niña. I didn't mean to upset you," the old woman said, more anxious than ever to set things straight. "I'm sure your man is a *good* man. I was never married, either."

Manuel glanced up into the old woman's eyes, understanding what had happened. "She'll be all right. Don't worry."

The coyote paced back and forth, angered by the disruption. He consulted his watch and peered through the brush at the train station below. The old stationmaster hobbled out from his office to look for a sign of the train. The old man checked his watch, and the coyote his. "Yá es la hora," the old man said. "Now is the time."

The coyote told the refugees, "Yá es la hora."

Ana began to recover. She could see again and watched a cloud slide across the blue sky.

"Do you want a cup of water?" Manuel asked. She nodded her head yes.

"Don't drink too much!" the coyote barked. "That's all the water we have left until the train stops again."

Ana pushed herself up on her elbows, and Manuel and the old woman helped her sit up. She took a sip of water, conscious of the coyote's warning. In the distance, a whistle blew. An old steam engine painted bright red grunted as it towed a long line of freight.

"All right, everybody! Come here!" the coyote ordered. "When I tell you, I want you all to run down to the far side of that station. Quickly, so no one will notice you. Stay there until I give the word. Then, follow me. Do *exactly* as I do. We are going to be catching the train. Do you understand?"

The refugees nodded their heads.

"If you cannot run or keep up, it is best if you remain behind so the others will not get caught," he said, staring directly at Ana.

"I can make it," Ana said. Peligro sneered.

With its iron wheels screeching and steam hissing, the old steam engine slowly rolled to a stop. The frail stationmaster lumbered over to the engine and handed the brakeman a mailbag while they exchanged greetings. As the stationmaster's back was turned, the coyote cried "Yá!" and bounded down the hill out of view of the train. The refugees followed close behind.

They huddled together on the south side of the station, Ana and the old woman slipping out of sight just as the stationmaster turned and began the long trek back to his office.

"As soon as the train begins to move, follow me!" the coyote ordered, spitting the words out between his teeth.

"What about the old man?"

"Don't worry about him. He'll be asleep in a minute. Just do what I say!"

There was a blast of steam from the engine. Sputtering, it slowly lurched forward, groaning under the weight of its cargo. The coyote gave the signal and raced toward a freight car, built like an open wooden shoebox. The refugees followed, scaling the walls of the car and leaping into its bed, laden with steel bars and trash.

"Get down!" Peligro ordered, and the refugees fell down on the hot steel bars.

The train gradually picked up speed, racing past wood shacks and plots of beans and corn. When Peligro peered over the side of the freight car and signaled all was clear, the refugees breathed a sigh of relief. They took turns sharing what remained of their meager water supply, taking care not to spill a drop.

As the afternoon wore on, the steady click-clack of the train rocked many of the refugees to sleep, though there was little comfort to be found on a bed of steel bars stoked by the sun. When it became clear that their journey on the train would be a long one, men made their way to the back of the freight car to urinate. The women bore their discomfort for as long as they could. But soon they, too, made the trip, going in groups of three or more, forming a half-circle to provide them some privacy. Señora Chavez suffered the most under the circumstances, feeling a loss of dignity urinating in public—especially in the presence of men. Compelled to preserve some measure of pride, she used a discarded coffee can to collect her urine, eliminating any evidence of her humiliation by discreetly dumping her waste over the edge of the car.

Hours passed, and the sun began to drop, the walls of the freight car finally providing shelter against its glare. The coyote checked his watch and attempted to calculate their whereabouts. He spotted a familiar landmark and gestured to Manuel and another young man to come to him. "We're going to be stopping soon, but just for a few minutes. We'll have to get some more water. Listen! There's a pipe and a faucet next to an old building and a water tower. I'll point them out to you. You two are the most athletic, so I want you to get us some water. You won't have much time—just a couple of minutes. Get the water bottle and whatever other containers you can find—and move fast! We'll be there soon!"

Manuel and the other young man did as they were told, then waited for the coyote's instructions.

"Okay," the coyote said, pointing his finger at a barely perceptible object in the distance. "We're going to stop there. When the train slows, jump down and get as much water as you can— bien rápido! Fast! Watch for my signal to return!"

The young men strained their eyes as a building and water tower took form, growing in size every moment. The train slowed just as Peligro had said it would, and before it came to a complete stop, they leaped over the side, flying forward with momentum, stumbling about, searching for the containers dropped in their haste. The coyote was furious. He pointed at the faucet, his arm trembling, his face stretched by G-force, strychnine rushing through his veins.

Before the young men had completed their mission, a gush of steam blasted from the engine and the coyote gestured for them to return. They ran toward the freight car, juggling the cans and bottles they carried, precious amounts of water splashing out as they attempted to scale the rusty rungs bolted to the side of the car.

"Pass the water up first, pendejos!" the coyote cried. And as they paused to lift the containers over their heads, the train jerked forward, throwing Manuel to the ground. Ana watched in horror as he tumbled head over heels, the freight train rolling forward, struggling to pick up steam. Manuel leaped to his feet and made chase, coming within inches of getting a hand on a metal rung of the rumbling freight car, only to slip on the loose pebbles upon which the train tracks lay. The coyote viewed Manuel's struggle with unrestrained delight. He rested against splintered walls with his arms folded, smiling as the train pulled farther and farther away.

The train approached a blind bend, leaning into the turn. A buck crossing the track glanced up at the red steam engine. The engineer instinctively engaged the brakes—an act of mercy for Manuel, though one made too late to benefit the animal. Peasants working nearby stopped what they were doing and smiled at their good fortune. The delay was all the time Manuel needed to catch up with the freight car, seize the bottom rung of a ladder and climb safely aboard with the others. Ana embraced him and kissed him on the cheek. "Oh, I was so scared! I thought you were going to be left behind!"

"Yo tambien, mujer! I thought so, too! But here I am, thanks to God!"

The engineer reengaged the old steam engine, neatly butchering the buck for the grateful peasants who would find plenty of salvageable meat from the kill. They, too, believed God was smiling upon them.

The coyote brushed aside the entire incident with a wave of his hand. He demanded a can of fresh water, eager to quench a thirst not satisfied by the chain of events, despite the bloodletting.

"No! You shouldn't drink that!" Señora Chavez cried, waving her finger in the air like a grandmother.

"Está *bien*,vieja!" the coyote answered.

"No!" she insisted. "It's dirty!"

The coyote examined the contents of the can. "It's fine, vieja! It's just a little rusty! If you don't like it, then you don't have to drink it!" He tilted the can back and took a long, cool drink.

"But . . . I *peed* in that can!" the old woman confessed with great embarrassment. Immediately the coyote spat out the water from his mouth, coughing and choking as though he had been poisoned. The refugees laughed, delighted by the spectacle of the coyote suffering from his own arrogance. Only the old woman was troubled by what had transpired, her pride diminished by her revelation.

The train sped ahead, and slowly the laughter died down. The coyote tossed the can of water over the side of the freight car and gestured for the water that remained. With great scorn, he washed his face and hands, then drank. As twilight's shadows flipped past the refugees, and as the steady rhythm of track and train rolled along beneath them, the refugees waited patiently for their turn at the water, hoping that when it came there would be enough for them to have a sip and relieve their parched throats and chapped lips.

20

Amerio Mersola sat back in the easy chair in his den. Scowling, he peered around the room, trying to think of something he could do to pass the time. He stood up and strolled over to his library, half-consciously examining the titles of books displayed like war medals on rosewood shelves. Many were from his college days—textbooks on business and management—large, hardbound studies that he had never found to be too practical. Amerio Mersola believed such works danced around the real principles of business and management. Nevertheless, they looked impressive enough, displayed as they were, suggesting the decorum one might expect from a library at a prestigious university.

What stood out most in Mersola's den was the leather-bound *Library of Knowledge*, an engraved collection of the classical works of Western civilization. One day, when retired, Amerio Mersola planned to read all the books that were displayed there. He planned to retire to his den at night and immerse himself in the great works of the masters. Then he would read them *all*. But for the time being, there were more important things on his mind. And so he thumped his fingers against the bindings of the books, content with the knowledge that he had many of the greatest works ever written at his fingertips.

The phone rang, and Mersola rushed from the den into the kitchen where his wife was busy preparing dinner.

"Answer it!" he barked. "And remember—if it's the press, I'm not here! And I have no comment!"

Mary nervously wiped her hands clean, and as she did,

throughout the house, four phones rang simultaneously, including the one in the den.

"Hurry up!" Mersola said, unable to stand still.

Mary tossed aside her towel and picked up the telephone, though she would have preferred to wash her hands first. It was the press again. And once again, as she had done all day, she sweetly explained that her husband wasn't home, though not without suffering pangs of guilt; she was, after all, a devout Catholic, even if her husband was not. But she believed in standing by her man, even if it meant being less than honest now and then. Anyway, God would forgive her for telling a lie. But Amerio would never forgive her for telling the truth.

"I'm sorry, but my husband isn't home, and he has no comment," Mary said, doing her best not to let on how much she enjoyed the attention she was receiving. As her husband continued to issue orders, Mary plugged one ear with her index finger and listened intently as a reporter asked another question. Her eyes rolled back and forth like a cat clock.

"Just hang up!" Mersola insisted.

"I'm really very sorry, but my husband isn't home right now," Mary said, pulling on the receiver as if it were stuck to her head.

"Mary, just *hang up!*"

"I'm terribly sorry but . . ."

Mersola leaped across the room and quickly terminated the conversation, dispatching the reporter with a dial tone, his finger pressing against the white plastic disconnect button with such force one might have thought it was a pressure point in a wrestling match. With the dial tone, Mary was freed from the uncomfortable dilemma of having to lie to a reporter whose voice she recognized as that of a major television celebrity.

"Who was it this time?" Mersola asked.

"It was NBC News. They said they've been trying to reach you all day, but..."

"Shit!" Mersola turned his back on his wife and stormed out of the kitchen back to the sanctity of his den. He poured himself a shot of blended whiskey and opened a box of hand-rolled Cuban cigars, a gift from one of his foremen. Puffing away on the contraband, Mersola paced back and forth in his red-stockinged feet, pausing for a moment before a large relief map of California. He traced the Mexican border until he found Tijuana. "Jesus Christ! How the hell did it happen?" he wondered aloud. They were almost there! Shit! Must have been a bunch of *communists* behind it, he thought as he chewed on his cigar.

Amerio Mersola contemplated the miserable state of affairs that existed for hard-working businessmen such as himself. How could he be outmaneuvered by a bunch of illegal aliens and radicals? The country is going down the toilet! he concluded, his jaw set.

He glanced up at an antique clock that read four minutes to six. Chomping on his cigar, Mersola grabbed a remote control device and pushed one button, then another. Finally, a picture appeared on the TV screen, and he settled back into his favorite chair. It was three minutes to six.

"This goddamn thing!" he growled as he attempted to turn up the volume without success.

In three minutes the news would be on, and Amerio Mersola would see what he'd been dreading all day. Maybe I've been worrying for nothing, he thought. Maybe a celebrity has been murdered and they'll show clips from his most popular films. That would be *good*—as long as it isn't Bob Hope! Mersola poured himself another shot of blended whiskey and swirled it around in his glass, inhaling the fragrance with great satisfaction. Maybe all those phone calls were from cub reporters getting their feet wet. After all, who gives a rat's ass about a bunch of wetbacks?

Mersola pushed a host of different buttons without success, enjoying the challenge as he began to feel the effects of his drink.

Mersola tried numbers for which there were no stations. He accidentally increased the volume from mute to heavy metal. Soon he began to grow angry at the television and the remote control—so angry he gave them both a verbal warning: "You better work the way I *want* you to work or you're scrap metal! Goddamn it! Fourteen hundred dollars for a television and I can't even get the damn six o'clock news! I should have known better than to buy something made in Japan! Son of a bitch!"

Finally he found a station with the news. It was six o'clock exactly. Mersola sat on the edge of his chair as reporters joked among themselves, adding a little fluff to endless disasters. Mersola's heart beat faster and faster as he watched a torrent of homeless people, explosions, bloody bodies and burned buildings whirl past like a newsreel by prophets of the apocalypse. Commercials provided the only relief, a shot of morphine to numb the pain.

At 6:20, Mersola began to relax. Nothin'! he thought. Everything is all right. They're not going to show nothin'! Hah!

He paused to relight his cigar, then settled back in his chair and watched another commercial. Jane Fonda, outfitted in tiger-striped leotards, did deep knee-bends, smiling at the camera as she bent over suggestively. "You owe it to yourself to feel *good*," she cooed as a phone number appeared beneath her.

As the commercial faded away, a lovely Asian reporter appeared on the screen and with stark professionalism announced, "A hundred undocumented workers, all employees of the Mersola Shoe Factory, decided to take a bus ride back to Los Angeles from the Mexican border early this morning after a court injunction prevented them from being deported."

"Son of a bitch!" Mersola cried, leaping to his feet. He leaned toward the television set breathing heavily as though he had been doing aerobics. Antonio appeared on screen, a Lutheran pastor at his side. Reporters in the audience took notes.

"The raid by the immigration service clearly was a union-busting tactic," Antonio declared.

"You goddamn *pachuco!*"

"The trade union movement has a long history of organizing immigrant workers, going clear back to the days when workers from Ireland, Eastern Europe, Germany, and other European countries first came to the United States," Antonio continued.

Mersola could stand no more. In a fit of frustration, he smashed the buttons of the remote control device, and the television picture vanished in a blaze of color.

"So the union *was* behind the injunction! That bastard *lied* to me! God *damn* it! What's this world coming to? A union of wetbacks!" Mersola paced the floor and gesticulated like a madman. He issued condemnations of every institution that came to mind, with the exception of the Roman Catholic Church and the sacrament of marriage. He continued his harangue until he noticed his father peeking around the corner of the doorway, smiling impishly.

"Well? What the hell do *you* want?"

The old man's head disappeared from sight. Amerio Mersola stared at the space vacated by his father and listened as the old man pranced down the hallway, rubbing his hands together and snickering with delight.

"Senile old man . . . that's all I need!"

Mersola immediately resumed his pattern, pacing the floor, shaking his head back and forth and wondering how such a thing could happen in America. There must be something I can do, he reassured himself. *Something.* There *must* be. He scanned his thoughts and reconsidered his plans, not stopping at any particular juncture to examine what might have gone wrong, but searching instead for something he was certain he had in reserve—an idea that he had overlooked or an obscure law that had not been properly applied. In the back of his mind, he knew there was an answer: there always *was.* Always. After all, that was what made America great.

There were tiny explosions in his mind—flashes of light and strange designs, patterns in the inner eye. He pictured a dinner table, lasagna and a bottle of cabernet; he saw his daughters-in-law, picking at their food, saw smokeless candles and the Mediterranean Sea. Then he heard a voice—it was his older son. "Don't you think it's time you called that legal firm I told you about? They get *results*."

Amerio Mersola smiled. He picked up the phone and dialed a number he knew as well as his own. As the phone rang, his eyes zeroed in on the engraved letters of a leather-bound book that sat apart from the others on the rosewood shelves. Best business manual ever written, he thought, reaching for the fourteenth-century work. And a Western classic.

21

The offices of the Shoeworkers Union were busy that afternoon. Phones rang, clerks typed names on form letters, and an endless stream of people flowed back and forth from the coffee machine. Young men in three-piece suits, the local's organizers, flirted with young secretaries, boasting and strutting about.

Then Antonio burst through the front door. Immediately the atmosphere changed. A wave of expectation rippled across the complex, bringing an abrupt end to all conversations; even the office equipment seemed silenced by his sudden appearance.

As Antonio made his way though the maze of work stations, the initial shock of his arrival subsided. Everyone knew he had been fired, though the matter was supposed to be a well-guarded secret. So organizers and office workers alike did their best to conceal their apprehension; they tried to maintain a veneer of normalcy, chatting nonchalantly, nodding at Antonio as he passed. But all conversations focused on one topic: The Confrontation. Many people predicted trouble—possibly even violence, given the temperaments of the two men involved. A clash was inevitable, the office workers agreed, and it was just a matter of time before all hell would break loose.

Antonio calmly climbed the stairs of the open, split-level office building. With peripheral street vision, he saw featureless faces following his steps, fingers pointing, heads shaking. As he approached Brady's secretary, he reached into his pocket for a cigarette. "I want to talk to Don," he announced, turning toward the offices below. Heads cocked back into place.

The secretary nervously picked up her phone, pushed Brady's

extension and dialed. "Don, Antonio's here." She dropped the receiver gently into its bracket and, without looking up, said, "You can go on in. He's expecting you."

There was an anxious stirring in the gallery below. Like spectators at ringside, people seemed unable to stay in their seats.

As Antonio turned to close the door behind him, the secretary glanced into his eyes. She knew nothing of street fighting—all the signs and displays, the posturing and subtle moves involved (she was hand-picked by Brady for her job because of her ignorance of such things). Despite that, when she saw Antonio's eyes, she knew instantly that teeth would shatter and blood would flow.

When Antonio entered his office, Brady calmly lit a pipe. He knew what to expect. "Hello, Tony. Won't you sit down?"

Antonio said nothing.

Brady reached across his desk and turned on a radio—a precaution in case there was an effort made to tape-record their conversation. As he leaned back in his plush leather chair, Brady's eyes finally met Antonio's.

"You're pretty damn smart—I'll say that much for you." Antonio's eyelids narrowed.

"I watched your press conference. There's only one little problem, as I'm sure you know by now. You are no longer a spokesman for this union." Antonio took a long drag from his cigarette and blew a long column of smoke across Brady's desk. Brady smiled faintly, amused by the taunt. "You shouldn't have called those lawyers, Tony. I warned you about doing that. You left me no choice."

Cóme mierda, cabrón. Eat shit! Antonio thought as he took another drag from his cigarette. I could cut you up so bad you'd look like an artichoke! Thugs or no thugs—it would be *worth* it! Go ahead and *send* your henchmen to shoot out my windows again! I don't give a damn! I know how to shoot, too, motherfucker!

The radio blared an advertisement for Disneyland. Both men smoked silently and glared at each other.

Cool it, man, Antonio thought. No hombre. You could do it. But what about la gente? What about the union drive? You can *still* get his slimy ass, carnal! The people can vote the bastard *out*, man!

With a voice as cold as the joint, Antonio said, "What about the campaign?"

Brady puffed on his pipe. "Well, I just don't know, Tony. I just don't know. The local's wasted a hell of a lot of money already, thanks to you. I don't believe our membership will go along with spending more."

Antonio tilted his head back and jutted out his chin. "Well, I guess I'll have to go to the federation."

Brady leaned forward, accepting the challenge. Fucking greaser! he thought. I'd like to wrap a chain around your neck!

"The fed won't be happy to find out what's been going on around here, Don. They might even start auditing your books."

"Don't threaten me, Tony. You're smarter than that. Nobody's going to listen to some wet-behind-the-ears organizer who hangs around a bunch of radical lawyers and pressures the fed to do things. Besides, I've got no intention of pulling out of this campaign. So your little trick worked. But let me tell you something. You're out of the picture from here on in. You went over my head, used the union's name and resources without permission. And there's no one in *any* union who's gonna back you up for doing that!"

Antonio arched his eyebrows and smiled. His aloofness infuriated Brady.

"I'm warning you, Tony. Stay away from Mersola's. You're no longer under any jurisdiction to organize there or anywhere *else* in this local. And if you try to stick your nose into things, we'll *sue* you. And I will personally make sure that you'll never work for any union again. Do you understand?"

Antonio heard what Brady said. His tactics had borne fruit. But still, deep down, he felt he had been humiliated. Instinct told him to kick Brady's ass; to do anything less would mean Brady got the best of him. Nobody would ever accept that in his neighborhood. Still, there were other considerations. Other things were happening. So he smashed his cigarette out, shook his head in disgust and headed for the door.

"Don't you walk out on me again, you bastard!" Antonio opened the door, and Brady chased after him. On the floor below, everyone stopped what they were doing and watched.

"I mean it!" Brady said, stepping out into Antonio's path. "Don't show your face at Mersola's before, during, or *after* the election! Do you understand? Think about it, now. What good are you going to do all of your 'people' if you're blacklisted from every union on the West Coast?"

Antonio knew exactly where he would hit him and he knew where Brady would fall. He took half a step back and clenched his fists. He was not playing. Brady was a dead man. Blood raced through his body and his arms and shoulders swelled. There was a gasp from the gallery below and Brady flinched. But it was Antonio who backed down. *Blacklisted! From every union on the West Coast!*

There was a sigh of relief from below—a demonstration tempered somewhat by groans of disappointment uttered by a handful of union members who had come to the hall to file grievances. One union man shouted, "*Hit* the motherfucker!" But it didn't happen. And to everyone's surprise, Antonio turned and walked away.

22

José's wife, Doña Bertha, leaned back from the smoking barbecue pit and the sizzling thin strips of carne asada. With a long pronged fork and a quick snap of her wrist, she snatched charbroiled fillets and wrapped them in aluminum foil, replacing them on the grill with pieces of marinated beef like a blackjack dealer in Vegas. Charcoal hissed and spat as juices dripped into the hungry fire. Children surrounded the barbecue in eager anticipation, their arms limp at their sides, their mouths watering.

"No *creo* que tienen hambre," Bertha said, taunting them. "I don't *think* you are hungry."

"Si, Abuelita! Tenemos una *gran* hambre! Yes, Grandma! We are *very* hungry!"

José, Javier, and Antonio stood around sipping cans of soda while Sonia and the other women set the table with bowls of guacamole, home-made salsa and fresh-grilled tortillas. All around them, an autumn breeze raced about playfully, brushing through sycamore trees, carrying frisbees and voices and the aroma of hot dogs and hamburgers, shish kebabs and teriyaki.

Javier could not stop smiling. "It was beautiful!" he said as he slapped his thigh. "You should have *seen* the face of la migra when we were stopped in Oceanside! He looked like he was standing there *naked*! And the bosses. Híjole! When we went back to work, they didn't know what to do. Carnal—I'm telling you—the union is going to win by a landslide now!"

Antonio managed a faint smile.

"Ah, Antonio, Antonio," José said fondly. "We did it . . . we really did it." José glanced across the park at a carousel as it spun and flashed, bells ringing and a pipe organ flooding the air with military marches and melodies from another era. His grandchildren approached him and begged for money so they could ride the merry-go-round. José reached deep into his pocket and handed them each a dollar bill. As they raced off toward the music and the clanging and the bells, José turned toward Antonio and smiled. "All day yesterday, people at work kept stopping me and asking about the union. They wanted to know how to join."

José gazed at Antonio the way a proud father admires his son. Antonio did not know what to do; he rocked back and forth and rubbed his neck with his hand.

Doña Bertha signaled that the food was ready, providing a momentary distraction quickly seized by Antonio. He took a seat at the picnic table, soon joined by the other men, who waited to be served like children. Sonia and Cecilia brought them paper plates, stacked with carne asada, homemade beans, and hot roasted tortillas wrapped in aluminum to keep them warm.

"Aren't you going to eat?" Antonio asked the women.

"Do you think I got this way by starving?" Sonia replied, smiling as she slapped her broad thighs.

The men chuckled. "That's something to hold on to!" Javier said.

"And with me, you've really got to hold on!" Sonia declared, her eyes sparkling with mischief as both men and women laughed.

José and Javier made themselves tacos and quickly set upon them with enthusiasm. Antonio showed more restraint, conscious of the unfair division of labor. Yet his primary concern was how to go about breaking the news he brought.

"Antonio, would you like another soda?" Sonia asked, pausing with her hands on her hips.

"No, gracias. But Sonia . . . I can't stay long and I want to talk to all of you before I leave. Couldn't you join us? It is important what I have to say."

"What's wrong?" Javier asked, dropping his taco on his plate. "Nothing, really. It's nothing to worry about. But there have been some unexpected developments."

Javier did not like the way Antonio phrased his answer.

Sonia sat down, making room at the picnic by bumping her wide hips east then west, bouncing Javier and Antonio out of her way.

Antonio leaned back from his plate. "Look, I have to be honest—what I'm going to tell you isn't good news. But it isn't as bad as it might sound, either. It shouldn't really affect the campaign. But it's going to mean you are all going to have to work harder than ever before."

"Well . . . what is it?" Sonia asked, biting her nails.

"Pues—you all know I've been fighting Brady, the union president, for over a year now. Ever since I first became an organizer with this local. Brady never really wanted to organize at Mersola."

Though all three of them had sensed as much, it was the first time their feelings had ever been confirmed by Antonio.

"Why not?" José asked.

"He didn't want to spend the money, for one thing. And the federation has a public position against organizing undocumented workers."

It was suddenly very quiet at the table; the only sounds were the voices of children playing on the grassy fields, and, in the distance, an antique pipe organ playing *Semper Fidelis*. "See, he is also afraid that I will run against him for president in the next election—and that the people at Mersola could make the difference and vote me in."

"Right! That's a good idea!" José said, hoping there was nothing more to it than that.

147

"Pues . . . well . . . he fired me yesterday."

"What!" Javier exclaimed. "Then all we have done was for nothing!" Sonia and José were speechless. They held their chins in their palms and stared off into the distance.

"No, hombre, it wasn't for nothing. You can still win the election! You can make a union! The only thing that has changed is that I won't be able to help you. But you can still win! You are all experienced organizers now, and you can do it yourselves!"

"But why, Antonio?" Javier asked. "Why did they do it? The union must be with the company."

"The union is the *people*, hombre! It's not Brady or me. Es la gente. And the success you've had so far is because of what *you've* done—not some big shots in the union."

Javier could not accept what Antonio said. He wrung his hands and pulled at his hair, his expression revealing the sentiments of the others, who did their best to hide their disappointment. "Chingados! The fucking union sold us out!"

José finally came to his senses. "Antonio—even if we won the election, what good would it do to be in the union as long as Brady is president? He doesn't want us. You said yourself even the federation doesn't want us."

"Mira," Antonio said as he stood up and shifted from one foot to the other. "You can vote him out once you're organized. It took the farmworkers thirty years to build a union, and they're still struggling today. I don't know if we'll ever see the day when the people will be able to sit back and relax. I don't know if we'll ever *really* win. But one thing I do know—if we don't fight and if we don't try to win, then *definitely* we'll never change anything." Antonio gained momentum as he spoke, finding his rhythm, catching his wind. Still, they were not convinced. They watched him and listened; they *wanted* to believe him. They wanted to, but there was something missing.

"There's nothing magical about a union," Antonio continued, sensing he had not hit the mark. "Even if you win, even if I was still the organizer, your problems would not go away. Things should get better. But they could stay the same, too. The key thing is *organization*."

José began to understand. He nodded his head. But Javier was confused. "First you try to get us to organize a union, now you say it won't solve our problems or make things better. Which is it? I don't know what to think anymore."

"Mira," Antonio said, pointing his cigarette at Javier. "Let's say the union wins, okay? Then the company decides to fire you and the others who were active in the campaign. What can you do? If you have a union, but no organization, you can file a grievance. In other words, you fill out some papers and ask for a hearing with the company. At the hearing, they rule against you. At least, they almost always do. So you're out of a job. With the union and no organization, you can appeal the decision. If they rule against you at the appeal, then you can appeal again. That's what they call arbitration. They bring in the lawyers and the big shots. That will take you six months or more, depending upon your union officials. Now, what are you going to do when you're out of work for six months?"

"Púchica!" Sonia answered. "Find another job!"

"Eso! You can't afford to sit around and wait to get your job back. That's if you *can* get it back. Listen. It's important to have a grievance procedure. I'm not saying it is not good. But it's more important to have organization! Okay, let's say the three of you all get fired. If the people are organized and together, *then* what can you do? Everyone just stops working! You shut the whole damned place down until management agrees to put you back on the job! See? There's no production—people just standing at their machines until there is action. Or everyone walks out. *That's* where your real power lies. But you can't do it without organization. That's what is wrong with many of the unions today. And shit, if you have organization *and* the union, there's nothing you can't do. If management knows you're organized, they won't mess with you. Or at least they'll be more subtle. You can get a contract and negotiate what you want— make them agree to things on paper. And then, if they break their agreement, you shut the bastards down!"

"Híjole!" Javier said, wiping his forehead with the back of his hand. "Remind me not to ask you any more questions!"

Sonia stared at Javier as if to say, Please, little brother! Now is not the time. Then she turned to Antonio. "But how? How do we do it?" she asked.

"You've already *done* it! At least you've got a good start. Look—you have a general meeting scheduled next week. How many people do you think you can get to come?"

"Well," Sonia replied, counting out loud. "Maybe fifteen."

"And you, José?"

"Twenty or twenty-five," he answered firmly.

"Javier?"

"Bueno. Let's see. There is my roommate and me—that makes two!" José and Sonia could not help but laugh. Antonio rolled his eyes, a clock ticking in his mind, every moment important. But he was brought back to earth by Javier's foolish grin.

"Okay, seriously, Antonio. You want me to be serious, right?" Javier continued. "You want me to bring people to a meeting of a union that doesn't want us. Okay. I can bring fifteen—I think." He couldn't help but grin. The whole thing seemed ludicrous to him.

Antonio turned to Sonia. "Why don't you ask Rosa to come?"

"Vaya, pues, if you say so. But I don't think she will."

"I think maybe she will surprise you," Antonio said, smiling so mysteriously he tripped Sonia's female intuition. "You see? Between the three of you, you've got close to fifty people. Fifty-one, counting Javier's roommate. Those fifty probably know another hundred. See what I mean? Once they see that the union is something good for the people, you'll be able to build your organization quickly."

Javier rolled his eyes. "Mira, Antonio. Maybe José knows about this sort of thing, him being old and all. But I don't know anything. I think we are going to need your help. You make it sound easy. But we can't do it without you."

"I'd like to help, but I can't. Brady threatened me, and he doesn't joke around. He's got a lot of influence. If anyone sees me anywhere near Mersola even after the election, I'll be in big trouble."

"Well, we're going to be in big trouble, too."

"Don't be that way, Javier," José said. "Antonio has done a lot for us. He's done all that he can."

Sonia nodded her head half-heartedly in agreement.

"Look. I can still meet with the three of you secretly. As long as no one finds out. And if there's an emergency you can always call me. I'll be around, don't worry."

Javier wasn't satisfied and Antonio could see it.

"Look, you can win this election. And after you win, you can vote Brady out. At Mersola's, there are over four hundred people. That would make it the biggest place in the local. We could elect a new president and get people organized. But first you have to win the election. You've come this far, and you've got nothing to lose."

Javier eyed Antonio with suspicion.

"And we can have breakfast together before work in the mornings, whenever you want." Antonio's voice was slightly solicitous, as if he were *trying* to convince them. It was a new sound for him—not tight, sharp or confident. His hands did not move with precision, and for the first time they could remember, he appeared to be self-conscious.

A breeze rustled through the sycamore trees; a leaf the size of a large hand scratched across the rutted wood tabletop. Javier and Sonia glanced into each other's eyes, unable to hide their doubts. Antonio understood instantly and fumbled to light a cigarette.

José began to fidget. The others could feel things slipping away even as they listened to the voices of children and the music of the carousel. They turned to José for help, and he could feel the weight of their gaze. He cleared his throat and began to speak, slowly and with deliberation. "When I was riding the bus to the border, I thought about many things. I worried about my family. I thought we'd lost everything. Then I remembered what a padre told me once in México during a long drought. The rain didn't come and we didn't have much of anything to eat, much less to trade or to sell. We were feeling like everything was lost, like there was no way out. Then the old priest grabbed me by the back of my neck and looked me in the eyes and said, 'No matter what you lose, you must never lose hope. Only when you lose hope have you lost everything.' And just as I remembered his words, the bus turned around and we were brought back to our families, back to work. Who would have thought that would happen?

"The people at work are all for the union now. Especially after the bus was turned around. They see that we *did* something, we *won* something. I don't think we can throw that away. Deep down in my heart, I believe we must not give up! I believe we can win. But even if we can't, whatever happens, I know one thing for certain—we can't give up hope."

Javier jumped to his feet and reached to shake José's hand, while Antonio glanced at his cigarette and smiled. Sonia was so excited she held her breath until she turned red.

But it took some time for things to get back in sync.

Javier had a question: "Bueno. I just want to know one thing. How are we going to tell the people about Antonio being fired? Maybe they'll think the union is a sellout, which, in a way, it is."

"But—" Sonia began.

"I know, I know," Javier interrupted. "I understand that now. But we are going to have to explain what is going on. And it is not going to be easy. What are we going to do? Tell the people to vote for the union even though the union president is a sellout? We must explain to them what is happening. We can't lie. Maybe we should get another union."

"It's too late for that now," Antonio said. "No other union can come into the factory until a year after the election. And no union *would* come in now with the election just a short time away."

"But we've got to tell the people the truth!" Javier insisted.

"Just tell them there's politics in the union and once the people are *in*, they can straighten it out. But stress the need for organization and the difference a union can make. Like benefits and wages. Keep the issues straight. Tell them the union isn't perfect. But most of all, tell them that the *people* are the union."

"Híjole! All of that?" Javier asked. "I'm going to sound like a politician! No wonder those guys in the union wear suits and ties!"

"I know it's a lot to say," Antonio conceded. "But the people have to know the truth. They've got to know everything or they will get confused. Anyway, just do the best you can. When the people ask about it—*if* they do—then I think you've got to tell them what is happening."

"Púchica!" Sonia interrupted, a little exasperated. "Slow down, Antonio! You've read too many of those fancy books! I'm getting confused. Now, what are we supposed to do?"

Antonio gazed down at the grass and took a drag from his cigarette. "I've been talking too much—"

"Well, don't stop now!" Sonia insisted.

"Okay. You've got Brady trapped. He can't stop the campaign now. But he *can* let you *lose*, which is what he plans to do. What we've got to do is organize ourselves and put pressure on him at the same time so he can't wreck the drive. You're going to need a bilingual organizer because none of his men speak Spanish. You'll need one at the factory gates and at meetings.

That's where you have some leverage. Maybe you'll be able to get one from another local if we do things right. That would be to our advantage because he wouldn't be one of Brady's men."

Antonio paused to see if everyone was following him. Satisfied that they were, he continued. "Next Monday, at the union meeting, demand he hire someone as a bilingual organizer. At the meeting, it is very important you speak up and take the lead. You'll be able to speak with authority because you are all original members of the organizing committee. Be sure you mention that. You've got to talk about the union and what needs to be done, because if you don't, Brady will bore the people to death. He'll probably launch into his 'I supported Pete Chavez for Congress' speech. That's what he usually does when he is speaking to Latinos. Anyway, Brady does not speak a word of Spanish. He doesn't even know how to order a burrito. You can make concrete suggestions about what needs to be done. Otherwise, Brady won't do anything. He'll wave his hands and say he is behind you, then leave. Now, he has to have somebody there to translate—probably some guy who is a bilingual organizer from another local. I'd be surprised if he could find anybody else on such short notice. It would have to be someone who he could control, and I don't think he's thought that far in advance. You never know—but still, I doubt it. It would have to be a used-car salesman, or something. So most likely, you'll have plenty of opportunities to take the lead. So volunteer to do things and make concrete suggestions. It will be difficult for him to turn you down. He would look too bad. Do you follow me so far?"

23

Low gray clouds slipped across the sky and it was warm and humid. Dirt streets were muddy from a storm the day before and many intersections were flooded, mucid pools stretching from corner to corner. Children ran about shoeless, their dirty faces gaunt but smiling as they played with their toys—grasshoppers they had captured and tied with thread to prevent escape, abandoned tires and rusty cans.

Ana, Manuel, and the other refugees huddled together in a tiny hotel room in Tijuana, guarded by two coyotes. Behind thin, stained walls, rats scurried about; cockroaches boldly darted across the scabrous wood floor and up walls, disappearing into cracks and holes in the rotting woodwork.

But the refugees sat motionless, listening to the rats and a woman next door who groaned and laughed wickedly. When Señora Chavez moved away from a particularly aggressive roach and the floorboards popped and creaked, the refugees grimaced.

There was a knock on the door—a distinct knock. It was Peligro. Smirking and drunk, he entered the room, a woman clinging to his arm. His companion—wearing a red mini-dress so tight it looked like she had been dipped in hot cinnamon—smiled and licked his fingers. Peligro put his finger to his lips, slapped the woman on her buttocks and dismissed her, quietly closing the door as she left.

"Get your things together," he whispered. "We'll be leaving soon. Now. You must all walk in pairs. Choose a partner. You are to follow me—but don't stay too close. I don't need ten shadows. I'm not giving you a tour of downtown, you know. Whenever I stop, stay where you are, but look like you are shopping or something. But don't fall too far back. Otherwise, you will be left behind. Understand?"

The refugees nodded their heads.

"Okay, now, get your things together—quietly."

As the refugees gathered their things, the coyote peered through smoke-stained windows until he spotted the prostitute across the street. She gave him the all-clear sign, smiling shamelessly as she peeled her dress above her thigh. The coyote licked his lips, then turned to the refugees.

"Do as you are told and you won't get caught. Stay out of the streets—they're very muddy, you know. Now, let's go—you, then you, you and you," he whispered, assigning Ana and Manuel the lead spot.

The refugees obeyed his instructions, following him two-by-two out of the hotel, abandoning their room to the rats, roaches, and rot.

Once out on the street, they moved from block to block, not knowing where they were or where they were going, gradually making their way downtown.

Soon the streets became boulevards, crowded with tourists shopping for bargains. Doormen solicited Americans and others who had money to spend, encouraging them to enter bars and clubs, promising them the best entertainment in town. One such establishment drew Peligro's interest.

"Watch a puta get screwed by a burro!" the doorman crowed.

The coyote could not pass up such entertainment, though he had seen it all before. He paid the doorman ten dollars and slipped in through a faded red curtain in time to witness the show's finale. Inside, a young Mexican woman heavily painted with makeup—her childlike body adorned with studded leather straps and nothing more—entertained tourists as they drank and howled without restraint.

Just two years before her performance, the little girl played with her first doll, a gift from an American charity. Now, under the glare of bright lights, in a smoke-filled room jammed with men shouting taunts and pitching dollar bills on stage, the young woman prepared to be mounted by an ass.

Outside, the refugees were thrown into a panic. They remained where they were, strung down the boulevard in pairs, unaware of the depravity around them, fear having struck them with tunnel vision. Though rattled by cheers that boomed from the clubs, the refugees were otherwise oblivious to the manic scene around them, their eyes focused on the red curtain where Peligro had disappeared.

Before long the coyote reappeared, bent over in laughter, amused as he was by the young woman's performance, by her audacity, and, most of all, by her great misfortune. The refugees, seeing him, breathed a sigh of relief, ever fearful of imminent detection by Mexican federales. They struggled to keep Peligro within sight as he plunged back into the crowd, moving quickly down the boulevard with ease.

Then, suddenly, Peligro reversed course. He signaled a cab and as it skidded to a stop grabbed Ana by the arm. "You've got to go with me so I won't look suspicious," he said.

"No!" Manuel protested, holding Ana back by her other arm.

"Do you want us all to get caught?" Peligro asked between his teeth, smiling at passers-by as if to assure them there was no problem. "Let go of her. She will be fine. I give you my word. I just need to look like I've got a girlfriend."

"No! Get someone else!" Manuel said. One of the other coyotes pressed a knife against his ribs. Still, Manuel would not let go of Ana.

"We are all going to get caught by the federales," Peligro said calmly. "Don't look, but we're being followed right now. Do you want to get us all caught?"

"I don't care!"

157

Peligro's men broke Manuel's grip on Ana and forced him to the ground while Peligro dragged her into the cab. One of the coyotes turned toward a gathering crowd of tourists and explained in broken English, "He drink too much. No problem. Too much drink."

Peligro gave instructions to the cabby and the taxi spun away, weaving. "Where are we going?" Ana pleaded.

Peligro leaned over and whispered in her ear: "Don't talk! Don't say a word! The driver will recognize your accent and turn us in. He makes good money doing such things."

Ana closed her eyes and silently prayed. Please, Lord, please! Don't let anything bad happen!

Traffic thinned as the taxi escaped downtown, the cabby following the coyote's instructions into rolling hills on the outskirts of town, hills of dilapidated houses with chicken-wire fences caging fowl and goats—a maze of dirty roads riddled with potholes and dissected by gullies cut by a decade's rain.

"This is far enough," the coyote told the cabby. He yanked Ana out of the taxi, grabbed her bag and paid the driver in dollars, including a large tip. "C'mon, baby," he told her for the benefit of the driver. "Your papacito is going to be very good to you."

The cabby laughed. "Make her scream!" he yelled before spinning away.

"Where are we going?" Ana cried. "And where are the others?"

"Shut up! You are becoming a big headache for me." As he led her up a hill, the sun setting and casting shadows, Peligro's voice softened. "Don't worry. You are safe with me. I will take good care of you. And you'll be back with the others soon."

Night was falling as the coyote pulled Ana past houses planted on dusty hills, dwellings where the poor burned candles for light while the better off among them moved in the shadows of a single bulb hanging from a frayed cord. Through the parchment-like windows, silhouettes slipped back and forth like phantoms. Children ran in and out of doorways that never closed; crickets sang and old mangy dogs scavenged about for food. Soon the moon rose over the hills, shrouded by wisps of clouds.

Peligro maneuvered Ana through the doorway of the biggest house in the barrio, the front room of which was a neighborhood market. There were crates of wilted vegetables and fruit there, along with barrels of beans and rice, and cartons of Mexican cigarettes. The coyote greeted the storekeeper who emerged from a back room where a color television blared; several children from the neighborhood sat and watched a program in Spanish, having paid the shopkeeper ten pesos for the privilege. Outside a helicopter passed overhead, its rotor blades silencing crickets and dogs, searchlights swooping randomly across the dirt streets, rooftops and barren hillsides.

The coyote left Ana standing amidst the crates and barrels while he spoke with the storekeeper privately, the neighborhood children run off like beggars. Soon Peligro returned with a salacious grin and a bottle of Coke. He led Ana into a small laundry room with clotheslines strung from one wall to the next, tied haphazardly to water pipes and windowsills. A large slanting stone sink sat in one corner where clothes were washed by hand, boxes of detergent and sundries stored in dusty stacks against the wall opposite. A battered sofa covered with bedding occupied what little space remained.

"Stay here for a while. You'll be safe here," the coyote said, the muscles of his face twitching. "You must be thirsty. Here—drink this."

"What is it?"

"What does it look like? It's just Coca-Cola. Go ahead. Drink it. I'll be back in a while. Relax. I've got some business to take care of. There's a toilet out back if you need it. Don't worry. I'll be back soon."

When she was sure the coyote was gone, Ana smelled the Coke and immediately poured it down the sink. She paced back and forth in the tiny room and wrung her hands. "Please, God. Please help me!"

Another helicopter passed overhead, and in the front room, Ana heard the shopkeeper say, "El mosco está buscando pollos—the fly is looking for chickens."

"Hay Dios," Ana sighed. "Por favor!"

Ana sank deep into the battered sofa and pulled at her hair. She heard the coyote's voice just outside the door and frantically searched for a place to hide. But there was none. Bolting through the door, Peligro announced: "See? That wasn't long, was it?" Ana cowered in the corner. The coyote glanced at her empty Coke bottle and smiled. "The federales are all over the place. But don't worry, chamaca. You are safe here with me."

"Where are the others?"

"Don't worry. We'll be meeting up with them soon, when it is safe. Trust me. You do trust me, don't you? You know, you are a very special person to me. Why do you think I asked you to come and not one of the others?"

Ana began to pace again, wringing her hands and pulling frantically at her hair. "But when? When are we going to join them?"

"When it is safe," Peligro said, attempting to conceal his growing impatience. He picked up the empty soda bottle and examined it. "Did you drink your Coke?" he asked. Ana did not respond. He took a step toward her. "Don't be frightened, mi linda. You are going to be all right. And when we get to Los Angeles, you can stay at my house, if you like. I have a big house with four bedrooms." Peligro watched her from the corner of his eyes, weighing her response. "And your cousin can stay there, also," he added, as he wrapped an arm around her waist.

Ana covered her face with her hands. With a sudden jerk, the coyote pulled her close, forcing her face next to his. Ana struggled against his grip, broke free and ran to the other side of the room.

"Where's Manuel?" Ana cried. "Where are the others?"

"What's the matter with you? Are you a child? Don't you understand anything?" The coyote regained his composure and forced a smile. "Did you drink that Coke I brought you? Don't you want another one?" Ana held her chest and breathed heavily. "Don't worry, mi amor. I told you. I won't hurt you. I just want to show my affection so you will know how much I care for you. That is all."

Slowly the coyote made his way toward the corner where Ana stood leaning against the wall, her eyes darting frantically around the room.

"You've never been with a man before, have you? There's nothing to be afraid of, really. Nothing." Once within reach of her, he pounced upon her, forcing his unshaven liquor-and-to-bacco-reeking face into hers, licking her lips. Again she fought him and again she escaped, wiping her face with the back of her hand and spitting on the floor. She began to cry, gasping for air between sobs, her knees buckling, her eyes rolling back as she grew faint. "Please, God! Please!"

Incredulous, the coyote stared at her, his eyes wild and vicious. Ana readied herself for blows. But they never landed. Instead, the coyote snorted and whipped his body about as if possessed by a demon. "What's wrong with you? Stupid bitch! What did you think? That I was going to make the tiger love? Shit! Fucking little whore!"

The coyote stormed out of the room, slamming the door behind him. In the market just outside he smoked a cigarette and swallowed a shot of tequila offered by the shopkeeper, who, as host, felt responsible for the coyote's displeasure. Peligro, in a rare concession, assured him he was not to blame.

After a few minutes, the coyote returned to the laundry room. Ana was still trembling and feared for her life. "Okay, let's forget the whole thing," he said. "Okay? Let's pretend it never happened. If you know what is good for you and your cousin, you will say nothing. Understand? Bueno. Then, let's go. It's time to meet up with the others." Ana hesitated.

"Oh, so now you want to stay here? Fine. You stay here, woman. But I won't come back for you. Understand?"

Ana took a deep breath, straightened herself up and stepped out the door. She walked through the market, past barrels of beans and rice, past wilted vegetables, and out into the moonlit street. The coyote moved quickly and Ana struggled to keep up as he raced down dark streets and around winding paths that seemed to Ana to lead nowhere.

A cloud covered the moon and suddenly everything was dark. They were in a canyon where there were no houses, no lights, and no shadows. Yet Ana could feel the presence of someone other than the coyote. Words were whispered and Ana had the sensation of being blindfolded.

"Wait here!" Peligro told her. "Don't move. Just wait here. I'll be right back."

"But where are . . ."

"I said wait here, cabrona! Don't you understand anything? And be quiet!"

Ana stood straddling a rock in the darkness, trying to focus her eyes ahead, trying to see something—anything. The thick cloud cover broke briefly and she mapped a path in the direction she last heard the coyote. She took a step forward.

"I told you not to move! Shit! All right. The others are just ahead. Follow me. And be quiet!"

Ana tried to follow him, but he moved too quickly. The moon disappeared and she stretched her arms ahead, groping in the dark, frightened she might lose her way. "Where are you?" she whispered. But there was no reply. Ana paused and cocked her head, listening for the coyote's footsteps. She heard a dog howl in the distance and a baby cry. But the coyote was gone. Her heart pounded as she squinted in the dark. She took another step forward and tumbled headfirst into a gully, landing atop a heap of garbage and trash. The back of her head began to throb and she felt the heat of decomposing vegetables and fish bones on her back. Yet somehow it felt good, and she took comfort in its embrace. As the rotting garbage seeped into her shoes, her head grew light and began to spin.

Ana felt warm and wanted, like a child being tucked into bed. She was no longer frightened, though she did worry about her shoes. She remembered an Easter Sunday when her mother gave her a wonderful gift—brand new white shoes with straps and tiny buckles, shoes that smelled like new leather and polish. Take good care of them! her mother had cautioned her. Your father worked hard so we could save enough money to buy these for you! And then she smiled with a mother's love, her eyes moist, content to see her daughter possess what she had never had. It was the happiest day of Ana's life! And that night she took her new shoes to bed, holding them close to her heart like a doll.

"Ana?" someone whispered. She lifted herself out of the garbage, remembering where she was.

"Estoy aquí! Here I am!" Manuel honed in on her voice and in the faint moonlight spotted her in the gully. He slid down the bank and helped her up, brushing away wet papers and rotting vegetables, which clung to her like parasites.

"What *happened*?" Ana was still in a daze.

"Did the coyote do this to you?"

"No, Manuel. No. I'm all right. I'm just a little dizzy."

"What happened?"

"I fell."

"Are you going to be able to walk?"

"Yes, yes. Don't worry. Where are the others?"

"Over there," he said, pointing with one hand and helping her up with the other.

Though her head ached and she was still lightheaded, Ana

stumbled along a path, holding Manuel's hand. As they approached the outline of what appeared to be a large boulder, Ana could hear Señora Chavez wheezing.

"Where were you?" the coyote asked Ana, feigning concern, though it was Manuel he watched.

"She fell into a gully, thanks to you," Manuel said. Peligro's smirk was masked by the darkness.

"I wouldn't be surprised if all the chingados federales in Tijuana show up any minute with all the noise you were making," Peligro whispered. "The two of you have to think of the others before you do things on your own. Now listen! We have to move fast. We're behind schedule. The moon is coming out again, so we will be easy to see. Follow me! And be quiet!"

The refugees followed him down a trail in the dim moonlight until they reached a deserted shack. There a stranger waited impatiently.

"Dónde chingado andavas, cabrón ? Where the fuck have you been?" the stranger asked.

"Never mind," Peligro replied. "What says El Lobo?"

"There's moscos everywhere. The federales are out tonight. But everything else is like ice."

"Good." He turned to the refugees. "You people follow me. And don't make any noise!"

The refugees followed him up a hill in single file. Then, as if of one mind, they froze. In the distance were two faint headlights. Instantly they bounded down the slopes of a steep ravine, skiing in the powdery dirt until they reached the trough, scurrying for cover in the resinous plants that thrived there. Moments later a jeep stopped where they had made their descent, kicking up a cloud of dust that rolled over and concealed one made moments before by the refugees. Federales leaped from their vehicle and scanned the ravine with flashlights, the beams crisscrossing the backs of Salvadoreans who had become invisible—as much a part of the terrain as the rodents and lizards that nested there. The refugees could *smell* the federales; they could see their eyes in the dark. But their fear was momentarily overcome by their new-found powers, instincts that were as real to them as the taste of dirt and the feel of spider webs. They were invisible, and they knew it.

"Chingados! They got away. Okay, let's go!" one of the federales said. "They must be further down the hill somewhere." Then, as quickly as they had appeared, they were gone.

The coyote began to climb the slope of the ravine, the refugees close behind. Only Señora Chavez had a tough time of it, coughing and spitting, while the others, though frightened, felt strangely emboldened.

Following a trail imperceptible to them half an hour before, they hiked until they reached another abandoned shack far up the hillside, well hidden from sight. They ran into the darkness of the shack and silently fell to the floor, catching their breath and dumping stones and dirt from their shoes.

"It's all right now," whispered the coyote. "That was close. But that's nothing compared to what's ahead. Don't get too confident! Soon we'll be crossing la frontera. Some of you might not make it." Though it was too dark to see, everyone knew he was staring at the old woman. "And if you think you can make it without me, it is better if you leave on your own now. I don't have time to risk my life for a bunch of Indios who think they know everything. Just remember—a lot of people have died trying to cross the border. Now. Who wants to try it alone?" There was silence; even those who had felt strong were stripped of their confidence. "Vaya, pues. Just remember one thing—a lot of people have died. Now. Better get some sleep. We'll be leaving in an hour or so, and you are going to be up all night."

"Hay Dios miyo!" cried Señora Chavez. "All *night*? I don't think I am going to make it! Hay Dios, I'm sore and . . ."

"Shut up, vieja!" snarled the coyote. "Do you want to get us all caught?"

24

It was evening and a rain fell upon Los Angeles, creating as much havoc as a natural disaster.

The city built on a fractured desert plain had learned to cope with its permanent state of drought, diverting water there from rivers and deltas in more hospitable regions of the country. It was rain that confounded Angelenos. Streets became oily and slick, freeway arteries clogged by traffic accidents caused by motorists unaccustomed to the hazards of wet raceways.

Most folks would have preferred to stay at home that night, where they could take long hot showers, eat a stew or soup, and curl up in front of the television set. It was not a good night for fundraisers, Tupperware parties, or PTA meetings. And it was the evening scheduled for a general meeting of the Mersola workers' organizing committee.

As raindrops streaked past the gunmetal-gray halos of streetlamps, an old smoking Buick clattered to a stop in front of the Carpenters' Hall, a building rented for the union meeting.

"Híjole, José! Adelante!" whined a young worker trapped in the back seat of the steamy automobile. "Hurry up before Chuy farts again!"

"I think I'm stuck," Chuy grinned as he struggled to free his two-hundred-pound frame from the grip of wet clothing and plastic seat covers.

"Why did you bring us here, José?" the young man complained. "And on a night like this? You campesinos don't mind getting all wet, do you? You're used to that sort of thing. All I can say is that this meeting better be good! I could be home, all nice and cozy, with my old lady watching TV instead of being tortured by some fat Mexican!"

Chuy finally escaped from the back seat, and the workers organized by José bounded up the steps of the building for the sanctuary of its tall, churchlike doorway, laughing at each other's feeble attempts to stay dry. As they made their way indoors, they were immediately greeted by other workers, animated and in good spirits despite the fact that they were soaking wet.

Inside the hall, Javier bit his nails and tapped his feet. He had arrived early, hoping José would be early, too. Javier was lost without him. And as José joined the throng gathered near the entrance, Javier rushed to his side, as restless as a child at a birthday party waiting for his turn at the piñata. "Mira, José! There are a lot of people here!" José smiled and nodded his head. "Bueno, José. . . what do we do *now*?"

"Just move around and talk to the people you know, like we planned. When the meeting begins, sit somewhere in the middle of everything along with your friends."

"Move around and talk with my friends," Javier repeated, trying to concentrate. "Bueno, José. I'm going to start now. Okay?"

José nodded patiently.

"Bueno . . . I'm going to—"

"Vamonos, pues!" José interrupted. "Let's go, then!"

José approached a group of people he recognized while Javier rubbed his hands together in eager anticipation. "Bueno," he said, not having noticed that his friend had moved on. "I'm going to start now, José . . . José? Hombre! Where did you *go*?"

As Javier searched the room, Rosa slipped into the building. She moved quietly and with reverence, like a Catholic attending Mass. Rosa spotted Javier and hid her eyes; she circumvented the crowd gathered in the aisle and took a seat in the back row, folding her hands on her lap.

Sonia burst into the hall with a large group of friends from the factory. Javier moved quickly to her side, uncomfortable being alone. He craned his neck and glanced around the room, poised for flight the moment he spotted José.

"Oh, Javier," Sonia smiled, her gold-filled front teeth flashing. She turned to her friends. "This is one of the *other* men in my life. He's young, you know. I like them that way. They don't get tired so easy!" Sonia's friends laughed and whistled. But Javier was preoccupied.

"Bueno," he answered stiffly. "Mucho gusto. Nice to meet you."

Three Anglos in suits appeared. They had the tense mannerisms of secret service agents.

"They must be from the union," Sonia whispered to Javier. "We'd better take our places."

Sensing the meeting would soon begin, people scrambled for seats. Javier finally spotted José in the crowd and climbed around a dozen people so he could sit beside him.

Two more men in suits appeared, conferred with those who had preceded them, then signaled someone outside. There was a brief commotion, as if a fight had broken out. Then Don Brady swept in, greeted by spontaneous applause. Though most of the workers had never seen him before, they knew instantly who he was—he had a celebrity's smile.

Brady strolled down the center aisle, waving and smiling at the crowd, flanked by an entourage. As he made his way toward the podium, a small light-skinned Mexican peeked in through the large double doors of the hall. It was David, wearing a new blue suit and a sheepish grin. He stepped inside and paused momentarily to collapse an expensive umbrella, striking a pose as if a spotlight heralded his arrival.

"What's *he* doing here?" José asked, pointing in David's direction. David approached the gathering at the podium, proud and self-conscious; he was where he had always wanted to be—at the front of the hall, behind the table, in the limelight. Brady shook David's hand, flashed his denture grin and encouraged David to step up to the microphone, which he did with a certain arrogance, thumping the mike and blowing into it.

"What the . . ." José said under his breath.

"Buenas noches. This is the general meeting of the Shoeworkers Union, Local 305, held for the workers at the Mersola factory," David announced in Spanish. "As you know, the union has been conducting an organizing campaign there, and we're here to tell you about the union. Oh, by the way. I should introduce myself to those who don't already know me. My name is David Gomez, former employee of the Mersola factory and the new bilingual organizer for the Shoeworkers Union."

"What are we going to do now?" Javier asked José. "What about our plan?"

"So, they hired that cabrón," José replied, shaking his head. "Well, there is nothing we can do. He is bilingual and a lot of people know him."

"You mean a lot of people *hate* him. He tried to sell the whole factory life insurance that was worthless. And have you forgotten what he did at the last union meeting? He almost ruined everything!"

"Welcome to our first meeting!" David continued. "We're very honored to have the president of the union with us tonight. He has taken time out from his busy schedule and driven all the way over here in the rain just to be with us tonight—to show he is one hundred percent behind us!"

"With a knife at our backs," Javier muttered.

"So, let's show him our appreciation! It is a great honor for me to introduce to you Señor Don Brady!"

There was a thunderous ovation, and though Brady did not understand a word David had said other than his name, he stepped forward and waved to the crowd.

José, Javier, and Sonia sat glumly in their seats.

When the ovation died down, Brady launched into his tried-

and-true trade union speech: "It's really great to see all you union brothers and sisters here tonight—and I tell ya, I'm damn proud to be here."

The workers listened politely.

"You know, nowadays, inflation and unemployment are killing the working man. And what's worse, there's a great attack upon our unions. All the great legislation that labor has worked so hard for over the years is being overturned by politicians in Washington, backed by big corporations who just don't give a hoot about the working man." The workers continued to listen, though they did not understand a word.

"Seeing a big crowd like all of you here on this cold, rainy night proves that the labor movement is not dead! In fact, it's healthier than ever!" Brady waited for the expected applause, but only three people responded. The majority squirmed uncomfortably. Brady's men glared at the crowd while their boss grew visibly uneasy.

"Of course, not *all* the politicians are controlled by big business. In fact, right here in East Los Angeles, we've got Pete Chavez, a great Congressman our union helped to elect!"

The crowd began to fidget.

Brady turned to David. "Maybe you should translate some of this," he said. David stepped up to the microphone and waited for Brady to cue him.

"Think we'd better start again, this time on a different track," Brady whispered. He took a deep breath. "You know, it's high time people stood up to men like Mersola!" Brady stepped away from the microphone, and David translated what he said. There was a roar of applause, many of the workers climbing upon their chairs and thrusting clenched fists into the air.

Brady was stunned. His eyes lit up as he watched the ovation, his entourage patting each other on the back and grinning. It had been a long time since Brady received a warm welcome from working people, and pride got the best of him. He wrapped

---

171

his arm around David and asked, "How do I say hurrah for the union in Spanish?" David told him, repeating the words three times until he got it right. Then Brady shouted, "Viva la unión!"

The crowd echoed back, "¡Que viva!"

José saw an opening and yelled, "Viva la clase obrera! Long live the working class!"

And the people shouted back, "¡Que viva!"

Sonia, excited by the chanting, cried, "Viva la huelga! Long live the strike!"

And again the crowd answered, "¡Que viva!"

Brady began to grow uneasy. He turned to David and without moving his lips asked, "What the hell are they shouting about?"

David answered, "Oh, they're chanting hurrah for the strike."

Brady frowned. "No, no. We don't need any of that! There's not going to be any strike. You'd better put a stop to that shit *right now*!"

David hastily returned to the microphone. He held his hands in the air to silence the chanting. "We have to quiet down now. There are a lot of things to talk about. And there isn't going to be a strike. So no more chanting, please!"

The people sat back down in their chairs, silenced by the chastisement. David turned to Brady for instructions.

"David, I want you to explain to everyone that they've got to be careful they're not mislead by a bunch of troublemakers! They could be spies for the company trying to disrupt our meeting, you know, trying to give the union a bad name." David translated dutifully and many of the workers glanced at José and Sonia.

"Well," Brady continued. "I've got to get going. Tell them I have to leave, that I am very busy conducting union business, but that I'm behind them and they're gonna win. Tell them all that, will ya, David?"

David did as he was told, and the people applauded politely.

Brady grabbed his umbrella and, with four of his men flanking him, paraded down the center aisle, smiling, waving, and shaking hands as he made his way toward the tall double doors at the hall's entrance. Sonia and José sat stoically as the union president passed. He nodded at them and, under his breath, told one of his aides: "Find out who those two are—tell David to get me a list of troublemakers."

Brady made his exit, and all eyes turned back to David and the two organizers who remained behind. They conferred with each other briefly. Then David cleared his throat and began to speak, while the others handed out several legal-sized pads of paper among the workers, passed row-to-row like collection plates.

"We're passing around paper to make a list," David explained. "Make sure you write down your name, address, and phone number." He stepped away from the podium and watched as the workers struggled with the notepads.

It was a monumental task to collect the workers' names and addresses, since many of them could barely write. When everyone had provided the relevant information to the best of their ability, David stepped back to the microphone. "Okay," he said with an almost flippant lack of enthusiasm. "Make sure you tell your friends about the union and get them to vote on election day. There's less than a week to go. And make sure you vote! We'll be in touch with you. Entonces. Thanks for coming tonight. Muchas gracias. Buenas noches."

José, Javier, and Sonia turned to each other in shock. Initially they did not know what to do. Finally, José leaped to his feet: "Aren't you going to talk about the *union*? And aren't you going to see if there are any questions?" An affirmative murmur arose from the audience as people shook their heads, confused by the proceedings, not sure what to make of things.

David was embarrassed by his oversight. But he was also irritated. "Are there any questions?" he asked sarcastically. The workers turned to each other and whispered: "What is there to ask questions about? They haven't said anything!"

Javier jumped up and cleared his throat. "I have something to say," he announced stiffly. "Bueno . . ."

"*Muy* bueno!" David chortled, drawing laughter from some of the younger workers.

Javier cleared his throat again. But he was unsure of himself. "Bueno," he said, though he tried not to. Again there was laughter, though many in the audience were disturbed by the treatment Javier was receiving.

He stared at the audience like a superstitious boxer who lost his good luck charm. He did not know where to begin; he stood dumbstruck, his arms dangling limply at his side. The crowd began to turn against him, unable to bear the sight of a champion who had lost his nerve. And suddenly the auditorium seemed very large to Javier; he became confused and disoriented. David leaned against the podium and smirked, poised to strike a mortal blow.

José rose to his feet. "I think what the brother is trying to say is that there are many important questions the people have about joining the union."

Javier shook his head and pointed at José. "Eso!" he declared. "That is it!"

David attempted to interrupt, but José would not permit it. "For example," he continued, "most of us working at Mersola get paid just the minimum. Everyone knows that is not enough to raise a family. Isn't that right, brother?" José asked, turning to Javier.

"That's right!" Javier said like a man overcoming a speech impediment.

José took his seat and whispered to Javier, "Go ahead, hermano! Just say what you think!"

"That is right what Don José said," Javier continued. "The people want to know—they have a *right* to know—about the benefits of joining a union. Will we get overtime pay? Now we don't. Will we get sick pay? Now we don't. Will the union . . ."

"I'm sure everyone knows the union is in favor of all of those things," David interrupted, overpowering Javier with his amplified voice. "They wouldn't waste their time coming here tonight in this bad weather if they didn't know the union stood for all those good things."

The audience was stunned by David's rebuke. Why won't he let the people speak? they asked each other. What kind of a union is this?

"We need a union—now we've got one," David continued. "But what we have got to do now is make sure everyone votes yes in the election! We don't need a lot of talking by show-offs. We need action! We need votes!"

A handful of people were swayed by David's self-assured manner, and clapped their hands in approval. But most of the workers were confused.

Sonia stood up, and those who knew her held their breath. "We all have a right to speak here, no? There is no one here who is better than anyone else. We are all just working people trying to make a living for our families. Isn't that what unions are all about? Pues—there are a lot of us who don't know about union benefits. Or what our rights are. A lot of us don't know. That is why we are having this meeting, no?" The audience nodded their heads in approval. "We should all feel free to ask questions. After all, we—all of us here—are the union!"

This brought on a loud ovation, but David moved quickly to contain it, gesturing to the crowd to simmer down, insinuating they had violated a canon of union law. When they were under his control, he asked derisively, "Is there anybody here who does *not* know what a union is all about? Please raise your hand if you don't know."

The workers turned to each other in astonishment, embarrassed by the question.

Before Sonia, José, or Javier could speak, David said, "Well, I'm sure you are all tired and cold and wet and want to get home. We really appreciate you attending this meeting tonight. You can be sure the union is one hundred percent behind you and will do everything it can to make your lives better. I know you all want to go home to your loved ones before it starts to rain hard again. So, unless there are any more questions, we'll adjourn this meeting. And don't forget! Vote for the union on election day! And tell your friends to do the same! Hasta la victoria! Until victory!"

Javier, José, and Sonia sat limply in their chairs as people picked up their things and filed out of the auditorium. As they made their way outdoors, bracing themselves against the rain, the workers from the Mersola shoe factory turned to each other and asked: "Is this what it is like to be in a union in the United States?"

25

"Levantense! Ya nos vamos!"

The refugees shook themselves from a short, deep sleep.

"Get up! It's time to cross the border!" the coyote whispered in his usual state of agitation.

Manuel sat up and forced his eyes open. He thought he was at the bottom of a dark pool and instantly held his breath, prepared to push off the bottom, prepared to swim to safety. Then he remembered. Pale light seeped in around the frame of a door and there were forms all around him. "Ana. Where are you?"

"Shut up, cabrón!" the coyote snarled. "Do you want to get us all caught?"

Ana bolted upright, blinking in astonishment. She searched the shack where bodies lay like cadavers coming back to life. "Where am I?" she asked.

"You are at the border, mujer! We are going to cross now!"

"I said shut up, goddamn it! Stupid fucking wetbacks! Don't you know *nothing*?"

Ana stared across the room and attempted to focus her eyes on the coyote. She could hear him as he scratched his chin and his groin and she could smell his breath. And though it was dark, Ana could see him bare his teeth.

"We are going to cross now," the coyote continued. "Get your things together. If you are wearing any jewelry—even a watch—take it off. It reflects light. Also—this is important—if a helicopter passes overhead while we are outside, drop to the ground and do not move! Understand? And don't look up!"

The refugees gathered their belongings together with ceremony, like soldiers before a battle. "If la migra catches you, tell them you are from México. Understand? Don't tell them anything else! Nothing! Say you are from México and you saw some people and you followed them to get across the border. You don't have a coyote. Entienden? You don't know me or anyone else. Now. We have to move fast. Do what I tell you and by morning, we'll be on the other side."

Peligro opened the door and peered outside, across the road, and beyond at the mountains—mountains dusted with moonlight, steep desert hills intersected by fragile trails, littered with abandoned clothing and bleached bones—mountains of boulders and sagebrush and rattlesnake dens. Then he listened. And his eyes glowed yellow in the dark.

"Yá! Alístense! Get ready!" he said, turning his head just enough for his voice to carry, his eyes fixed on a point in the distance.

Manuel turned to Ana and smiled. "Are you ready?" Ana nodded her head.

"Hay Dios miyo," Señora Chavez groaned. "Please, God! Help me to make it across the border!"

"Apúrate!" the coyote ordered just before he made a dash toward the mountains. The refugees hesitated just long enough to take a deep breath, then raced to keep up with him, sprinting as if under fire. Across a clearing they ran, lungs heaving, hearts struggling to pump blood to arms and legs still sleeping, out of sync, rebelling against such sudden movement. They ran through sticky monkeyflower and thistle, around mescal and cactus, tripping on jagged rocks and holes dug by kangaroo rats, traps in the darkness—all of them, young and old, running madly toward the mountains, seeking refuge in its canyons, boulders and sagebrush.

As they ran, they felt the mountains swell beneath them; they felt them grow, heaving up from deep within the earth, rupturing upward as they had in the beginning. Up the mountainside they ran until they too were part of the mountains.

Soon the coyote slowed the pace, allowing the refugees to catch their breath. He followed a trail only he could see, moving them steadily along on a timetable only he understood. Up one hill and down another they moved until they knew not if they were traveling north or south, lost in another world where they were truly aliens.

An hour passed, though the refugees knew nothing of time. Then, suddenly, the coyote froze, signaling everyone to do the same. "Get down!" he ordered. Instantly they dropped to the ground. Ana lay with her ear to the earth, now well accustomed to its smell and taste. And the earth rumbled.

Half a mile away, on the backside of the mountain, two immigration jeeps climbed the steep hillside, their searchlights like lasers cutting lines in the earth. They knew the mountain well and could feel the presence of intruders; they, too, paused in the darkness and listened.

The coyote climbed up on one knee and searched the horizon, while the refugees tried desperately to remember how to be invisible. But their hearts were beating too fast, their thoughts were too rational, and they were too close to where they wanted to be.

Instinct told the coyote it was safe to proceed. He waved the refugees ahead, satisfied they had forgotten the magic they had nearly mastered. They were frightened, he knew—and that was good.

Señora Chavez wheezed mournfully as Manuel helped her ascend the crest of the mountains. In the distance, bright lights glistened. "That's the United States," announced an old man who had made the trip before. "See, señora? We are almost there!" Manuel said. "Keep going! We are going to make it!"

The refugees marched through the night, their skin torn by thorny brush as they slid down dusty hillsides, crawled on their hands and knees and scrambled up invisible switchbacks. They climbed and ran and prayed, forming unspoken words with dry chapped lips. The moon slipped in and out of clouds like a woman unable to decide what to wear. And when the moon was clothed, the refugees fumbled blindly in the dark, grasping for the touch of those next in line. When they grew weary, when pushed to the limits of endurance, they thought of their families back home and moved on.

The travel took its toll on Señora Chavez. She fell behind and paused to rest on a boulder, laboring to catch her breath, sputtering words between gasps: "Please, dear God! Take me home! Please . . . take me."

As the line of refugees careened around the brink of a cliff, word passed rapidly from back to front: "We need a rest. The old woman can barely breathe!"

"What?" the coyote said when the news reached him. "Are you all *crazy*? We can't stop now! Where is the old woman?" he demanded as he swung past the refugees, clutching their arms and their clothing, moving hand-over-hand around the line poised on the precipitous cliff. Señora Chavez had become delirious. "Hey, immigration! Here I am!" she shrieked. "Come and get me!"

The coyote leaped past the last refugees in line and slapped his hand over the old woman's mouth. "Shut up, vieja! Do you want to *die* here?" Peligro turned to a coyote who had been attempting to reason with the old woman. "Get everyone moving again. I'll catch up with you in a minute."

The coyote obeyed, bounding past the column of refugees, defying the law of gravity as he passed. He assumed the lead position at a particularly dangerous juncture of the journey—a mountain trail so delicate one might have thought it was carved with a stick, a crag so high and perilous Death called from below with its sweet, alluring voice.

There was no time to hesitate. Manuel followed a rhythm that begged for no interruption, movement punctuated by a steady beat—a life force compelling him to move on.

As the trail dilated, the line of refugees increased their speed. They snapped around a bend in the trail, moving faster and faster. Panting for breath, they were led down a dusty slope, sliding feet first, headlong, rolling, tumbling, following the lead man. Then, finally, the pace slackened.

Ana caught her breath, and the thought of Señora Chavez returned. Manuel's thoughts caught up with him, too. They turned to each other. But it was too late. And they knew it.

At the saddle of the mountain, the refugees came to an unkept road that slanted toward a valley below. As they filed down the road, Peligro appeared from nowhere and raced past them to the front of the line. Ana and Manuel's hearts leapt ahead of the rhythm of their pace. They couldn't face each other. There was nothing they could do. It was better to lose themselves in the movement forward, to obey the commands of their lungs, to follow their instincts, their minds just another organ of survival.

The road dissolved and the column of refugees cut downhill through spikeweed, winding around the trail like a Chinese dragon dance. They moved quickly until halted by a barbed wire fence.

The coyotes moved to a section of the fence hidden by a large thorny bush. They removed an anchor, which held the bush in place, revealing a section where wires had been carefully spliced, creating a crawl hole.

"Don't touch the wire!" Peligro said. "It's a trap!"

The refugees cautiously slid through the opening, their eyes darting about, ever mindful of the unknown danger, Ana and Manuel the last to pass through the portal to the United States.

They followed the lap of the mountain until they reached a railroad track that lay upon a long bed of pebbles. "Listen!" Peligro said.

"There is a bridge ahead. Run as fast as you can across it! There will be someone waiting for you on the other side. He'll tell you where to go next. All right! Move! Quickly!"

They ran toward the bridge, up the black pebble railroad bed, leaping from tie to tie in a midnight game of follow-the-leader. As they ran, the moon modestly slipped behind a cumulus silk screen. Yet its light continued to shine, deceiving the refugees, pursuing them as it does young children. The refugees paused momentarily to witness the spectacle, watching as the moon appeared to swell, turning night into day.

Suddenly a fierce wind arose, and the sky erupted in a mad frenzy, whipping angrily above them.

"Get down!" Peligro shouted, and the refugees dropped to the tracks, trestles and tar. A helicopter swooped down on them, rotor blades hacking the sky into pieces that fell around them. The refugees lay motionless as the helicopter descended, a dusty column of light running across their backs and leaping to a roadway beneath the bridge. Then, just as suddenly as it had appeared, the helicopter wheeled back into the night, leaving behind a cloud of dust and a terrible silence.

"Run!" Peligro shouted, and the refugees raced across the bridge. On the opposite side a man appeared from hiding and directed them toward a large pepper tree still oscillating in the wind.

"Hurry!" Peligro cried, his voice quivering like the leaves of the pepper tree. "There's migra all over the place!" He turned to his connection. "Is it safe to take the road?"

"Safer than standing under a pinche tree!"

Peligro regained his composure. He signaled the refugees to follow and sprinted down the dirt road.

Soon the desert gave way to a small community, paved roads lit by streetlamps, resinous weeds usurped by trimmed hedges and watered lawns. The refugees entered the sleepy suburb by way of a dead-end street, a borderland still contested by desert winds. Herded across a gravel lot, they stepped past a plywood door peeled open by a shadow, into an abandoned building that smelled like charcoal. Inside, they leaned against burned walls and struggled to catch their breath.

"All right," the coyote sputtered. "We're going to spend the rest of the night here. Be quiet! Don't cough or sneeze or nothing! These two," he said, pointing at men in the shadows, "are going to stay here with you. I'll be back in the morning. As you can see, it is almost dawn now." The refugees gazed up at the sky, visible through a large gap in the roof. Faint pink brushstrokes colored clouds as they raced eastward. "You had better stay where you won't get wet—it's supposed to rain tonight. Now find yourselves a spot and get some sleep. I'll be back soon." The refugees did as they were told, some taking shelter beneath the scorched remains of a pool table warped by heat and a thorough drenching; others camped under the overhang of a bar, once crowded with patrons tossing down dollar bills and hard liquor.

Manuel spotted a cardboard box untouched by the blaze that had destroyed the club. He fashioned it into a blanket and wrapped it around Ana and himself. The two cousins snuggled close together against the night as they had a thousand times before, young children sharing the same bed.

The night was still for a time—a silence soon broken by the gentle tapping of rain that fell upon the charred roof, the pool table, and the brows of those within its reach.

But the Salvadorean refugees were not troubled by the rain; they took comfort in its song and scent. One by one, they yawned, closed their eyes and leaned against their neighbors' shoulders, as if members of the same family—lulled to sleep by the rain, and by visions of their true families back home, in another world, far away.

26

Sonia slapped a pupusa between her hands until the corn masa was nearly as flat as a pancake. She tossed it beside a stack of others already stuffed with cheese and chicharrones, ready for the skillet. Then she checked her soup. Steam billowed up from the pot, filling the kitchen with the aroma of chayote, beef, plátanos, yucca and cabbage.

"Ummm," she smiled as the steam caressed her face, pleased with the feast she prepared. Sonia dropped the lid back on the pot and it startled her, clanging like a bell. Her heart jumped: It's them! It's them! They are here! Realizing her mistake, she shook her head and said to herself: Tonta! It's not the phone at all. Hay Dios miyo. But *when*? They were supposed to arrive this morning! Oh, God. I hope everything is all right.

Yandy, Sonia's teenage daughter, lay stretched out on the floor in the living room nearby watching a sitcom, her legs swinging idly back and forth.

Sonia scooped up another handful of corn flour, rolled it into a ball, slapped it flat and filled the center with grated cheese and fried pork rind. The phone on the wall rang and she jumped.

"I'll get it!" her daughter yelled, leaping to her feet.

"No, niña!" Sonia protested, wiping her hands with a towel. "Maybe it is Manuel! Turn down the television, would you please, mamalinda?" The phone rang again. Trembling, Sonia picked up the receiver. "Hello?"

"Umm. Un momento—aquí está. It's for you, Yandy!" she cried. Her daughter dashed to the phone. "Please don't talk too long," Sonia said, holding the receiver ransom until Yandy agreed. "We have got to keep the line open."

Yandy nodded her head, and Sonia returned to the lavish dinner she was preparing for her brother and cousin.

The screen door slammed shut. It was Kike, Sonia's son. He headed straight for the kitchen. "What's for dinner, Mamá?"

"Pupusas. *And* sopa," she said, an eyebrow arched, both eyes dancing. "When Tío Manuel and Ana arrive, I know they will be very hungry,"

"How was your day, Papi?"

Kike grimaced, embarrassed by his mother's pet name for him. "Okay, I guess. When do we eat? I'm starving!"

"When your uncle gets here. Would you do me a favor? Would you go down to the corner and buy an avocado? And some soda if you want. Get a *big* bottle. Ana and Manuel are going to be very thirsty. There's some money in my purse."

Kike jerked his body about in protest, one that Sonia ignored. She had other things on her mind. As her son stormed out the door, Sonia called to him, "And be careful, Papi!"

"Ahh!" The screen door slammed shut.

Kike swung down the street, brooding over the way his mother treated him. She's always telling me what to do, he thought, his grievance formulated in English. She doesn't understand. . . t'ings are *different* here. It's not the *same*. Not *eve-en!*" Kike liked the sound of the words so much he repeated them out loud. "Not *eve-en!*" They sounded good.

A beautiful teenage girl crossed the street at the corner just ahead of him, walking in the opposite direction. Kike slouched and swung his arms at his side. He thought for an instant he saw her smile, though he was at the age where the difference between a smile and a sneer was often difficult to discern: in the barrio, as often as not, they were one and the same.

Kike's head swiveled and his eyes locked on to the girl's every move. A white Cadillac aggressively yanked to a stop at the corner and blocked his view, tinted windows hiding the passengers. There was something menacing in the manner in which it stood its ground. But Kike thought nothing about it and turned the corner, still thinking about the girl, hoping to get another glimpse of her, fantasizing about a future encounter where he would know what to say and what to do.

The Cadillac turned left, and Kike glanced back over his shoulder just in time to see the girl as she furtively glanced in his direction. She feigned indifference to mask her embarrassment and turned away, leaving Kike in a state of complete confusion.

The sound of tires skidding to a stop in gravel made Kike turn. Ahead of him, in a cloud of dust, both driver and passenger doors of the white Cadillac opened in unison. As two white men in tailored suits and sunglasses climbed out, Kike watched the scene unfold as if he were in the front row of the cinema, wondering who they were, what they were doing there and what would happen next. By the time he realized he had a part in the script, he was face down in gravel, his mouth full of dirt and stones, arms pinned behind his back.

"What!" he protested, thinking the men must be cops. "I ain't done nuh-ting!"

The driver grabbed a handful of hair and yanked Kike's head back while his partner dug his knee deep into his spine.

"Now listen carefully, you little fuck!" the driver said almost whimsically. "This is what in America we call a verbal warning. Understand?" Kike peered up at him with one open eye. The driver shook his head impatiently. "Comprendo? Tell your mama no union. Got it? No *union*." Kike nodded meekly. The driver slammed Kike's face into the gravel while his partner applied carefully calculated force to his wrists. The two well-dressed men stood up and brushed the dust from their hands, calmly glancing around before leaving Kike with their version of "Have a nice day" — two solid kicks to the solar plexus. They climbed back into their Cadillac, backed out of the gravel lot and sped away.

Kike clutched his stomach and writhed in pain. A plump Guatemalan dropped her groceries and ran to his side, her long braid dangling from the back of her neck like a rope. "Está bien? Está bien, patojo? Are you all right, young man?" Kike could not answer. The storekeeper—a small Asian man—abandoned his cash register to come to Kike's aid. "You okay, niño? You need hospital? You want I should call police?"

"No!" Kike coughed, still gasping for air. A small crowd gathered as he fought back tears and struggled to sit up.

Back home, Sonia called to her daughter. "C'mon, Yandy! You've talked long enough! We have to keep the line open!"

Sonia's husband, Raúl, sat in a battered easy chair, watching the evening news in Spanish. "Twenty-seven indocumentados were discovered dead in a locked van today near the Mexican border with California," a reporter announced in Spanish. Sonia rushed to her husband's side; they listened and watched with dread. "They were believed to have been deserted there by coyotes frightened away by immigration officers," the reporter continued, as footage was shown of the grisly scene. "It is believed most of the undocumented workers were from the same village in México."

"Pobrecitos," Sonia moaned. "Poor people."

As she watched the report on television, Sonia did not notice the screen door swing open; nor did she see Kike as he propped himself up in the doorway. Down the hallway, Yandy, still on the phone, cried, "Kike! What happened? Mamá! The cholos beat up Kike!"

Sonia rushed to his side. "Hay Dios miyo! What have they done to you? Oh my God! My boy!"

Raúl helped his son into the easy chair, while Sonia embraced Yandy, who had begun to sob at the sight of her battered brother.

"Calmense!" Raúl told Yandy. "Calm down, would you?

Now, what happened, son? Are you badly hurt?"

Kike shook his head no, yes, then no again. He fought back tears. "These two gabachos, dressed up real fancy, in a fancy car." He held his side while his father examined his ribs.

Sonia calmly stepped into the kitchen put a pot of water on to boil, glancing over the counter that separated the kitchen from the living room, watching as her husband examined Kike.

"It's all right, son," Raúl said, looking into Sonia's eyes with love and reassurance. "He is going to be fine, mí amor."

As husband and wife nursed their son, Kike told them what had happened. "Two white men in fancy suits and sunglasses drove up and grabbed me and threw me into the dirt by the Chinese store. They twisted my arms behind my back and kicked me."

"Did they say anything?"

Kike gulped, glancing at his mother as if afraid she would be hurt by his words. "They said to tell my mother this is a warning. To tell her no more union."

Sonia and Raúl's eyes met again. Everything became clear. "Did they say anything else?"

"No. That was it. Well. They called me a bad name."

"What did the car they were driving look like?" Raúl asked.

"What *difference* does it make?" Yandy blurted out.

"It makes a lot of difference!"

"Why? Why does it matter? It's all because Mamá is doing that union thing. That's all there is to it! First she was going to get fired, then she was almost deported. Now this!"

Sonia dropped her eyes.

"Mira. Don't blame your mother because some men beat up your brother. She is doing the right thing. Just because some bad people don't want her to do it doesn't mean she shouldn't. And remember—what she is doing, she is doing for all of us!"

Yandy was not convinced and glared with resentment at her mother. Raúl became angry. "Look. If you want to be upset, then be upset with me! Back home, I was doing the same thing. That's why we had to come here. You are too young to remember."

"Your father was in the Bloque Popular," Sonia explained in a whisper. "That's when they came."

"When *who* came?" Kike asked.

"The White Hand."

"The White Hand? *C'mon!*" Kike said as if they were telling him a children's story.

Sonia and Raúl shook their heads.

"Serious," Raúl continued. "You don't remember. You were both too young. We've tried to protect you so you could grow up and be happy. Trouble-free. Maybe we made a mistake. But now it is time you both know. In El Salvador there are secret organizations in the army and the treasury police. The death squads. One of them is called the White Hand. They call them that way because they warn you before they kill you. They put a white hand on your door."

"You mean Kike got beat up by the White Hand?" Yandy cried. "You mean we have to move again?"

"No, I don't think so. But we did back home. We had to leave the country. That is why we are here."

"¿Es verdad? Really?" Kike asked. Sonia nodded gravely.

"But that sort of thing doesn't happen in this country!" Yandy interjected. "They don't *allow* that here. Not in America!"

"Humph!" Sonia replied, her voice ringing with sarcasm as she collapsed in the easy chair.

"Are you saying those men were from the army?" Kike asked his father.

"I don't know, son. Possibly from the government. Or the company. I don't know."

"But why would the government beat up Kike?" Yandy asked, still skeptical. "The union drive doesn't concern them!"

"If you had been older when we were in El Salvador, you

wouldn't ask foolish questions like that," Raúl replied.

Sonia sat impassively on the easy chair, her eyes glazed. "La migra, the government, death squads. And now this. I thought we'd left all our problems behind." She took a deep breath. "Manuel and Ana are supposed to be here tonight! What should we do? What if those men are watching us right now? Oh, God! Why do you let things like this happen?"

27

Tires skidded across gravel. A car door popped open then slammed shut. Then there were footsteps. There was the sound of a güiro, then another slammed door. The footsteps drew nearer. Ana and Manuel held their breath.

"Hey, it's me," a voice whispered. "Open the pinche door!" A board was pried open and the coyote slipped into the burned-out bar. "Listen! There is a van parked right outside the door. This side is open. Here is what you've got to do. One by one, you move *quickly* and get inside. You have to lay on top of each other."

"I know which one I'd lay on," one of the coyotes smirked.

"Shut up, cabrón! Now listen. Keep down so no one can see you. And so everybody can fit. Entieden? Okay. We're going to Los Angeles now. It is a long drive. Once we are past Oceanside, there is no problem. And they usually don't even check today. Anyway, don't worry. We are going a different way. Don't talk or move in the van until we tell you it is safe. That should be in a few hours. It won't be real comfortable, see, but after this, you'll be in Los Angeles. All right now, let's go! Vamonos!"

One by one the refugees ran to the van, Ana and Manuel the last to leave, having learned from experience the disadvantages of being at the front of the line. Once everyone was inside, the coyote slid the door shut, popped the van's hood and pretended to examine the engine. After a few minutes of the charade, the coyotes climbed into the van and sped away.

They traveled east, whirling around mountains of black stones. Occasionally the slate moonscape gave way to cactus and homesteads rooted among the rocks. But such signs of life were dwarfed by the huge piles of stones, which looked like the result of a gigantic excavation.

As the sun rose, so did the temperature. Soon it was well over one hundred degrees. The refugees thought they had taken a detour through hell on their way to Los Angeles; they were pressed together like packed fish, squirming and cooking in the sweltering heat. Yet no one complained.

There was no other road to Los Angeles as safe as that through hell—a route even immigration agents avoided.

After two hours, the van veered northwest and followed a road traveled by rock hounds and migrant farmworkers from Calexico. Soon they pulled into a small gas station with neon beer signs in the window and a hand-painted sign that read LAST CHANCE TO WET YOUR WHISTLE.

"Stay down—I'll be right back," the coyote whispered to the refugees through the curtain dividing the cab and the cargo bed.

Peligro sauntered into the store. The owner sat back in his chair as if the mammoth folds of his body and neck had been poured there. He rested a massive arm atop a water cooler that bellowed out cold air unable to escape the atmosphere surrounding him. As the coyote approached, the shopkeeper looked him over, gauging whether he would be worth the trouble of getting up. He remained seated.

"E-speak E-Spanish?" Peligro asked, doing his best to appear friendly and harmless. The shopkeeper slowly shook his head no; he formed a tight-lipped smirk and squeezed his eyes shut.

"You have-a the pay phone?"

The storeowner lifted his hulking arm and lazily pointed toward the back of the store. Still sizing up the coyote, he revealed a growing, if lackluster, interest in his personal business. He turned his large concrete head in the direction of the van parked on the gravel out front. For a moment, it appeared that he might stand up—he made a slight movement, which did not escape the attention of the coyote. After whispering a few words into the phone and abruptly ending the conversation, Peligro adjusted his trousers, pulled a six-pack of beer from the cooler, and waited at the cash register.

"That's six dollars even," the shopkeeper said. "Just leave it on the counter."

There being few persons in the world who resent impropriety more than a thief or a charlatan, the coyote bitterly swallowed his pride, left six dollars by the register, smiled his gambler's smile and said goodbye. As the shopkeeper lifted his head to check the denominations of the bills on the counter, the coyote quickly snatched a copy of *Penthouse* magazine and stuffed it under his armpit, an act of personal redemption unnoticed by the pile-of-a-man on the chair.

"Don't try to steal from a thief," the coyote said to himself in Spanish as he mashed his way across the loose gravel toward the van and its cargo of sweltering refugees. Once behind the wheel, the coyote spun away from the store, creating a cloud of dust that hid the van from the shopkeeper's view.

Sweating profusely, the shopkeeper waddled from his chair to the money left by the coyote, rang up three dollars on the register, pocketed the difference and leaned against the counter to catch his breath. "Sittin' kinda low," he wheezed, spotting the van as it emerged from the cloud of dust. He glanced at the magazine rack and arched an eyebrow. "Don't ever try to hustle a hustler," he said, his cheeks inflating like a bellows as he reached for a telephone beneath the counter.

The coyote threw the magazine at his partner, sitting comfortably in the passenger seat. "Here. This is for you, you horny bastard—compliments of a pig."

As they raced down the highway, the coyote's partner licked his lips as he leafed from one page to the next. "Look at all this panocha!" he howled.

"You'll be able to buy as much of that as you want tonight,

if we're lucky," the coyote sneered. "The word is they are not checking at San Clemente today."

"All right! It's coca and panocha tonight!"

The coyote grinned, opened a can of beer with his teeth and drank it straight down.

Within an hour, the temperature dropped. Mountains became hills, hills ravines and marshland. Giant billboards appeared advertising restaurants and service stations. Peligro spotted a highway patrol car waiting on the shoulder of an on-ramp. "Get rid of those cans," the coyote ordered. "That's all we need is to be pulled over by a pinche chota."

They cruised down the highway, gliding across the swells of the road like a toboggan on packed snow. The highway straightened as it approached a bridge spanning a dry river-bed. Then, without notice, traffic suddenly slowed. The coyote spotted immigration vans on the north side of the bridge, yellow lights flashing. But it was too late to turn around without drawing attention.

"Son of a *bitch*!" Peligro sputtered as he applied pressure to the brakes. "All right now—be cool. It's a visual inspection. Roll your windows down," he ordered his partner as he did the same. "Okay. Now open the curtain."

"What? Are you crazy? What if they see what's back there?"

"Just open the fucking curtain and be cool! If the curtain is closed, they're going to want to take a look for sure!"

Peligro turned the radio to a rock 'n roll station and leaned back in his seat, slowing the van down until it nearly stopped.

Immigration agents glanced inside vehicles and scrutinized people's eyes, one by one waving travelers past the checkpoint. The coyote soon moved to the front of the line.

"Don't act like you are happy to see him," Peligro whispered to his partner between his teeth.

An agent leaned toward the passenger side of the van and peered through the curtain toward the cargo bed, though he could not see the refugees from where he stood. The coyote nodded his head with feigned respect. The agent wasn't buying it. He checked the van's plates then signaled Peligro to pull to the side of the road where half a dozen immigration agents waited. Peligro did not hesitate; he gunned the engine and the souped-up van lurched forward, screaming past the roadblock and down the highway, burning rubber in first and second gear. Seven agents leaped into four patrol cars and made chase.

A short distance down the road, the van slid to a dusty stop on the highway's shoulder. "La migra!" the coyotes shouted. "Everyone make a run for it!" They bounded up the brush and oak-covered hillside without stopping to open the cargo door. They knew that the refugees' attempts to escape would divert the immigration agents as they scampered away to safety.

Manuel immediately crawled across the backs of other refugees, past the bucket seats in the cab and out the passenger door. He popped the cargo door open and yanked Ana out of the van. They raced across a clearing and down the steep slopes of a ravine, into a thicket of oak and bay.

The other refugees struggled to climb out from the van, barely able to move—sore and hamstrung from the long journey through the desert and from the weight of bodies pressed against theirs.

Those who could move lumbered up the hillside, following the coyotes as they disappeared into the brush. But they did not get far before immigration agents arrived at the scene. Those who had succumbed to cramps and fear were quickly handcuffed. The women sobbed and the men cried, too, as clouds of dust drifted across the scene like smoke from cannon.

Agents shouted unintelligible commands into bullhorns; one, ignoring regulations, fired warning shots into the air. The pandemonium was soon heightened by the pulsing rotors of a helicopter, which hovered over pockets of refugees as they cowered in hiding spots on the hillside, shielding their eyes from the whirling dust.

Ana and Manuel followed the trough of a ravine up its seam, toward the hills it sliced open. Agents thrashed along behind them, cursing roots, holes, and thorny brush. Most of all they cursed Ana and Manuel, who ran without pause, their faces flushed, eyes wide open, hands bloody and trembling. They ran with the madness of instinct, driven forward by shouts and screams that grew more and more faint behind them.

Eventually they reached the crest of the hill. Panting, they crawled into a thick cluster of lupine and thistle, lying face down in the dirt, impervious to thorns, rock, and rattlesnake skin. They listened as they had learned to do, their ears to the earth; but all they could hear was their hearts pounding.

Soon the pressure of blood on their eyes subsided and they could see the sky and hear the wind. Birds sang and prepared their nests for the night. The helicopter whirled off toward another battlefront, and the last of the refugees were loaded into government vans bound for detention camps. Occasionally a distant voice was blown up the hillside, muffled by the trees and bent by the wind—a voice issuing orders in bastardized Spanish.

"I wonder where we are?" Manuel whispered.

"I heard the coyotes say something about San Clemente," Ana replied. "Is that close to Los Angeles?"

Manuel did not answer. Surveying the hillside, he tried to get his bearings. "Well, I think we have only two choices. Either we hide up here tonight, or we try to find our way back to the highway and see if we can find someone who will give us a ride."

"But they might be looking for us down there."

"Well, yes, but we can go farther north. But I don't think we should stay here. Sooner or later, we have got to go back down."

Ana closed her eyes and thought. "Do you still have Sonia's phone number?" she asked.

"Yes, I think so. Yes. You've got the right idea. We'll find a phone and call her. Maybe she can get another coyote for us. But first, maybe we should find a place to spend the night. A place where there is water—and where it is safe."

They crawled out from beneath the lupine and thistle; they could perceive every movement, hear every sound, recognize every scent; they had never felt so alive. Ana spotted something: "Look! Over there! See how green it is? There is water over there."

Ana and Manuel climbed down the hillside toward a grove of trees in the distance, veering north with every step—a precaution to make certain they would not end up where they had started.

Soon the sun began to set. But Ana and Manuel continued to hike in the cool shadows of twilight. They reached a lemon orchard. Trees ran away from them in perpendicular lines, shadows strobing between rows like an old silent movie.

In the darkness before moonrise, they gathered together a handful of lemons and dug at the tough rinds with bare fingers; they squeezed the fruit between their palms, stomped on them and smashed them against a tree, but without success. As the misty night fell around them, Ana and Manuel groped about on their hands and knees, searching for something they could use to break open the fruit. They were getting desperate; they had not eaten for more than a day, nor had even a sip of water for twelve hours. They were parched and dry, and a night in the grove would be difficult enough without something to quench their growing thirst. So they searched through dead leaves and soil with a growing sense of urgency, digging and thrashing about until Ana unearthed a long rusty nail. She lifted it up in the air and, like a shaman offering a sacrifice, stabbed the lemon once then twice. She yanked out the entrails and handed them to Manuel before savoring a strand herself.

As the cousins sat in the lemon grove in the dark, they took turns at their dinner, passing it back and forth, squeezing juice and pulp into mouths chapped and dry. And though their lips burned, it was good. They celebrated the feast with grunts and groans, relishing every morsel, savoring every drop, momentarily content and only vaguely aware of the significance of their first taste of life in North America.

28

Machines pounded and hissed and wheezed in the dim yellow light of the Mersola factory. Sonia sat glued to her bench, working a giant stapler, fastening formed pieces of cardboard to wooden heels. She pulled a long worn lever three times in succession, quickly spun a heel around, pulled the lever again and again and again, then stacked her finished work on a pile to her right. With the efficiency of a computerized machine, she reached for another piece, inspected it to make certain it was in good condition, then set it on the saddle, pounding another staple deep into the shaped wood, then another and another.

José approached her bench with caution, mindful of the whereabouts of the foreman. "Is everything all right?" he asked.

Sonia did not take her eyes off her work. She rotated a heel on the saddle and pulled the lever with more force than necessary, pounding one, two, three staples in a measured row. José arched his bushy eyebrows in astonishment. "Qué te pasa?" he asked tenderly. "What is happening?"

"Nada!" Sonia replied curtly—fighting instincts, feigning indifference—stacking another finished piece on the pile. José leaned forward and gazed deep into her eyes. But Sonia resisted. Any other man would have felt the sting of her rebuff and walked away. But José could feel her suffering, the lines of his own face a map of hardship endured. He offered her his hand— scarred and callused and warm—and smiled his grandfather smile.

A foreman rounded the corner and struck a pose, his head tilted back as if he had uncovered a crime in progress. "Don't you have something to do?" he asked with condescension.

José returned to his workstation. Sonia never missed a beat on her stapler.

The foreman scratched his chin and smiled smugly. Then he remembered Sonia and the reason he left the comfort of his air-conditioned office and the coffee-cup pleasure of the sports page. "Sonia, there is going to be a meeting in fifteen minutes. Over by the time clock. It's mandatory everyone attend—even *you*."

"Yes, sir. I'll be there," she assured him, though with minimum enthusiasm.

The foreman stared at her for a moment as though he wasn't quite sure he heard her correctly. He shrugged and sauntered off to the others in his department, anxious to make the same announcement.

Word spread and the workers began to file toward the time clock, many passing Sonia's bench on their way as she dutifully pounded staples into shaped wood and cardboard. An old man stopped momentarily to chat with her. "What kind of wonderful news do you think they have for us *this* time?" he asked, expecting sarcasm.

"I don't know. Anyway, what does it matter? As long as I get paid, I don't care," Sonia said, much to the old man's chagrin.

People gathered in concentric circles by the time clock, the drone of machinery replaced by the clatter of gossip and anticipation. Amerio Mersola appeared, clad in a cowboy shirt and Levis, accompanied by other men who normally wore suits, men who had been instructed to dress casually for the meeting. They watched Mersola's every move, anxious to smile when he smiled and frown when he frowned—all of them members of upper management, high-paid sycophants.

An attractive young Chicana in a red pantsuit commanded Amerio Mersola's immediate attention.

"Is everyone here?" he asked the plant foreman, who nodded obediently. Deferring to the young woman, Amerio Mersola asked, "Shall we get started then?" She smiled her approval.

Mersola cleared his throat and awaited the crowd's complete attention. "I've got some great news for all of you today," he announced, pausing for the foreman Pete to translate his remarks into Spanish. "Meet Linda Garcia. She's an immigration attorney I've hired to help you. I understand many of you may be in need of legal assistance in immigration matters," he continued, reading from a prepared statement. "So, in keeping with our company's policy of responding to our employees' needs, I've hired Miss Garcia."

"*Ms.* Garcia," the young attorney interrupted, nodding like a monarch.

"Excuse me," Mersola said, twitching. "*Ms.* Garcia."

"How do you say 'miz' in Spanish?" Pete asked another Latino foreman.

"Can we continue now?" Mersola asked, still twitching. "Yes, sir, Mr. Mersola, sir."

"Good. As I was saying. The immigration raid that occurred here recently was—most unfortunate," he said, checking his prepared statement to be certain he used the correct terminology. "Personally, it saddened and upset my entire family. I know what you went through was a difficult experience for all of you. But now that we have an attorney to help you, I feel quite confident we won't have to go through such an ordeal again."

Amerio Mersola licked his lips, savoring every word, confident they would have the desired effect. Pete translated, going so far as to mimic Mersola's gestures and movements. And the effect was overwhelming; the workers were jubilant, responding to Mersola's announcement as if it were the answer to their prayers—a cease-fire in a terrible war. Only a handful revealed any cynicism.

Javier dropped his head and laughed bitterly, while José pondered the implications of Mersola's new tactic. Meanwhile,

Sonia, consistent with her new attitude, betrayed no emotion.

Foremen leaped into action, quickly distributing leaflets that were snatched up with unbridled enthusiasm.

"The flyers you are getting have Ms. Garcia's office hours here at the company, as well as her phone number at her office," Mersola continued. "I hope now we can put the past behind us and all come together like a family again."

Mersola took a step back, waited until the translation was complete, then asked, "Okay?" A chorus of voices answered in unison, "Okay!" and many workers clapped their hands in appreciation. Satisfied, Amerio Mersola nodded his head and started back toward the executive offices, his entourage in trail. Only Ms. Garcia remained behind, anxious to mingle with the masses.

Following instructions, the foremen let workers bathe in their euphoria—though not without some difficulty, drilled as they were to eke out the last drop of production from those in their charge.

Rosa returned to her station, not one to take advantage of newfound freedoms. She stared across the cement floor of her department at Sonia, who was already back at work. Rosa knew something was wrong but did not know what to do. She knew Sonia was troubled—but she was raised to mind her own business and not to interfere—to respect the wishes of others; she was raised with the values taught all peasant girls in Jalisco. Still, she could not help but gaze across the aisle at Sonia, knowing deep in her heart that something was very wrong.

Sonia pretended not to notice Rosa's concern and quickly reestablished her stapling rhythm, her arms, hands and fingers extensions of a machine.

The day dragged on slowly, Sonia a model worker, Rosa preoccupied with worry, the drudgery of work broken only by a buzzer announcing the beginning and end of coffee breaks. But in the afternoon, something unusual happened: all the foremen were summoned to a secret meeting in the executive offices. In a day full of surprises, the workers wondered what would happen next. Half an hour later, their questions were answered. The foremen burst out of the office doors and swarmed into the factory. Everyone knew something was going down.

Pete could barely control himself, so anxious was he to perform his assignment. He sidled about from one area to another as if he could move unnoticed. Avoiding Sonia, he approached Rosa. "Qué tal, mi amor?" he asked. Rosa shuddered. "What's wrong, baby? Do I make you nervous?" Rosa focused on her work and shrugged her shoulders. "That's all right, mi amor, you'll come around some day. I can promise you that. By the way, I've got some news you might be interested in." He bent over and whispered in her ear. "You know that raid by la migra that picked you up? Do you know who was really behind that raid?"

Rosa leaned away from Pete's face, turning to Sonia for help. "It was the *union*!"

"Mentira!" Rosa replied. "That's a lie!"

"No, no, baby! It's true! The *union* called in immigration! I've seen proof! Besides—why would I lie to a beautiful woman like you?" Pete wrapped his arm around her waist and Rosa politely removed it.

"All right! Don't believe me! You'll find out!" he said and stormed off. It wasn't long before he spotted Meche, a portly Mexican who had the habit of wearing low-neck blouses and cut-away bras. He slithered up to her, smiling and gazing at her breasts with admiration. Meche blushed as Pete came on to her, never lifting his eyes from the cleavage he interpreted as an invitation. He digressed briefly from his proposition—just long enough to announce the news—then quickly returned to his preoccupation, pushing his luck and getting his hand slapped. Spinning away from Meche's bench, he laughed bawdily, eager to share his adventures with another foreman. Meche used the opportunity to confer with Rosa.

"Did he tell you?" she asked.

"Yes," Rosa answered. "But you know that man has never said an honest word in his life."

José, who had been observing Pete's maneuvers from his workstation, took advantage of his absence to find out what was happening. Meche told him what Pete had said, her voice strained by a growing disdain, which suggested to José that he, too, was somehow responsible for the immigration raid.

"That's a lie what he told you!" José said. "Why would the union call in la migra? Didn't you see Antonio on the television?" Meche was not convinced. "It was the *union* who called in the immigration lawyers who turned the buses around! This is just a lie invented by the company to confuse people."

"I'm not so sure," Meche replied caustically. "I don't really trust unions. They just try to use people. Like that Antonio. He used to come to the gates every day. Now he has disappeared!"

Rosa's eyes met José's. Across the aisle, Sonia, with her poker face, struggled to overhear the conversation.

"You know something, Meche?" Rosa asked softly. "The union— thanks to José and Antonio—took care of my children when I was picked up by la migra. The company didn't do that—it was the union. Do you think the union would do that if they were responsible for getting me arrested?"

"Pues, well . . . I don't know. Anything is possible. Maybe. But whatever happened to Antonio, anyway? I haven't seen him since he was on TV that day. Why is that?"

"It is a complicated thing," José sighed, deep furrows cutting across his face. Rosa closed her eyes and listened. "The truth is, he was fired by the union president. Now—before you make up your mind about anything—we've got to understand the union isn't perfect. Nothing is."

"But Antonio *was* the union," Meche said, impressed by her own rhetoric.

"No, señora. *We* are the union. There are some big shots who *think* they are the union. Isn't that the way it is with everything? Aren't there always some people who think they are more important than others?" José took a deep breath and watched Meche, unable to hide his emotions. "We'll make a union—all of us here at the factory. And when we do, we'll vote in people we can trust. And if they don't do the job, we'll elect someone else. It won't be easy. Nothing that matters is. But things will be better—you'll see. We can do it if we stick together! Mira! Look at what the company is doing! They're trying to trick people. Don't you think it is strange that Mersola suddenly cares about our problems with the immigration? He knew we didn't have papers when we were hired. That's *why* we were hired! He thought that way he could push us around and there would be nothing we could do about it! Now, with the union organizing, he is scared. Now he might have to pay us for overtime and pay for medical insurance. He is afraid of the union—he is afraid of us organizing!"

Meche listened, but was not convinced. The company version of the truth was so much easier to accept. She didn't have to lift a finger. Everything would be all right if left alone.

"Think about it, señora. Do you think Mersola would do this if the union wasn't here? Do you think—"

"All right, José, enough of your propaganda!" Pete interrupted, having crept up behind the three workers without being detected. "This is the last time I'm gonna warn you. Next time, I'm going to write you up! Now, get to work, old man!"

José returned to his workstation, his thoughts still whirling. Rosa bowed her head and plunged into her work, expecting the worst, her hands trembling.

"Don't listen to that old man," Pete warned Meche. "He's only out for himself. He doesn't give a damn about you or your family. He wants the union to win so he can become a big shot union steward! Then he won't have to work anymore."

Meche nodded meekly, blaming José for the reprimand.

Satisfied that he had driven his point home, Pete approached another workstation, where a young woman smiled bashfully as he advanced. Pete leaned across her bench to tell her a joke. The young woman's eyes glistened as he spoke, her head propped up by open palms. She had admired Pete for a long time, though from a distance. He had all the traits she admired—he was tough, important, and—well, he was a *man*. The young woman was enthralled by his presence and listened intently, as if he were reciting sonnets, every word sweet as a gardenia. And as she listened to him make his beer-bellied pitch, her machine sat idle, throbbing with an electric pulse. But Pete wasn't the least bit concerned by the loss of production in this case; he had met a woman who appreciated his wit and charm. She could take the day off as far as he was concerned—as long as she spent it with him.

Meche glanced at the lecherous foreman, then at Rosa. Across the department, José was watching the scene unfold. And though he did not speak, she could almost hear him say, "See? See how things are?" But Meche refused to acknowledge any impropriety; she preferred to accept things as they were. Change was an unknown and ideas that suggested change were dangerous.

And as she thought about things, it was *José* she resented, not the foreman. Blood raced through her veins, and she felt restless and angry. How *dare* he tell me what is wrong and what is right! she thought. If he knows so much, how come he is working while the foreman can do as he pleases?

Machines hummed and pitched and pounded; the air grew stale and smoky; the dim yellow lights flickered, an electric web stretched to its limits. Sonia reached for more cardboard and wood, pounding rows of staples with a lever worn by the contours of her hand. Rosa stitched another sole on her machine. And for the workers at the factory, life quietly slipped away.

Finally the buzzer sounded. It was time to go home. People reached for their jackets, lunchboxes, and cigarettes. A long line formed at the time clock, folks taking turns to punch out. And as they waited, they calculated bus fares and transfer points, planned dinners, and thought about their favorite TV shows. One by one, they filed out into the light of the setting sun, determined to overcome all obstacles that awaited them, anxious to get home as fast as possible. They wanted to be home where they could follow their own schedules and meet their own deadlines. They wanted to be with their loved ones; they were desperate to touch somebody, to feel something—to be home where what they said and what they thought mattered. And as they left the factory, they fought with others who had the same needs and the same desires—all of them jockeying for position, arguing over bus seats and right-of-ways like refugees battling in breadlines.

José made his way through the crowd to Sonia's side as she raced toward the bus stop. Once he caught up with her, he struggled to overcome his anxiety. "Have you heard the latest lies?" he asked.

"I was at the meeting," she replied coldly, increasing her pace.

"No. I mean the other lies."

Sonia attempted to appear indifferent.

"Now they are saying the union called in the immigration."

Sonia stopped so suddenly a worker walking behind her nearly ran into her. She turned to José, indignant and full of fire. Then she remembered her son and her manner instantly changed. "Oh, really? Well, I can't help it if people believe things that are not true."

"What's wrong?" José asked. "You've been acting strange all day!"

"I'm sorry, Don José, but I am really in a hurry! I have to get home."

Sonia bounded down the street toward her bus stop, José still at her side.

"I know something is wrong, Sonia. I just want to help you, if I can. We are friends, no? Is there something I can do?"

Sonia shook her head in an effort to free herself from the tenderness of José's voice. She tightened her lips and increased her pace another notch. "What is it, Sonia? What are friends for if they can't help each other when they have problems?"

"It is nothing, Don José! Really! I am sorry! It's just that—well—I cannot be involved in the union anymore! I'll vote for the union, but I can't be *involved*! I just can't! I hope you will understand."

José fell a step behind as they hurried down the street toward the bus stop. As motorists honked their horns and engines roared, Sonia fought back tears.

"Did I say something to offend you?" José asked.

"No, José. It is nothing like that. It is my family. My younger brother and cousin are coming from back home. And I can't have any more problems now. They'll be here any day!"

"But nothing is going to happen!"

A tear streaked down her cheek. "They beat up my son! They beat up Kike!"

"What! *Who* did? When?"

"Two men. They told him it was because I am involved in the union! They told him . . ." Sonia covered her face with her hands.

José wrapped his arms around her shoulders. "It's all right," he assured her. "Everything is going to be all right. Why didn't you tell us? We've got to do something about this!"

"No! Please! My family! We have been through enough! Please! Don't tell anyone about this!"

"But Sonia, your family is already in danger."

"Please!" Sonia begged. "I'm sorry. But please leave me alone!" Sobbing, she ran down the street to her bus.

José watched as Sonia stepped on board, overcome as she was by powerful emotions, torn by circumstances totally out of her control. The bus roared away into the night, wrapping José in a foul blue cloud. He watched the bus jostle with traffic, yellow arrows flashing left, then right, caught as it was in a web of traffic. When the bus was no longer in sight, he reached into his pocket for a handkerchief, which he used to wipe away dust and carbon and tears from his eyes.

29

Sonia lit a match to ignite a burner on the stove. She poured a little oil into a pan, heated it until it began to pop, then added slices of onion to fry. When the onions began to brown, Sonia scooped in a generous amount of cooked black beans, smashing them until they were almost a paste. It was a traditional Salvadorean dish she prepared, one that would be served with fried platános—a type of banana—and a sour cream. Frijoles fritos con platanos y crema—even the words tasted good.

Sonia had been preparing special meals for several days, hoping Manuel and Ana would be there to enjoy them. But crossing the border was not like going on a vacation. Sonia knew first-hand about such things. Still, she was worried. She had not heard a word from her brother and cousin since they left El Salvador.

The phone rang, and as she had done for the past few days, Sonia dropped what she was doing and rushed to answer it.

"Hallo? Yes? Yes, okay. Yes? Yes—you can pass it to me. Yes. I will—how you say? It is okay. Tank you berry much." Sonia waited a moment while a connection was made. "Hallo? Manuel? Qué pasa? Are you both all right?"

Sonia's husband and daughter instantly joined her near the telephone. She motioned for a piece of paper and a pen.

"Hay Dios miyo! Donde están? A *donde*? San Antonio Park? South of San Clemente? In the mountains? But *where* in the mountains?"

Sonia listened, grimacing with every word, as Manuel gave details about what had happened.

"We'll get a coyote for you," she assured her brother. "Don't worry. Now tell me exactly where you are again."

Sonia wrote down their whereabouts as it was described by Manuel and repeated it back to him twice to be sure. But there were few names, few significant details. He described a tunnel where "a cement river runs under a big fast street"—their hiding place. It was close to the main highway, she surmised— "the one that runs north and south." According to Manuel's description, there was "a big white place where people buy gasoline for their cars, with bright lights and a big sign." Sonia asked the name of the gas station and wrote it down. She told her brother that if nobody had come for them by morning to call her again. She taught him how to say "Collect, please" in English—just in case—while reassuring him that everything would be all right. Then, with a heavy heart, she said goodbye and hung up.

Sonia was instantly deluged by questions from her husband and daughter. She patiently shared what little she knew, answering most of their inquiries with an emotional "I don't know!" Then, together, they sat down and considered what they should do next.

"Why don't we call the coyote who brought Tía Irma?" Yandy asked, desperate for a quick solution.

"How much will they want?" Raúl, a practical man, asked.

"I don't know," Sonia sighed. "I hope we will have enough." Sonia searched in a cluttered drawer for a piece of paper and, upon finding it, quickly dialed a telephone number. Without asking for a name, she identified herself as a friend of someone the coyote knew, then stated her business cryptically. Her family watched her expression, hoping for good news.

"They are near San Clemente," Sonia told the coyote. "Yes, south of there, near a park. Near San Antonio Park." She covered the mouthpiece with her hand. "How much money do we have?" she whispered.

Yandy ran to the cupboard and retrieved a cereal box where

they hid their cash while Raúl counted what he had in his wallet. They tallied it up. "One hundred and twelve dollars," Raúl announced.

"The rent money is underneath the carpet in the bedroom," Sonia whispered, still covering the mouthpiece. "There should be two hundred dollars there—I've already saved half of it."

Sonia uncovered the phone and replied, "*How* much? Well . . . let me make a few calls and I will call you back." She slammed down the receiver and turned to her family. "They want three hundred dollars in advance!"

"In advance!" Raúl said. He couldn't believe it. "No, we can't do that! Those guys are trying to make a good business. Remember the last time we paid the coyotes in advance? When Samuel was in Tijuana? When he was stuck there in a hotel and they wouldn't let him out? Púchica! They said they went there, but he was gone. And we never got the money back! No, if we do that, then they don't even have to try to find them! Pinche ladrones!"

Sonia plopped down in the big easy chair. The pressure of the past week was beginning to take its toll. "What are we going to do? We should have been prepared for something like this!"

"I thought those coyotes we hired were supposed to be the best. Isn't that what your friend Meche said?" Raúl asked.

"Well, it doesn't matter now. We can't just call them up, you know. They're not going to go back and get them." Sonia considered all the options, though there were few. They had not prepared for such a setback, though they knew deep down they should have. There were just too many things happening at once.

"If only we knew someone who could just drive down there and pick them up. Someone who could pass through San Clemente without any trouble. Hay Dios miyo. What are we going to do?"

Raúl sat back in his chair and scratched his chin. "Antonio!"

Sonia blurted out.

"What?"

"Antonio! Maybe he would do it!"

"You mean the guy from the union?"

"Yes!"

"Be realistic," Raúl said. "Why would *he* take a chance and drive down there? Besides, he hasn't even been around since he was fired by the union. Aren't *you* the one who told me he is afraid he won't get another job as an organizer? Isn't that what you said? That he was *afraid*? Now do you think you can just call him and ask him to do something as risky as this?"

"But he told me once that if there was ever anything he could do for me, not to hesitate to call him."

"Oh, sure! But that was back when he was working for the union! This is different, you know. Why would he do such a thing? For money?"

"No, Raúl. I don't know. I can offer to pay him. I will do that, of course. But if he agreed to help us, I don't think he would do it for money. Would you take money from a friend?"

"No, of course not! But what makes you think he is your friend?"

"I don't know. But anyway, we have to try. I have to ask. We can't just leave Manuel and Ana hiding in the mountains like animals. We have to do something! Do *you* want to drive down there and pick them up?"

"I would—if we had a car—and if I had a license."

"So what are you saying? We need to *try*. What have we got to lose? They can't take the bus up here, you know!"

Raúl thought about what she said, then reluctantly agreed.

Sonia returned to the drawer filled with bills, birth certificates, and other important papers. She rummaged through it as before until she found Antonio's business card, his home phone number scrawled on the back. Her family watched her as she dialed the phone, flinching when she said, "Hallo? Antonio?

Soy Sonia. Bien, y usted? Qué bueno. Look, Antonio. I've got a big problem and I need your help."

30

Antonio rounded the curve of the off-ramp, his headlights illuminating cats' eyes and beer cans along the side of the road. At the stop sign, he leaned forward and checked for landmarks, and by the misty blue light of a streetlamp, paused to carefully reread directions written on the back of an envelope.

The blaring bright lights of a gas station dominated the barren landscape, a giant sign proclaiming MOBIL, in plastic red, white and blue. "I hope this is it," Antonio said to himself as he stepped on the gas and maneuvered his car into the station.

"What'll it be?" the attendant asked, poised between the regular and unleaded.

"It'll be a cold day in hell before I spend another night like *this*!"

"I heard that!" the attendant replied.

"Listen, man, is San Antonio Park close by here?" Antonio asked as he surveyed the dark countryside.

"This is it, man. You lookin' for somethin'?"

"Well, this is it, I guess. Would you fill it up for me and check under the hood?"

"Sure thing. Regular or unleaded?"

"Unleaded. And look, man. Where's the head?"

"Round the back, man. Door's unlocked." The attendant switched on the pump and searched for the car's gas spout.

"Thanks, buddy," Antonio said as he spun around toward the bathroom, fading out of the bright buzzing light of the station and into the dark of night. Antonio casually glanced over his shoulder; the attendant had his back to him, bent over the engine, checking the dipstick. Antonio pivoted in a right angle and headed toward the highway, elevated on a high mound. In the darkness, the highway looked like a dike holding back the sea, waves of light rolling past, roaring with the voices of men lost forever in the deep. Pausing momentarily to adjust to the dark, he squinted his eyes and searched for signs of a tunnel.

"Oye! Manuel!" he cried, softly enough so his words would roll into the folds of thunder emanating from the freeway. "Soy un amigo de Sonia. I'm a friend of Sonia's. I've come for you."

A faint form took shape in the drifting light of the gas station. It was Manuel. He approached with caution.

"Are you all right?" Antonio asked.

"Sí, hombre. I am all right."

"And Ana?"

"She is all right, also."

"Okay. Mira. We have to move fast. My car is over there," Antonio said, pointing. "See the phone there by that big light? I'm going to pull my car next to the phone and leave the door open so you can get in. I'm going to make a call. Watch me. I'll signal you when it is clear. Then you both need to run and get in the back seat. And when you are inside the car, lie down until I tell you everything is okay. Understand?"

"Yes, I understand," Manuel answered. Then he disappeared back into the dark.

Antonio walked back toward the bathroom then veered toward the service area and his car.

"That's better," he told the attendant, adjusting his pants.

The attendant smiled. "That'll be eight bucks, sir. Cash or charge?"

"Charge. No—you'd better make that cash." Antonio paid him with a ten-dollar bill. "Can I have a dollar in change? I've got to make a call."

"No problem, sir. The pay phone is over there."

"By the way," Antonio said. "Where is Ridge Road?"

220

"That's the next turnoff if you're heading south. Can't miss it." Antonio looked in the direction the attendant pointed.

"Okay, thanks. Take it easy, man," he said as he climbed into his car.

After driving around the gas pumps, Antonio parked his car beside the phone as planned, unlocked the passenger door and jarred it open. He flipped off the overhead cab light and walked to the pay phone, where he pretended to make a call. When the attendant was out of sight, he motioned to Manuel and Ana, who ran to the car and quickly climbed inside as instructed. Antonio continued the charade for a moment, then, when he felt all was clear, closed the passenger door, climbed into his car and sped away.

"Is everything okay?" he asked his passengers, barely moving his lips.

"Está bien, hombre," Manuel answered, whispering from the floor of the back seat.

"After we pass San Clemente, you can get up. I just passed that way not long ago, and there weren't any immigration agents there. But, just to make sure, you had better stay down for now. Sorry."

Ana and Manuel glanced at each other in bewilderment.

"I guess you're pretty used to having to hide," Antonio said. "That attendant seemed like a good guy, but I just couldn't take a chance. There are a lot of lies told about undocumented workers in this country—blaming them for unemployment, high taxes, and so on. So it is better not to take a chance. But you'll see. Most people are pretty decent."

Ana and Manuel were puzzled. They had thought they had to hide so they wouldn't get caught!

Antonio passed the checkpoint at San Clemente without incident and drove on, casually checking the highway ahead and behind for any signs of immigration agents. When he felt it was safe, he suggested someone get into the front seat with him.

Manuel quickly climbed into the seat, suspicious of Antonio's intentions.

"It must have been very hard for both of you these past couple of weeks," Antonio said, glancing at Manuel. Manuel nodded, showing no emotion. "Well, I hope things will be better for you now. This is a good country. The people here are, for the most part, buena gente—good people. The working people are. Some of them are confused, though. Rich people like for them to be that way. They like to keep people confused and fighting against each other." Antonio glanced at Manuel to gauge his reaction. It was an organizer's trait he could not overcome. But Manuel said nothing and showed nothing; he had learned that much during his journey from El Salvador.

"See, throughout the history of this country, whenever there have been difficult times—especially economically—one group of people or another have been made scapegoats. They have been blamed for all the problems. Especially when jobs are scarce. In the past, the Irish, Italians, Jews, and Chinese have all been blamed for our problems. At one time or another, just about every immigrant group has been blamed. And black people—they are always being shit on! And they didn't even choose to come here! Their ancestors were brought here by force as slaves! You know, some people have even been killed when things were bad. But what people have to do is *unite* instead of *fighting* each other. Then people like you won't have to hide like some kind of criminals. And we can change things so there is enough for everyone! If all the poor and working people get together, then there is nothing we can't do."

Manuel stared at Antonio for a moment, stunned by what he said. He was exhausted, running on adrenaline and little more. Yet, despite what he had been through since leaving his wife and son, what Antonio said still rang true. And despite the danger of speaking to a stranger he had no reason to trust—a man reason told him under the circumstances he should *not* trust—he could not remain silent. It had been so long since he had been able to say anything—even in private! He cleared his throat and began to speak, despite a precautionary kick under the seat from Ana meant to discourage such an indiscretion.

"You know, you remind me of a man I knew in my country. He was a leader of my sindicato—my union. Before the government smashed them. You talk just like he did. Not about exactly the same things—but still, a lot alike. He always talked about the workers uniting."

"Pues," Antonio smiled. "Maybe that is because I am a union organizer."

"You are?" Ana asked, leaning between the bucket seats. "De veras? A union organizer and a *coyote*?"

Antonio laughed. "I'm not a coyote. I'm a friend of Sonia. We've been working together organizing a union in the factory where she works."

"Do you see that?" Manuel asked Ana. "Sonia never told me she was doing that! But it doesn't surprise me."

"Sonia is a good organizer," Antonio said. "But it has been very difficult. The unions in this country aren't the same as many of those in México and Central America. Most of them are very weak right now. And there are a lot of vendidos—a lot of sell-outs."

"Oh, but there are many *bendidos* in our country, too," Manuel assured him. "A lot of them have joined the government. A lot of them get killed, too. When they turn against the people. Ah, but the *good* men . . . they *never* live to be old men. Like Miguel. The man I was just telling you about. He was killed by the death squads."

Ana leaned back in her seat and covered her eyes.

"He was killed by one of the leaders of ARENA—one of the rich people's parties back home. They are the same ones who murdered the Archbishop Romero—while he was saying mass! Ah, but Miguel, just like the Monseñor, he was a beautiful man!

Really! He told the people the truth, and fought for us. So they killed him. That is what they do to good men, no? They shot him when he was on his way home—they splattered a wall with his heart and guts. Blood splattered all over a brick wall. But then, los muchachos—the guerrillas—they named it a 'mural of the people.' And everyone used to leave flowers there. Then, after a time, the army bulldozed it down. But we will not forget him. No. We will never forget what he did for us."

Antonio fumbled for a cigarette, offering one to Manuel and Ana. Manuel accepted, anxious to be filled by the emptiness of smoke. Antonio pushed in the car's cigarette lighter and when it popped out, handed it to Manuel, who initially did not know what it was, having spent little time in an automobile. When he felt its heat and saw its glowing red coil, he laughed and lit his cigarette before passing the lighter back to Antonio.

Manuel settled back into his seat and gazed out the car window. "Yes. Miguel taught me many things. Sometimes I wish I could be more like him. He showed me it was better to die like a man, fighting for what was right, than to live afraid. When things got difficult, Miguel did not run away to protect himself." Manuel blinked and reflected upon his own life.

Antonio was stunned, unexpectedly cut to the bone by Manuel's remarks. He shifted in his seat restlessly, unable to remain still, wondering if Manuel and Ana somehow knew.

A bar of light from the rearview mirror crossed Antonio's face and for an instant he saw his own reflection. He was startled by what he saw. There in the rearview mirror was a man he did not recognize—a man who was weak and frightened. Antonio looked away and tried to shake loose the image of the man. But he couldn't, and he felt as if he couldn't breathe.

Then it was dark again. Antonio cracked the car window open, leaned over and took a deep breath, sucking in the cool night air. It was all just a hallucination, he thought. That's it— just an optical illusion. Too much stress, too much pressure. I am not like that. He smashed his cigarette out in the ashtray and stepped on the gas. The wheels of the car gripped the pavement, tires sizzling in the night. And for the duration of the trip, Antonio never looked back.

31

Exactly twenty-five minutes after waiting their turn to punch out for lunch, a buzzer sounded, warning workers they had five minutes to return to their jobs. During that five-minute span, they were required to wait their turn at the time clock, punch back in, return to their stations, stow their belongings and engage their machines. The moment the buzzer sounded again, they were to pick up where they had left off before lunch. "You're not being paid to wash your hands, pick your teeth, or dilly-dally," the workers were reminded daily by foremen. "When you're at lunch, your time is your own—within certain guidelines, of course. But when that second buzzer sounds, you're on the clock—and your time belongs to the *company*."

For every minute a factory worker was late, ten minutes' pay was deducted from their next paycheck. It was company policy; late one minute, work nine minutes free. Those who habitually broke the rules were subject to even stricter discipline, ranging from a written warning to suspension from work for a week. Ultimately, one could lose one's job for being a minute late. Those were the rules, lauded by management as "fair" and "impartial" —though they did not apply to any other employees of the Mersola Shoe Factory.

Meche stormed out of the business offices of the company, where she had spent her entire lunch break. She stood in line at the time clock, shaking like an out-of-tune automobile at a stoplight. When it was her turn, she jammed her card into the aging contraption three times before it registered a stamp then rumbled away, red-faced, to her work station, muttering a string of

Spanish expletives along the way.

As Meche brewed and bubbled at her bench, Sonia and José returned from lunch. Sonia picked her teeth and smiled as they waited their turn at the time clock.

"Oh, Don José, it was so good to see them again after so many years! We stayed up until two in the morning, talking."

José beamed and nodded his head, his eyes sparkling. As the two of them strolled toward their respective workstations, Meche stood at her bench, waiting for Sonia to return. And when she did, Meche raced to her side, steaming and sputtering.

"How do you vote for the union?" she demanded.

Sonia was taken aback. "I thought you didn't trust unions?" she replied, still picking her teeth.

"Ah! Well! That pinche Mersola! He changed my mind!"

Though relieved by the arrival of Manuel and Ana, Sonia was still hesitant to plunge back into the role of organizer. But she was curious what caused Meche's sudden change of heart. With restraint, she asked, "What happened?"

Meche took a deep breath. "That pinche güero Mersola told us he hired a lawyer to help with la migra, no? But what he *didn't* say was that just to talk to that cabrona would cost us fifty dollars! And—can you believe this? If she *does* anything to help you, it will cost four hundred dollars! That chingado! Huh! Does he think I am stupid?"

Sonia felt like laughing. But she didn't.

"Do you know what, Sonia? He and that fancy puta lawyer can both eat shit!" Meche shook her head in indignation. "You were right, Sonia. You and José were so right. And I tell you something. I'm going to tell *everybody* what Mersola did to me! And do you want to know something else? That son of a bitch is in for a surprise next week when we have the election!"

Sonia was not impressed by Meche's bitterness. Yet she could not help but smile.

While Meche vented her rage, Javier struggled nearby to get back into the flow of work. It was always difficult for him to return from lunch or break, though he took great pride in his work. He was, after all, from a long line of shoemakers, his father and grandfather having enjoyed the reputation of gifted craftsmen in their village in México. Javier had learned at an early age how to make a pair of shoes from scratch. But there was little craft in making shoes on what was essentially an assembly line—not for one who had mastered the process from beginning to end.

But there was more to it than that. Something had happened to Javier during the union drive. His exposure to organizing had awakened other instincts in him, new desires—though his skill as an organizer was about as limited as his function on the assembly line. Still it was work with meaning that he sought: a job which, when complete, brought satisfaction. And so he ventured away from his work area, though the buzzer had just announced the end of lunch and he ran the risk of being disciplined by a foreman if caught somewhere other than where he was supposed to be.

Javier spotted an old man operating a machine that sliced leather into strips. The old man focused on the material, turning his head cockeyed, peering through thick cataracts, smoking and sweating and adjusting the machine until it was set just right.

"Hey, old man! You going to vote for the union next week?" Javier asked, glancing from side to side with caution.

The old man finished his cut, wiped his forehead and took a puff from his cigarette. Exhaling, he answered, "Well, I don't know."

"Why not? Do you want to work the rest of your life in this pinche fabrica making the minimum?"

"I make more than the minimum," the old man mumbled, squinting his eyes against the curling smoke of his cigarette.

"Really? Hey, that is wonderful! How much do you make? Three twenty-five an hour?" Javier asked sarcastically.

The old man coughed. "Three *thirty-five.*"

"Three *thirty-five!* Hey! That's a *lot!* Hombre! You'll be able to retire soon on that! Híjole! Not bad for ten years at this pinche place!"

"Twelve," the old man said.

"Twelve! Oh, excuse me!" Javier laughed. "I know you must be a very happy man! They are treating you so *good* after twelve years in this place! But really, old man. Con respeto. With respect. Don't you think you deserve more than that? Bueno. And wouldn't it be nice to be able to retire with a pension? Really, you can be honest with me. I am not talking bullshit."

"Pues. They say the dues from the union would mean we would have less money for food. I like to eat, you know, muchacho. That is one of the things I like best."

"*Who* says? That pinche viejo Mersola says, that son of a bitch! He comes strolling in here with his fancy clothes and hundred-dollar shoes telling us we're like his family! Do you think he would pay his family the minimum? Excuse me! Three thirty-five an hour?"

The old man laughed, his laughter raspy like a smoker's cough. "We're making that thief rich! We're . . ."

"*There* you are! I've been looking for you!" Javier's foreman interrupted, with a twisted grin, his voice slurred with restrained anger. "I'm not paying you to brainwash people, you know!"

"The truth is—you're not paying me shit!" Javier answered with defiance.

"What did you say?"

"You heard me!"

The old man turned back to his machine and prepared to make another cut. But he cocked his head to listen, anxious to know what would happen next.

"Either you get your ass back to work or you're going to be one sorry wetback!"

"What are you going to do? Fire me? Hah! You know you can't right now. That would be a bad idea. The big boss might not like it! You could be in a lot of trouble firing me just one week before the union election." Javier turned and began to walk away, hesitating just long enough to fire off one more salvo: "I was on my way to the bathroom, you know. Are you going to follow me there to see what I am going to do?" His question unanswered, Javier sneered and strolled away.

The foreman was speechless. The old man glanced at him then turned away, doing his best to keep from laughing. Feeling naked and absurd, the foreman made a hasty retreat, anxious to return to the sanctity of his office, his right hand whipping uncontrollably behind him, fanning the air as if it had a life of its own.

Javier soon returned from the bathroom; he grinned audaciously at the old man, winked, clenched his fist and held it tight against his ribs. The old man smiled and awkwardly clenched his fist as well, his fingers white from the power of his grip.

As Javier swaggered back to his station, the old man watched in admiration. His eyes twinkled as he whispered to himself: "*La unión!*"

32

It was a beautiful morning, dawn an explosion of light in a turquoise sky. Autumn winds whisked leaves into cartwheels, and the air smelled clean and good.

Workers arrived early that morning at the Mersola factory. They gathered together throughout the plant, debating issues of the union campaign like college students in coffee shops.

For the first hour of the workday, foremen raced around frantically, trying to restore order. They told people to go back to work, to return to their stations—commands that were largely ignored. Frustrated and hoarse, the foremen finally gave up; they stood together like a football team witnessing the final moments of a game that was lost.

José and Javier listened in on the discussions, startled by the sudden outpouring of support for a drive that only a week before had seemed doomed. When Javier attempted to answer a question in one debate he was interrupted by three other workers making the same point he wished to make.

"I don't know if I should be happy or mad," Javier confessed to José.

"Be happy," José beamed. "This is what we have been fighting for."

"Bueno, José. You are right. But if I am happy too often, I am going to get mad."

Sonia refrained from campaigning for as long as she could. But after a while she too was swept away by the festive atmosphere and joined in, plunging right into the thick of things with more verve than before. It was time to go for broke—and she knew it.

Break time approached and few shoes had been made. The foremen continued to stand around in groups, brooding and plotting revenge, preparing hit lists and detailed dossiers for future reference. Their time would come—of that much they were certain. And when it did, those who had defied them would pay. In the meantime, they would watch—arms folded—and wait.

At 9:00 a.m., the buzzer sounded. A catering truck careened around the corner toward the factory gates, right on schedule. The owner leaped from the cab and lifted long metal doors, revealing a cornucopia of food. A tiny Mexican woman in an apron stained by beans and blood peered through the window of the truck's kitchen, carving knife in hand, trembling in anticipation, psyched up by the benzedrine demands of her job. Cheap cuts of beef and slices of bacon fried on a griddle; burritos de chorizo y huevos, wrapped tightly in aluminum foil, were stacked in a pyramid behind a glass door with a stainless steel knob. A pot of pinto beans steamed on a burner. Everything was ready.

But the normal crowd of hungry workers shouting orders and waving dollar bills did not materialize. The owner of the hot food truck checked his watch and thumped it with his finger to make certain it was working.

Finally, two customers arrived. They raced to the coffee spigots and drew Styrofoam cups of the bitter brew, softening its punch with packages of sugar and tiny plastic cups of non-dairy creamer. Faced with economic ruin, the owner asked, "Where *is* everyone?"

Smiling like born-again Christians, they patiently explained, "Today election day!"

Meanwhile, inside the factory, the debates raged on. Workers were oblivious to the yellow-faced factory clock with its arms sweeping past minutes and hours. For once, its burden fell on management, who yearned for the day to end, anxious to be finished with what, in their minds, was a circus-like spectacle destined to entertain simple minds, then pick up and move out of town. Things were particularly difficult for the foremen, who were selected to perform the unpleasant task of telling workers the hour and location of the vote. Barely able to restrain their disgust, they did as they were told, notifying workers that the voting would begin at noon in the employee parking lot. Word passed swiftly through the factory, and before the foremen could complete their task, long lines of workers had already formed at the polling place.

A government man stood guard beside a locked ballot box, an American flag adding to his authority. He viewed the long lines of workers with contempt, and though he was physically frail, he did his utmost to appear to be tough.

Javier rode to the polling place with a dozen other workers on a forklift expropriated for the trip. They arrived like revolutionaries in a liberated zone, workers cheering them and shouting accolades. Javier swaggered to the end of the line, a conquering hero proud to wait his turn. When he finally emerged from behind the curtain of the voting booth, he displayed his marked ballot to the crowd, who roared their approval. The government man wasted no time abandoning his post. "No campaigning in the vicinity!" he whined. "That's not allowed! Definitely not allowed!" Javier looked at him and laughed, not understanding a word he said, amused by his gestures and shrill voice. He stuffed his ballot into the padlocked box and stepped to the side to observe the voting, pointing at the government man and laughing.

Many workers required assistance to mark their ballots, barely able to read Spanish, much less English. Having foreseen the problem, volunteers—recruited from management—instructed workers where to make their mark. Javier watched from a distance with suspicion.

An old office worker and employee of Mersola's for twenty-three years chased Javier away like a grandmother running children out of her kitchen. As Javier turned to leave, he bumped into a man he hadn't seen for a long time.

"Hey! Como estás?" he asked. "What are you doing here? I thought you got another job somewhere else?"

"No, hombre. I'm still here!" the well-dressed man replied. "I'm just working in a different department now, that's all. You know how it is."

"De veras? Which department? I thought you were some kind of big shot, going to college and all that."

"No, brother, no. Yeah, I went to school, you know. But I still have to pay the *bills*, hermano. So I'm working in the . . . in the mail room, you know. At night. During the night shift. Wow, man. It's really fucked *up*." Before Javier could ask any more questions, a young woman in a slinky dress nuzzled up to the man, locking her arm with his. "Are you ready now?" she asked him, her eyes and voice as smoky as musk.

"I've got to go now, bro', duty calls," the young man said with a macho grin. Javier nodded his head and watched the young couple stroll away.

"Okay! Time to go! Leave! Let's move!" the grandmother office worker told him, shooing him away again with her hands.

"Okay. *All right*, lady!" Javier said as he laughed and danced out of her way. "Take it *easy*! Híjole!"

"Hey! Javier! Hey, what's *hap*-pen-ing?" a Chicano factory worker asked with a sneer. They shook hands, a fairly complex ritual between partners in the barrio; there were three different grips involved, hands slipping back and forth like the pieces of a Chinese box puzzle; finally, the greeting was consecrated by the bashing of clenched fists, knuckles-to-knuckles.

"Oye, bato, you know Smiley and Juan, no?"

"Seguro, Jesse!" Javier replied.

"Hey, carnal! This is a great day, no? Un día para la *raza*!"

Jesse said, bobbing his head. "Hey, hermano. I've waited a long *time* for this day!"

"Yo tambien, hombre! Me, too!"

"Hey, sabes qué, like, when will we know the *results*, man? You know, we want to *celebrate!* "

"Well, they say sometime around five o'clock, they are supposed to know. That's what they say."

"Oh, wow, man! You mean we won't know until *tomorrow?*"

"No, Jesse. Like I said, they say we will know around five o'clock."

"But I'm not going to stick around this pinche place until five, you know. I've got better things to do! Like watch TV or something."

Javier laughed. "No, Jesse. A lot of people are going to wait at la cantina across the street. We're going to wait there to get the results."

"You mean the *wetback* bar? Hey, Javier, I was just *joking*, hombre. You know that."

Javier clenched his teeth. "That is where we are going to wait, to get the results, you know."

"You mean to *celebrate*, no? Yeah, all *right*! We're going to *partee*! Okay, carnal! We'll be there! Won't we?" Jesse asked his friends.

"Símon!" they answered in unison. "Of course!"

"Está bien, hombres!" Javier replied. "Miren. I have to go now. I'll see you all at the cantina then."

"Be there or be square!" Jesse said in English.

"Sí, hombre," Javier answered, not certain what he meant.

Jesse and his friends leaned back against a wall and soaked up the sun, checking out young women as they waited in line to vote. "There's nothin' like an election to bring out the chicks!" Jesse said to his friends.

"Símon!" they answered again in unison.

Javier, in the meantime, spotted José and made a beeline to

his side. José was in the middle of a discussion with several other workers, patiently making a point. Javier nudged his way into the thick of things.

"But you see, compañeros, this is only the beginning. If we win today, we still have to get a contract, you know. And we might have to strike to get one . . ."

"La huelga, pues!" Javier interrupted. "We'll strike, then! And shut this place down!"

"We might have to," José continued. "Hopefully not. But we might. It is better to be prepared just in case. But listen. We might lose the election, you know. I don't think so. I just have a feeling we are going to win. But if we don't, that is not the end of our struggle. That is not the end. We have to stick together, no matter what happens."

"Claro!" the workers agreed, though of course the prospect of losing troubled them.

"But we are not going to lose, José!" Javier interjected. "My whole department voted for the union—everyone I've *talked* to voted for the union—and I've talked to just about everyone!"

The workers beamed at each other and nodded their heads in approval.

A woman in her sixties watched and listened quietly as if she were not really there, her deep-set eyes milky and vacant. Old beyond her years, she mashed her gums, and a faint expression of awakening flashed in her eyes as though her soul, lost decades before, had returned for a brief instant. Possessed by the spirit, strange words escaped her lips: "Vamos . . . vamos a *ganar?*" she asked feebly, turning to José. "We're going to *win*, aren't we?"

José embraced her with a smile as soft as a child's blanket. "Sí, señora. I think so. I think we are going to win."

The old woman smiled a toothless grin, rocked herself back and forth as her mother had rocked her, and glanced at Javier, embarrassed by her own happiness. Javier cleared his throat and coughed into his fist.

The buzzer sounded, announcing the end of lunch. Though there was no real pressure for them to return to their stations that day, Javier took off, anxious to breathe the stale air of the factory again. The other workers in the crowd vanished just as quickly, leaving José, the old woman, and her ghost.

"We . . . we *are*, aren't we? We are going to *win*?" she asked again. "Sí, señora, we are," José said.

33

Across the street from the shoe factory was Beto's Cantina, sitting cockeyed as if dropped there from a dusty village where peasants grew corn and beans, raised children, and died poor.

In the afternoons, workers sauntered out of the sun and into its cool darkness, buying beer and dropping quarters into the neon-like jukebox blaring scratchy rancheras and traditional Mexican ballads.

Men drank there; the few female customers propped their heads up with fingers woven together and waited for someone to buy them a drink. They smiled easily, their eyes deep and serene—and to the men who sat beside them, their dark coarse hair smelled like chocolate.

Afternoons passed slowly in the cantina, men drinking until they staggered out, women always disappearing mysteriously. But it was a good place to lose time—there were no demanding foremen, no bill collectors or landlords pressing for the rent, no paintings of the Virgin of Guadalupe, no crucifixes or palm fronds. It was a place where men could buy what they did not need, shoot pool, smoke and talk with whores.

Yet despite the occasional gales of laughter, there was no pleasure there. In every bottle of beer was the subconscious memory of invasions and foreign armies, conquistadors bringing deliverance and murder, ancient pyramids robbed of gold, cathedrals built of straw and mud, and revolutions—revolutions toppled by thorough, bloody counterrevolutions.

The cantina offered no promise of life after death. Those who went there knew that when they left, they would have less than when they arrived. All the cantina could offer—all it did offer—was a brief moment of intoxication where the reality of the moment was bearable. And for that brief instant, for the fleeting rush—for the opportunity to laugh at the ghosts of the past—men gathered and drank and spent what they did not have. And when it came time to leave, they left a part of themselves behind.

No one knew why Beto's Cantina was chosen for the victory celebration; there was little festive about the place. Rancheras hung in the air like cigarette smoke, the singers telling tales of unfaithful women and unrequited love. Those who frequented the bar sat bent over their beers, gazing deep into the amber, recalling dreams as ephemeral as the pleasure they felt there.

Yet things were different that afternoon. As the shoeworkers streamed in, filling booths and bar stools until the mirrors were steamed up, the atmosphere became charged with exuberance. Gone were the forlorn rancheras; the newcomers to Beto's Cantina played pulsating cumbias and tropical salsas instead—music for dancing.

The cantina's regulars did not mind the intrusion; in truth, they welcomed it. But they were confused by the sudden change. Most of all, it was the presence of so many *women* that confounded them—women much like their wives, women who normally would never set foot in a cantina, conscious of the stigma attached to those who did. Yet things were strangely different that afternoon and the old rules did not apply. It took some adjusting on the part of the regular patrons of the cantina—and not a few sternly worded warnings. Yet once the ground rules were established, men and women joked and laughed and sipped beer together as equals—an experience as unique and astonishing as the victory celebration itself.

José and Javier were among the first of the shoeworkers to arrive. They sat side by side, ordered two beers, and turned at exactly the same moment to see each new figure that appeared in the shadowed doorway.

Javier lifted his glass to José in a toast: "Hasta la victoria! Until victory!"

José smiled and they clinked their glasses and drank.

"Bueno, José. I've waited a long time for this day." Javier searched the room. "Are Sonia and Rosa going to make it?"

"Rosa can't come—she has four young children, you know. But Sonia will be here."

"That's good. Then everything is all right now?"

"Yes, everything is fine. She is even bringing her brother and cousin. That is why she will be a little late. They just arrived a few days ago, you know."

"Well, it is good they're going to come. They can relax and take it easy for once. Eh, José? They can have a few beers and celebrate with us, no?" Javier gulped down what remained in his glass. "Hey, hombre! Dos más cervezas, por favor!" he called down the bar. "Two more beers please!"

"Take it easy, Javier! We've got a long wait still! You'll be asleep in the corner before we get the results!"

"Don't *worry* about it, José! I can *handle* it, hombre!"

The bartender dropped two more beers in front of Javier, who paid and wasted little time gulping down half a bottle. His eyes already red and full of mischief, Javier turned to the crowd and cried, "Viva la *unión*!"

Turning from conversations as if they had been waiting for that moment, workers answered in unison, "Que *viva*!" With a shit-faced grin, Javier stood up and shouted—louder than before, "Abajo con *Mersola*! Down with Mersola!" and they answered, their voices booming, "*Abajo*! *Down* with him!" Satisfied, Javier turned back to the bar, two-dozen conversations picking up where they had left off. He finished his beer and called to the bartender for two more. José shook his head.

As the bartender dropped two more bottles on the counter, Sonia, Ana, and Manuel arrived, smiling uneasily, having heard the chants as they approached the bar. Sonia spotted José and, with her brother and cousin in tow, plowed through the crowd. When she reached the bar, she tapped Javier on the shoulder and scowled playfully. "Was that you who made the chants?"

"Of course!" Javier grinned.

"I should have known."

Ana and Manuel stood behind her, not knowing what to do with their hands. Sonia turned to introduce them. "This is my brother, Manuel, and my cousin, Ana. This is Don José, and *this* is Javier."

Ana and Manuel grinned. They had heard many stories about him. "Fellow wetbacks!" Javier said in greeting, his words beginning to slur. "Welcome to Los Angeles, where all the streets have Spanish names and the people ask you why you don't speak English!"

All laughed, Javier shaking José's outstretched hand. "Bartender! Three more beers, please!" Javier shouted as he pushed the beers already on the counter toward the newcomers. He reached for a wad of dollar bills in his pocket.

"No, no, gracias," Ana said, waving her finger in front of her.

"No? And you, Sonia? Don't you want a beer?" Sonia grinned and reached for a bottle. She felt she was committing an indiscretion and enjoyed it. Javier handed a bottle and a glass to Manuel, who accepted graciously.

"Bartender! Bring me a Coke, please!" Javier shouted down the counter. The bartender scowled and cursed him under his breath.

"Here's your pinche Coke!" he said angrily, slamming it on the counter in front of Javier. "That will be five dollars! Is there anything else I can get you?"

"No, gracias, that's all for now." Javier paid him, though he left no tip. "What's wrong with *him*?" he asked as he handed the soda to Ana. Ana smiled shyly and shrugged her shoulders.

As the five of them drank and talked, an effervescence rose

up in the cantina and gently caressed the workers, kneading their backs and shoulders, tight and sore from a day's work. They reveled in the warmth of a hundred bodies and listened to music and laughter and the clinking of glasses. Ana and Manuel turned to each other and breathed a sigh of relief, intoxicated by the unexpected security they felt there.

Javier turned to José: "You know, I feel *good*. Good for the first time in—well, I don't know how long. You know what I mean?" He focused his red eyes on José. "Bueno. I usually feel *mad* all the time," he continued, involuntarily clenching his fists. "You know? I just feel mad—like I want to hit someone or put my fist through the wall or something. But today—today is different. I feel like we have *done* something—like I *am* somebody, like I am a *man*. You know?"

José nodded, and thirty years flashed before him. And he remembered when *he* was young. He remembered a morning when his landlord pounded on the door of his apartment, demanding the rent. The rent! It was due on the first of the month. And it was Sunday morning—the first of the month. And José lived with cockroaches and mice, and the roof leaked when it rained, and the toilet didn't flush, and the faucets leaked under the sink. And still, there was the landlord, his fist pounding on the door, then standing there, his hand outstretched, eyes fixed with condescension. And José told him about the roaches and the mice and reminded him how he had asked him to fix the roof and the toilet and the sink. But the landlord insisted everything was fine, knowing José didn't have papers, knowing there was nothing he could do about it. José remembered how his children clung to his pant legs and watched—he remembered their wide, frightened eyes. And there was no milk in the refrigerator, and there was no food. So he lied and told the landlord he'd just been paid Saturday and hadn't had the chance to cash his check. And his children shuddered as the landlord grew angry and told him he was a stupid fucking liar and that he had better have the rent ready first thing on Monday or else. José felt like grabbing the landlord by the throat and . . . but he couldn't. He had no other place to go. So he said nothing. And his children dropped their eyes in shame. Yes, José thought—he knew *exactly* what Javier meant.

As the two of them raised their beers for another toast, David, dressed in the blue suit the union bought for him, stepped through the front door.

One of the workers near the doorway asked, "Hey, David! Qué te pasa? Any news?"

David walked past him without answering.

As he made his way through the crowd, one by one, table by table, the people asked: "Hey! What happened? What was the vote?" Still, he didn't respond.

"Shhh!" someone hushed the crowd. "Quiet everyone! David is here! David is here with some news!"

The laughter and conversations settled down until there was only one voice in the cantina, as a cumbia blared in the corner, *Oyeme, Diosito Santo, tú de aritmética nada sabías?*

"Well? What was the vote?" Javier asked. David bowed his head; the people grew pale and frightened. "Did we win?" someone asked meekly.

David shook his head no.

Dime porqué la platita tú la repartiste tan mal repartida? the cumbia cried, drowning the gasps of disbelief.

"What was the vote?" José asked, his voice hoarse.

"Two hundred ninety-six to two hundred seventy-five. There are some contested ballots—but not enough to make a difference."

The workers could not bear to look at each other. They dropped their heads and struggled to fight back tears.

A profound anger gripped Javier—an anger sharpened by bitterness. He smashed his fist down on the counter, knocking over several bottles. "Those *chingados!*" he cursed, his blood poisoned, muscles tensed like bowstrings pulled taut. "They sold us out! That's what they did! The union sold us out! They *let* Mersola win the election!" Javier slowly turned his head. "If I could get my hands on . . ." He paused in mid-sentence when his eyes landed on David.

Aware of the danger, David shuddered and nervously brushed lint from his blue suit jacket. "Well, everyone, I've got to go now. There is something else I have to do. Sorry! But we can try again! Don't worry . . . maybe with the contested ballots, who knows?" David slowly backed up, following the wall with his fingers, making his way toward the door. "You all did a really great job! Really! Well, like I said, I have to go. Ciao!" He slithered out the front door, glancing over his shoulder to see if Javier was going to follow. But Javier had turned back to the bar and was concentrating on the illuminated bottles arranged in a cubbyhole, grouped by spirit. "Bartender! Give me a shot of tequila!"

Conversations slowly began again, though they were hushed and sober. People finished their drinks, extinguished their cigarettes and said goodbye to their friends, filing out the door one by one. Manuel moved to Javier's side, patting him on the back like an old friend.

"I know how you feel, compañero. In my country, we have been fighting for many years, in many different ways. Now there is a war and many people have died. I don't know how many more will have to suffer before we win."

Javier stared at Manuel, his eyes burning red. "Give me a gun and I'll go to your country. At least there, you know who your enemies are!"

"Hey, hombre," José said gently. "It is not the end of the world, you know. Remember what Antonio said—we still have organization."

"Antonio? Oh, yes, Antonio. Where is he now that we are all alone?" Javier swallowed his shot of tequila and wiped his mouth. "We've lost everything."

"No, hombre. Not everything. You shouldn't think that way. Mira. I'm going to call Antonio right now. I'm going to see him and tell him what happened. Want to go with me?"

Javier shook his head and smiled bitterly.

"Okay, my son," José said, pausing at his side. "Do you have a ride home?"

"Don't worry about me, José. I'll be all right. Go and see your *hero*. Just leave me alone!"

José took measure of him, not certain that leaving him was the right thing. But he knew that to insist would only create more problems. "I'll see you tomorrow, son. Mañana, no?" He waited for a response, but Javier only waved his hand and barked at the bartender:

"Hey, hombre! Bring me another shot of tequila!"

José knew there was nothing he could do, nothing he could say. Javier wanted to be alone, and that was that. So he squeezed his shoulder with affection and left, signaling Sonia she should do the same.

Sonia gathered her things together, shaken and confused as she led Ana and Manuel out the back door. Javier turned his back to them and ignored their departure. "Bartender! Where is that tequila?"

Slowly, those who had come to celebrate at Beto's Cantina stepped outdoors into the glaring light of the street. Gone was the freshness of autumn, smothered by a shroud of smog and the burden of defeat. The workers trudged down the stained sidewalk toward bus stops and parking lots, avoiding the shadow of the Mersola factory, which loomed across the street in the afternoon sun like the Bastille.

A young man who remained behind raised his glass in a toast. "Let's drink up! Tomorrow we go back to work! I only hope that bastard Mersola chokes on his pride!"

"And I hope the big shots in the union who are celebrating

with him do the same!" Javier added, before downing his drink and ordering another beer.

34

Amerio Mersola lifted his glass in a toast: "To our great victory! How sweet it is! Cheers!"

"Cheers!" echoed the guests gathered in his spacious home, crystal ringing as glasses touched in celebration.

A huge banquet table stretched across the Mersola living room, laden with roasts steaming beneath red heat lamps, salads and shellfish cradled in beds of crushed ice, all of it framed with fresh fruit and vegetables.

"More champagne for everyone!" Amerio Mersola declared. "And eat! Eat and enjoy yourselves!" Latino waiters in starched white jackets made the rounds, skillfully pouring champagne from heavy bottles wrapped in linen. Guests lined up at the banquet table, pointing their fingers as a chef with a tall billowed cap and sharp knife carved generous helpings of turkey, tri-tip beef, ham and other roasts.

Amerio Mersola had invited what he considered a broad spectrum of "folks" to his home to celebrate: there were business associates, gloating over the wisdom of advice freely given as they spread pate on Norwegian flatbread; local politicians, smiling over plates of veal parmesan; and the guests of honor—partners from a prestigious law firm and specialists at union-busting, who preferred pasta and green salad, their blood thirst apparently satisfied elsewhere. Not one to forget his friends, Amerio also invited his golf buddies, who stood about, hands in their pockets, distracted by the feast yet prattling on about the need to "nuke" Iran and restore American pride. Nearby, Linda Garcia glowed—the center of attention in a group of balding, middle-aged men willing to indulge her liberal views, their eyes revealing lewd and sordid thoughts.

All the guests felt quite comfortable in Amerio Mersola's living room, fitting in like the marble statuettes that adorned the mantle and glass bookcase.

All but the foremen, that is. They lumbered about in their clip-on ties and wing-tip shoes, ceramic-and-steel American flags pinned to their lapels in case there was any doubt as to their loyalties. After all, they were Latinos—each and every one. But first and foremost they were Americans—and patriots at that. They were also staunch Republicans, more devout in their beliefs than any businessman, their loyalty built upon *ideology*, not class or social position.

Still, they did not feel comfortable there. They dared not sit on the satin-covered French provincial couch. They refrained from smoking, at great personal cost, not wanting to dirty crystal ashtrays. They ate with great restraint, cautiously leaning over porcelain plates, conscious of the lush ivory-colored carpeting. When offered champagne, they accepted graciously, though they would have preferred a good cold beer. The foremen bore their discomfort gallantly, proud to be included on the guest list yet secretly anxious for the festivities to end.

Amerio Mersola spotted Pete as he struggled to balance a plate of food in one hand and a glass in another. "Is that all you're going to eat? Come on, now! Don't be shy! Nelson!" he called to the chef. "Make my friend Pete a plate, would you? And make sure he's well taken care of."

"Yes, sir! Mr. Mersola," the chef answered, twirling his knife like a samurai.

"Let me know if there's anything you want. All right?"

"Thank you, Mr. Mersola, sir."

"My pleasure. And keep up the good work!" Amerio slapped Pete on the back, while Pete panicked at the thought of champagne and potato salad on the ivory-colored carpet.

Scanning the room, Amerio Mersola spotted his older son. With some ceremony, he deftly moved to his side.

"Well, son, what do you think?"

"You did it, Dad. You really did it."

The proud father smiled and gazed into the distance.

"I have to say you were pretty confident, ordering all this food and all. What would you have done if you lost?"

"You don't think a bunch of wetbacks and troublemakers could outsmart your old man, do ya? Besides, I had a lot of help, you know." Lowering his voice to a whisper, he wrapped his arm around his son in an uncharacteristic display of affection. "I owe a lot of it to you, son. Those attorney friends of yours are pretty damn smart." Amerio kissed his son on the cheek, choking with pride and emotion. When it became clear all eyes were upon him, he cleared his throat. "Music! Dancing! In the Mersola house, when we celebrate, we dance! Right, son?"

Proud and overcome by his father's affection, Amerio's son smiled and nodded his head.

Together, they walked to the stereo, Amerio searching through a library of records until he found a vintage album that had survived the revolution in electronics.

"Play this for me, would you, son?"

Soon a scratchy Italian folk song blared from state-of-the-art speakers. Amerio set his glass down and clapped his hands, his expression suggesting that perhaps the others gathered there should do the same.

"Watch the look on your grandpa's face," Amerio winked, dancing across the room toward the old man seated stoically in his favorite chair.

Amerio did a few steps in front of his father, his eyes glazed with love and champagne, the music rekindling memories shared by the two of them. "C'mon, Papa . . . join the party. We'll play some of the old songs and dance—like the old days, when Mama was alive. Remember? Do you remember this song? It was one of Mama's favorites."

The old man sat scowling, his chin set, arms folded across his chest. But he could not repress the memories. His wife danced across his eyes, young and laughing, reaching for him, imploring him to dance. And Amerio could see her there. He smiled lovingly at his father for the first time in many years, his arms open, awaiting his embrace.

But the old man resisted, despite the pleas of his wife.

Amerio would not be denied. "Let me get you a glass of champagne, Papa. Eh? Would you drink a glass of champagne with me?"

"I'm not thirsty!" the old man snapped.

Amerio straightened, his patience tried by his father's stubbornness. But he shook off the remark and tried again. "C'mon, Papa . . . this is a big day for me. All my friends are here to celebrate. Aren't you just a *little* proud of your son?"

"Nope!"

Amerio was stunned. His muscles stiffened and the smile vanished. "What's wrong with you? Give me this one day, won't you? Why do you have to be so stubborn? Can't you let go of that shit for just one day?" The old man sat sullen, his head bobbing about like a string puppet. "Look. Everyone is having a good time. Why do you have to ruin it? What's wrong with you? You'd think this was 1937 or something. Times have changed—the unions have changed. And those 'people'—they aren't even Americans! They don't even belong here!"

"Huh!" the old man grunted. He pointed an accusing finger at his son. "Amerio. When you were a kid, you used to get into a lot of fights. Remember? You'd come home bloody, with a black eye—real mad. Do you remember that?"

"Yes, yes, I remember. But what has that got to do with the price of tea in China? All kids get into fights. It's natural. So what?"

"Yeah, well. Do you remember the time you fought Mark

Smith? The big kid who was such a bully?"

"Sure, I remember. I kicked the living daylights out of him!"

"Yes, that's true. I was proud of you, son! Yes sirree! You really taught that punk a lesson! But let me ask you something, son. Do you remember what you was fightin' for?"

"I don't know why you're bringing this up, after all these years . . ."

"Just answer me, eh? Do you remember or not?"

Amerio breathed a sigh of exasperation. "Okay, all right, you *made* your point! Now let's change the subject, all right? I know what you're leading up to—but it isn't going to work. That kid was too big for his britches and I had to teach him a lesson. That's all. End of story."

"He called you a wop! That was the whole thing in a nutshell, wasn't it? He called you a wop and said you'd better go back to where you came from. You got mad—and you had every right to be—and so you let him have it!"

"Okay, Papa! You told the story. Now can we come back to the present? Don't try to tell me that some kid calling me a wop and telling me I didn't belong here when I was born and raised here has got anything to do with this union thing! You're talkin' apples and oranges! Apples and oranges!"

The old man shook his head and smiled wryly. "Do you know why Mark Smith called you a wop?"

"You are the most stubborn, exasperating person I have ever known! You just don't know when to quit, do ya? All right. Okay. I'll play your little game. He called me a wop because I was Italian. There. Are you happy now?"

"Does that mean you're not Italian anymore?"

Amerio Mersola turned his eyes skyward. "Oh, Lord! Please! Why do I have to put up with this?" He looked back to his father, who, despite Amerio's perception, was not bent on tormenting his son. They locked eyes. "All right, Papa. Look. I don't have to listen to this. I'm proud of my heritage and you know it! Now don't give me this holier-than-thou bullshit! I don't need it! You've done good by me, haven't you? I don't hear you complaining. You've got your family, your grandchildren, your own room, your own television. What is it you want that you don't have?"

"Do you know where the word 'wop' comes from?"

"It's hopeless! You're gonna ruin this party! That's what you really want, isn't it? Now I told you once and I'm not going to say it again— that shit has *nothin'* to do with these wetbacks and their crooked union! That's all there is to it!"

"Well, I'm gonna tell you anyway. Then I'll shut up and you can have your damn party. I'm gonna go to my room and watch television and won't bother you anymore. When my Papa first came to this country—by himself, you know! Well, he couldn't afford to send for my mother, your grandmother. He came over in a ship, and it cost him his life savings."

Amerio rolled his eyes as if he had heard the whole story many times before.

"Now, listen to me, Amerio! If you want me out of your hair, listen and then I'll shut up! You can be sure of that! I never told you all this before . . . at least, if I did, I don't remember. So, anyway, he came over here to the United States of America on a big ship. And when he first got here, he stayed on Ellis Island for a while. That's where all the immigrants from Europe used to have to stay, you know."

"I know."

"Yeah, well, anyway. He didn't have nothin' but a bag of clothes, a razor and a Bible. That's what he always used to say. And you know what? He didn't have permission, either. So they took his passport and they stamped it W-O-P—without papers. See? Do you get it? Do you understand now? Your grandpa was an illegal alien!"

Amerio had *not* heard that story before. At least, if he had, he didn't remember it. His knees buckled and his face drained of color. For an instant, he felt like a kid again, rounding the corner of his block, spotting Mark Smith, the neighborhood bully—feeling that gut feeling you get when you know there's going to be trouble, but you're not sure if you're up to dealing with it. It's my *father* who makes me feel this way, Amerio reasoned. He knows all the weak spots, which buttons to push— he *knows* how to make me feel weak and powerless again. But I'm not going to allow that. I've worked too hard for too many years to feel that way again. Amerio glanced around his living room, at those he had invited to celebrate his victory. Though nobody had overheard the conversation with his father, Amerio felt like all eyes were on him. He cleared his throat and forced a smile. Only his father knew it was a front. "Look, Papa, let's not argue today. Eh? Not today. Today we celebrate. Like the good old days, eh? Like when Mama was alive."

35

How could it happen like that? How could we *lose*? There we were, a bunch of stupid wetbacks, *celebrating* like if we had *done* something. Celebrating, thinking we could actually *win*. We lost before we ever *began*—before the votes were counted. Long before any of that. What a *fool* I was for believing. What a fucking idiot! And now, they're all laughing at us. They probably celebrated last night. Making toasts and jokes about the stupid wetbacks who actually *believed* they could win!

Why is that? Why is it the rich *always* win? And why do the poor people *always* lose? Jesus Christ! Huh! You say you love the poor. Mentira! If you love us so much, why do we always lose? Why can't the rich lose for once? Answer me, Jesus! I bet Mersola was talking to you last night. Thanking you and saying, "I knew you wouldn't let me down! Thank you, God. Thank you Jesus! Thanks for everything! Have a nice day!"

That's the way things are, no? The rich always get their way. Like the stories they tell children. The most beautiful girl in the village is poor and wants to marry a prince. The poor girl marries the rich prince, becomes a princess, and everyone lives happily ever after. Even the poor folks are happy the way things turn out, though nothing has changed for them. There's a big party with free food, and everyone celebrates. Everybody is happy and wants to dance. Like me! I'm happy! I want to dance, too! Watch me, God! Look, Jesus! I'm dancing!

Javier danced around the sidewalk in front of the Mersola factory, shuffling his feet, his arms raised above his head. Folks on their way to work veered sharply from their paths to avoid him, unsettled by the spectacle of a man out of control.

That was good. Yes, God, that was good. I'm sorry I had to stop so soon, you know. But my head feels like it is going to explode. I don't want to make a big mess right outside the door of the big boss, you know. He would not like that. It's because I'm hung over, God. Really! If it wasn't for all those drinks I had last night when I was celebrating, I would dance some more for you. Honestly! I would! Well, maybe tonight. After work. Bueno. Maybe tonight after work you can make a little miracle for me. Not a big one! Just provide me with a few more beers. Or some wine, even! Turn some water into wine for me. Would you, Jesus? I know you can do it! Make me some wine!

No. I don't want any wine, Jesus. Or beer. I've had enough liquor already. You know that. But if you really want to make a miracle—if you really want to make this poor, stupid Mexican happy—let me meet up with an *army*! You know—a poor people's army. Like Zapata had! Bueno. And don't forget the guns! Yes, God. Just let me join some real-life guerrilleros! I don't care if I get killed. You can let the Yankees blow my brains out—if they can find any. That's all right. But let me take at least a land-lord or a rich man with me! Give me that one satisfaction, God! I'll go live in the mountains and eat only beans and tortillas— and fight! Like Zapata! That's all I ask. Let the rich and power-ful be defeated one time by the poor! Just *one* time in my life! *Por favor*! Then you can let them pop my eyes out with a spoon—as long as I get to see that first! At least then, when I die, I would go down like a man! Like *Pancho Villa*! But please! Not like this! Don't let me die with only memories like this!

Javier paused at the entrance to the factory to catch his breath. Workers plodded in past him, shaking their heads with scorn as if he had let them down.

Don't make me go in there, God! Don't make me! Como? What? All right. I'll go. I have no choice, no? It is there or the streets. Just one thing I ask. Don't put that foreman in my face!

260

I just could not stand it! I think I might *hit* him or something. I don't want to go to jail, you know. I have enough problems already.

Javier stepped through the factory door and everything smelled bad. And the air—he tried to breathe the air. But it tasted like dirt.

As he made his way toward the time clock, his head throbbed. And what he saw seemed like a memory—unreal, two-dimensional and flat. There was no substance to it, as if he were separated from reality by a clear plastic curtain, what he saw images of things that had been.

He punched in at the time clock at eight minutes to seven. Still, he was not there. Someone from the nightshift had left a Styrofoam cup on top of his workbench, half-filled with coffee and stewing cigarette butts. That was real enough. Javier gagged and held his head. The drone of muffled voices and machinery corkscrewed into his ears like some kind of deadly worm, the noise and dull lights and factory smoke spinning around him like demons, taunting him without mercy.

Look what they have done to me, God! Look! They're laughing at me now—laughing! Sons of bitches! I'm as good as dead and they are laughing!

Javier's eyes fell upon a plywood box that blocked the narrow aisle in front of his machine. He kicked it, but it stood its ground. Angry, he launched a merciless attack on the wooden box, tearing at it with bare hands, kicking it again and again, stomping and smashing it with his feet. Still, it would not yield. Javier paused for a moment, out of breath; he took measure of the box, his eyes blazing. Then he launched a final assault, employing every weapon at his disposal until the box was obliterated, pieces strewn about like dismembered limbs. When the devastation was complete, he fell back on his workbench, his fingers searching for support as he closed his eyes and waited for the world to stop spinning. Stop! Make it stop! Jesus Christ, *please* make it stop! And finally, it did. It did stop. And when he opened his eyes, things looked different than before. Javier glanced down at the cement floor and it was as if he was viewing an old war newsreel, shuddering in black-and-white. Confronted by his own atrocities, he struggled to get a grip on himself. Bright red drops glistened in the dull factory lights like the work of an abstract artist, red globules as cohesive as mercury. Javier marveled at their luster, so vivid and alive, spots of raw pigment in an otherwise colorless space. He looked into his palms and saw bold, crimson strokes. And then he realized — this is *my* work. Have I lost my mind? Why can't I *feel* anything? Why does everything look so strange? He squeezed his fists and watched as drops of blood fell to the gray concrete floor. Then his hands began to ache — and it felt good. Javier tilted his head back and squeezed his fists again and again. And he thanked God for the pain; it felt so much better than oblivion.

In time, Javier picked up the battered fragments of his anger and dropped them into a large aluminum trashcan. He wiped the blood from his hands with a rag and drenched the lacerations with iodine. The buzzer sounded and he switched on his machine, his blood and madness gently soaking into the porous cement floor.

Nearby, around the corner, past hoppers full of canvas and leather and cardboard, Sonia stapled heels together, slowly losing herself in the rhythm of her work. Yet things were not the same as before. They never would be. Sonia traced over the past few weeks of her life, pausing to examine bits and pieces, searching for an answer to a question she had yet to pose.

Across the aisle, Rosa worked steadily, as always, strangely serene and dignified. For all appearances, it was as if nothing had changed for her. But it had.

Among the factory's organizers, only José was animated that morning. He joined a group of workers who had taken to speculating as to who among them had voted against the union, their eyes flashing with accusations.

"We shouldn't blame each other," José interjected. "The company cheated us. Mira. Some people told me they had to ask for help from officials from the company when they voted. They can't read, so they aren't sure if they voted yes or no." But no one was interested in his insight. They preferred targets closer to home.

"El patron!" someone said, spotting a foreman as he rounded the corner. The gathering quickly dissolved.

The foreman was unable to hide his amusement as workers ran at the mere sight of him approaching. He spotted Javier working nearby and swaggered to his station, sneering. "Hey, big-shot union man. Qué pasa? What happened?"

Javier's body tensed and the muscles in his shoulders and back rippled; his hands grew cold and his face turned white as death. Get out of here before I rip your face off! Get out of here before. Javier had not said a word. Still, the foreman backed off. He forced up a nervous laugh and stiffly retreated to his office, locking the door behind him.

Javier gripped the sides of his workbench, fighting instincts, squeezing blood from his wounds. He exhaled all the air from his lungs, a frosty plume bellowing out as he stood frozen in anger and shivering in the cold.

José, witness to the confrontation, approached Javier. "Hey, mano—how are you doing? Are you all right?"

The warmth of José's voice broke the spell, and Javier could move again.

"Don't take it so *hard*, brother! You can't let him get to you. That's what he wants. Just remember—we did a lot. We've got to think about *la gente*—about the people. And remember, we've still got organization."

"Is that what Antonio told you?"

"Isn't that what you were telling the people yesterday?"

"Yesterday, I thought we were going to win. I was a fool for thinking that. I was stupid! They had things all worked out in advance—the union and the company. I *saw* them bring in outsiders to vote. I saw it with my own eyes! And I didn't realize what they were doing. There wasn't no one there from the union. No one!"

"Mira. Now is not the time to feel sorry for ourselves. We did the best we could. Remember what Antonio said—they'll be on our asses if we win, and, if we lose, they'll be after our heads."

"When are you going to quit that shit about Antonio? You talk about him like he was some kind of saint. Can't you see by now he let us down? Jesus Christ!" José shook his head, resisting Javier's conclusion. "I'll tell you something else, José. The next time that pinche cabrón foreman gives me shit, I'm going to kick his ass!"

"Javier! Hermano! It's me, your friend, José! Remember? Listen, my brother. Do you really want to hurt that guy? Pues, what happens if you hit him? Sure, you might feel kinda good. I remember when I was young—I used to feel that way all the time. But what good would it do? They'll just fire you. They might even put you in jail! How are the *people* going to feel if that happens?"

"I don't care how the *people* feel anymore."

"Well, then. What *do* you care about? Yourself? Is that why you organized folks? So you could get back at the boss? What about *them*? What about Sonia and Rosa? They have children, you know. They *trusted* you and stuck their necks out—not to try to get even with someone. They did it for their children! So they could have a better life! Now are you going to tell me you don't give a damn about them? I don't believe you. No, brother. Listen. We've got to stick together.

"Tonight we're going to have a meeting with Antonio. I know how you feel about him. But he wants to meet with us, see? He wants to help us to keep our organization together. Don't let Mersola and his men take that away from us, too. We're going to figure out what to do next. Can you make it?"

"No, amigo, sorry," Javier said with a weary shake of his head.

"Look, Javier. Try to make it tonight, eh? We'll be at Sonia's place at seven. Anyway—try not to give that foreman an excuse to fire you. The people feel bad enough as it is, you know. And it will just make things more difficult for you. Besides, we're not finished yet."

Javier stared at José in disbelief, and José flinched, struggling to maintain his optimism. A foreman spotted them and José quickly returned to his work area, the foreman close behind.

"The party's over!" the foreman said. "An old man like you had better start thinking about his job! If I catch you away from your work station again, I'm going to write you up. This is a verbal warning. Understand?"

José went about his work as if nobody was there, unaffected by the scolding. But Javier was livid. Go *hit* the cabrón! he thought. Who does he think he is? Go pick him up and throw him into one of those machines until his belly has holes for laces! What about the *people*? What about Sonia and Rosa? They have *children*. They *trusted* you!

The foreman strutted toward his office, sneering at Javier with greater arrogance than before. But this time Javier ignored him. Instead he watched the reaction of his co-workers: they dropped their heads and pretended not to see. But Javier could feel their pain. And for the first time, he knew their loss was more profound than his. They have *families*, he thought—they *trusted* you!

The yellow face of the factory clock glowered down at the workers; the agonizingly slow movement of its hands had the same tortuous effect as a medieval rack, stretching minutes into hours. And though the workers said nothing, Javier could hear their screams. He closed his eyes and covered his ears with his hands; still, the voices would not go away.

When the buzzer sounded announcing lunchtime, workers waited in line at the time clock, then stormed out the gates. They ate their meals on street curbs, on patches of parched grass, in automobiles—anywhere but the factory. Many made runs to the liquor store, buying beer and canned cocktails that they quickly consumed in cars parked a safe distance away. Those who drank ate peanuts and chewed gum to conceal the scent of alcohol on their breath; they could be fired for having consumed as much as one beer, though members of management often boasted about the number of drinks they had at company expense during their lunch hour, euphemistically referring to such cocktail parties as "working lunches." Soon—too soon—the buzzer sounded the five-minute warning. Workers quietly punched in and marched to their stations, engaging machines with acquiescence. Still, the foremen were not satisfied; they wanted revenge—and they had orders to exact it.

With Pete in the lead, a group of foremen gathered behind Sonia as she worked, snickering and making jokes she could not hear. Sonia continued to do her job, pulling the worn lever of her machine, apparently oblivious to the provocation. Not easily rebuffed, the foremen increased the volume of their taunts, probing for weakness, psyched up and ready to strike. Sonia stapled heels with a steadiness that annoyed the foremen. Her face revealed no expression, and she stared into the distance with a vacant gaze. Rosa glanced across the cement aisle, her eyes betraying a concern that did not escape the attention of Pete, under pressure to demonstrate his prowess. He signaled the others and sauntered over to Rosa's bench. "*She* was with them, too!" he said, with as much anxiety as a teenage boy. "She was at the union meeting. And I bet that shithead Antonio had fun recruiting *her*!"

Though Pete had lapsed into English, Rosa caught the gist of what he was saying.

"Well, will you look at *that*! I've never seen *her* get mad before."

"Maybe you hit too close to home," one of the foremen smirked.

"Maybe," Pete conceded, trembling with jealousy. "And maybe she understands more English than I thought. It's amazing how fast some bitches can learn—in *bed!*"

The other men grunted their approval, then moved on in search of *other* victims, laughing, scratching their buttocks and hitching their trousers over bloated bellies. Sonia and Rosa looked at each other across the cement floor, and like two sisters—raised in the same house, sharing the same memories—they both instinctively knew: it was just the beginning.

The foremen carried out their campaign with military discipline, for the most part, their objectives having been spelled out for them on chalkboards by supervisors and men from upper management. Authority and order had to be restored. Tactics to realize that goal were classic martial canon. First: break the will of the people; give them no rest, provide no retreat; teach them a lesson they would never forget. Second: isolate and eliminate their leaders; fire a barrage of rumors and innuendo so extensive few would be able to resist the conclusion that *some* of the charges *must* be true. Finally: divide and conquer; split the Mexicans from the Central Americans, those with papers from those without, the young from the old. By effectively employing such time-proven tactics, it would just be a matter of time before everything would be under control. Then it would be a turkey shoot.

In the unlikely case that the initial campaign fell short of its goals, a contingency plan was prepared. Rumors as to its details were circulated among the workers like leaflets dropped behind enemy lines. There would be mass layoffs; all jobs and classifications would be subject to review. Word of impending disaster spread throughout the factory. And it wasn't long before many began to blame the union and its supporters for their woes.

Foremen reveled in the new climate of fear, where a glare or a wave of the finger could cause panic. They disciplined workers for the most trivial offenses, reserving special attention for the organizers, who were watched and hounded. Except for Javier. After a careful review, he was considered a "unique case." Thought to be "potentially violent," foremen refrained from singling him out for discipline, even when backed by an army of reservists. The foremen discussed the matter in some detail and agreed: sooner or later, he would blow up and they would get him. It was just a matter of time.

But Javier's case was not the only deviation from the company battle plan. Though the foremen had been explicitly warned against targeting workers who had openly opposed the union drive, they did not feel compelled to observe strict military discipline. And so there was an unspoken oath—a brotherhood— among them that made allowances for minor infractions of company policy. After all, they had served in the military and knew how things were *really* done. Those who savored their ability to shatter people's nerves and draw tears did so with impunity. And on more than one occasion, even opponents of the union drive bore the brunt of their cruelty.

A small group of foremen spotted two young women foolish enough to exchange words as they worked. They swooped down upon the women with a virulence that surprised even Javier, who witnessed the assault from his station nearby.

"Get back to work!" one of the foremen ordered, glaring at the women. "You are not being paid to chitchat, you know!" The women tried to focus on their work, heads bowed, hands trembling. But they could do nothing right.

Javier watched what was happening from behind his machine: he watched as the men criticized and berated the women into complete submission. Soon the foremen felt the heat of his eyes on their backs, Javier staring at them like a wolf in the night. They made a hasty retreat.

Factory lights buzzed above Javier; machines grunted and belched and pitched. In the stale yellow light, he felt he was trapped—chained to a workbench for the rest of his life, imprisoned with no chance of parole. And as he raised his arms and moved his legs, he could feel restraints as they dug into his skin, tightening around his wrists, his ankles and his neck. And for a moment it appeared to him there was no escape. Javier turned back to the women and watched them dab the corners of their eyes with their bandanas, coughing and sniffing and fighting back tears. And he realized he was not alone.

The afternoon died slowly. The buzzer finally sounded and workers lined up at the time clock, shuffling forward a step at a time, waiting their turn to punch out.

José stood in line with the others, his jacket and thermos in hand. Javier tapped him on the shoulder.

"Bueno, José," Javier said. "What time did you say that meeting was going to be?"

36

An orange moon dominated the sky and a restless wind scattered fallen leaves. A pack of dogs rummaged through an overturned trash can, frail carcasses maimed by brushes with automobiles and barrages of rocks thrown by children. Yet despite the sorry state of the animals, Ana was scared. She knew what dogs could do—she'd seen them tear flesh from cadavers stacked outside the incinerator in San Salvador; she'd watched in horror as they gnawed the bones of men tortured and slain the night before—men whose eyes had been plucked out, limbs severed and throats slashed by the death squads.

Ana tucked the carton of milk she had bought under her arm and slowly backed down the driveway beside Sonia's apartment building. The dogs took one look at her and made a run for it, hobbling away, turkey bones clutched in their jaws, fear in their eyes. Still, it was Ana who was afraid.

Ana quickly climbed the stairs of the cubist building, grasping a wobbly wrought-iron rail until she reached the landing on the second floor. Flakes of glitter sparkled from crumbling stucco, illuminated by the bare porch light over Sonia's door.

Inside, Antonio and José sat stiffly in chairs that did not match, Antonio nervously thumping his fingers on the kitchen table. Sonia poured cups of boiled coffee for her guests, and Rosa prepared a platter of Mexican bread she had brought for the meeting.

As the battered screen door creaked open, Sonia glanced up and smiled. "José, Antonio—you both know my cousin, Ana."

"Yes, of course. I have had the pleasure," José answered,

standing with formality.

"Como estás?" Antonio grinned, leaning forward to shake Ana's hand.

"Bien, bien, gracias. Y ustedes?"

"And Rosa, let me present my cousin to you. Ana, this is my compañera, Rosa."

"Mucho gusto."

"Igualmente," smiled a bashful Rosa.

Ana immediately joined the women in the kitchen while Antonio and José returned to their chairs. But somehow, things were not right. José was not himself and Antonio could sense it.

"Sonia, do you need any help?" Antonio asked, grasping the arms of his chair, prepared to join the women behind the counter in the kitchen.

José awkwardly mimicked Antonio's movements, though the idea of helping in the kitchen was alien to him. He grasped the arms of his chair and waited to see what he should do next. He was relieved when Sonia replied, "No, gracias. We have everything ready now."

A sugar bowl, spoons and paper napkins were placed upon the table. Sonia filled a cream pitcher that she saved for special occasions with the milk Ana bought at the store, and Rosa placed a platter of Mexican bread at the center of the table, smiling with satisfaction.

"Aren't you going to join us?" Antonio asked.

"Sí, como no. Of course." Rosa sat beside José, her hands in her lap. She did not know what to do. It was a new experience for her, sitting with men at a dinner table. She glanced at Antonio and José and laughed nervously, while Ana busied herself with chores in the kitchen.

José concentrated an inordinate amount of attention on the sugar he added to his coffee, sprinkling each spoonful as if counting the crystals. Antonio watched, not knowing what to make of his silence. He turned to Rosa for a clue. But she blushed and played with her coffee cup nervously.

"Does anyone care for some cream?" Sonia asked.

"Yes, thank you," José replied, carefully pouring a small amount of milk into his cup.

Sonia plopped down in a chair, and the table rattled. "Ah, it feels good to sit down."

José smiled politely. "Yes. It feels good. That is true."

The organizers each continued to prepare their coffee as if conducting a ritual—slowly stirring in milk then tapping the sides of their cups several times with their spoons. Again, there was an uncomfortable silence.

"Umm . . . there's nothing like a nice cup of coffee," Sonia said.

José smiled and took a sip, setting his cup down and adding a little more sugar.

The quiet was painful.

"Have some pan," Rosa suggested, encouraging the others with a nod of her head and a smile.

Antonio and José each reached for a pastry, setting their choices down on paper napkins and carefully removing granules of sugar from their fingertips.

A television blared in the back room. The organizers sat and gazed at the tabletop.

Manuel quietly entered the kitchen, not wanting to disturb the meeting, yet unable to restrain his curiosity. His arrival presented an unexpected break from the tension.

"Ah, Manuel. Antonio, José, you both know my brother, Manuel."

"Good to see you again!" Antonio grinned.

"Won't you join us?" José asked.

"No, no, gracias, I don't want to interrupt. I just got bored watching the television, you know. I've been watching it for three days now. Go on with your meeting. I'm just going to help Ana in the kitchen."

Ana smiled as she dried a plate with a dish towel.

The organizers were disappointed. They turned to their coffee and pastry, glancing uneasily at each other.

"And Javier?" Rosa asked. "Is he coming?" Ana turned from her work in the kitchen.

"Yes, I *think* so," José replied. "He said he would be here. But you know Javier. He is always late."

Sonia nodded her head and feigned a smile. But Antonio was not convinced. He examined José's eyes. He had never known Javier to be late. Quite the contrary. He was usually early. So *that* is what is wrong, Antonio thought. It is Javier. Something is wrong with Javier. Antonio reached into his pocket for a cigarette. "I've been trying to quit, you know," he explained as he lit a match. The others nodded politely and Sonia brought him an ashtray. Antonio blew smoke rings which lingered in the air. And as Rosa sat stoically in her chair, it seemed to her a great distance separated her friends.

Finally, José broke the silence. "Well, Antonio, it is like I told you the other day. The union is going to contest some of the ballots—but not enough to make a difference."

José looked Antonio in the eye for the first time since they had arrived at Sonia's apartment. Antonio arched his head back as if troubled by a stiff neck, took a long drag from his cigarette and carefully prepared his response. In the kitchen, Manuel leaned against the counter and listened.

There was a knock on the door. "Javier! Come in! We've been expecting you!" Sonia declared.

Javier hesitated at the threshold for a moment, peeking inside to see who was there, his eyes red and full of mischief.

"Come in, compañero!" Ana said, blushing when she realized that she had perhaps appeared too happy to see him again.

"Javier? Have you been drinking?" Sonia asked playfully, her hands on her hips.

"Who, me? Why do you ask? Is it Holy Week or something?"

Sonia frowned. "Would you like a cup of coffee?"

"No, no, gracias. It keeps me awake, you know."

Ana grinned like a schoolgirl. But José and Manuel could not conceal their disappointment. Antonio smashed his cigarette out and calmly lit another, distancing himself from the others.

Javier was making the rounds, greeting everyone with a handshake and small talk. Antonio sat back in his chair and waited, smoking and watching everything out of the corner of his eye. The tension grew as Javier approached him.

"Antonio! Hey, hombre! I haven't seen you for a long *time*! Qué *onda*? What's happening?"

"Por aquí, hombre. This is it."

"I know what you mean. Well, it has been a long time, no?" They shook hands, arms cocked at right angles.

"It hasn't been *that* long, has it, carnal?" Antonio said.

"Pues, well, for *me*, it has seemed like a long time, you know. Bueno. A lot has *happened* since the last time. So what do you think? We lost, eh?" Sonia searched for something to do. She grabbed a dishcloth and began to wipe the kitchen counter, forcing Manuel to search for another way to pass the time. José got up from his chair and began to pace back and forth anxiously.

"Well, I wouldn't say that, brother," Antonio said. "No, not really. You all came very close to winning, you know. And you didn't get much help—not from the union—not from anyone."

Antonio's last words were an admission. He said them so everyone would understand as much. And it made him uneasy.

Javier searched his eyes. "That's it?"

The air became instantly ionized. Sonia wiped the dust from a glass figurine; she could hear the crystal crack.

"No, hombre, that's not it. You know. I think maybe you *did* win. Oiga. You did the whole damn thing yourselves! Without any help from the union. *Despite* the union. You self-organized. Man, if I was you, I would feel *proud*!"

275

Javier stared at him blankly. Only Rosa and Manuel seemed encouraged by his words.

José paced nervously about while Sonia continued to polish glass. "Antonio, I don't feel proud," Javier said. "I feel *bad*. *Real* bad inside. We were sold out. That's what hurts the most. Now they treat us like dirt. And the people—the people don't even know what hit them. No. I don't feel proud. I don't. And to tell you the truth, I can't stand the thought of another day like today."

With Javier's bitter words, the full weight of the defeat finally fell upon Antonio. Glancing around the room, he realized he was being blamed for their loss. It was true, he could have done more—though one man does not make a union. Anyway, it was too late. There was nothing else he could do—nothing he could say—to change things. So he sat, silent and humbled, too proud to ask for forgiveness, too tough to admit the pain he felt. He sat in his chair and stared at the tabletop. There was nothing else to be done.

José could not bear to see things end that way. "It's not Antonio's fault that we lost. He did more than most men in his position would have ever done. He lost his *job* helping us—what more do you want from him? We would not have come as close as we did to winning without him. And we would all be in México or El Salvador right now had it not been for him. So let's be fair. We did our best and we lost. That is all there is to it. What we have to think about now is what we are going to do next.

"We all knew this might happen. There was no guarantee we would win. I think we should keep going. We lost because of the sell-outs in the union, and because of the dirty tricks played by the company. So why don't we tell them? Why don't we *tell* the people what really happened? Let them know the truth?"

Sonia set the last glass figurine down and returned to the table, encouraged by José's suggestion. "But how? How would we do it?"

"Put out a leaflet like the union used to do!" José said. "Tell them everything! Then at least maybe they will stop blaming each other for what happened."

Sonia slipped back into her chair, her thoughts whirling; Ana and Manuel leaned across the kitchen counter, their heads cradled in their hands.

"But who would pass it out?" Sonia asked.

"We can!" Javier replied, a glimmer of hope rekindled in his eyes. "Anyway, we are all going to get fired sooner or later."

Sonia, José, and Rosa recoiled from the thought.

"The company can't just fire you like that," Antonio said. "They have to show cause. If they do fire you, then you can file with the labor board and charge harassment and termination for union activities. I know some good lawyers who could help. But look—don't give them an excuse to fire you. Passing out leaflets is probably not a good idea."

"He's right," José conceded. "We have to be careful. It is very hard to find work now. There aren't too many jobs. And it would be especially hard if a company found out we worked at Mersola's and were with the union drive."

"How would they find out?" Javier asked.

"They have their ways."

Resignation drifted across the table as everyone thought about unemployment lines and their families and relatives back home. Their enthusiasm was slowly sucked away.

"Well," Javier said, "maybe we should all quit and try to find another place where we could work together. Maybe we could even try to make a union again."

As Javier spoke, everyone knew it was over. There was a long, ponderous silence.

Rosa cleared her throat. "When my husband disappeared, I wondered how I was going to take care of my children. I was all alone, and I didn't have anything."

The others looked up, surprised to hear her voice.

"I just wanted to work and make enough money to feed and clothe my children. I only wanted to work. I went to the factory and I was afraid of the foremen and the supervisors. I was afraid of being picked up by la migra. I only lived for my children and stayed away from anything that might endanger them. Then the union came along," she said, smiling at Antonio. "I stayed away from it, too. I was afraid of trouble. Then there was the immigration raid. And the thing I feared most—being separated from my children—happened.

"On the way back from Chula Vista, I began to realize that trouble will come whether I hide and try to avoid it or not. Anyway, life is hard. So I thought to myself—if life is going to be hard for me anyway, I might as well stand up for the things I know in my heart are just. I should try to change the things that are bad instead of hiding from them. At least then, when times are difficult and things are not going well, I'll have my self-respect and dignity."

Rosa paused for a moment to collect her thoughts.

"I think I learned that if I really love and care about my children, then I have to do what I can to make the world a better place. We can't *ever* lose hope that things will be better....

"Since that bus ride from Chula Vista, since working with all of you, for the first time in my life, I feel strong. I've seen people stand up for their rights—I've seen it with my own eyes! I would never have believed I could ever feel this way."

Rosa glanced down at the tabletop and rubbed both hands against her face the way a mother reassures a child. She took a deep breath, then looked into the eyes of Javier, Sonia, and José, easily penetrating all their defenses. "Don't you see? Things are different now. We just cannot let things go back to the way they were before. We just can't. I d o n ' t care if they call me names and talk about me. I don't care anymore. But whatever happens, as God is my witness—I will *never* let them take away my dignity again!"

José smiled his warm grandfather smile and beamed with pride. Sonia and Ana wept. Rosa had touched them all. And as Antonio and Javier fought back tears, Sonia understood and embraced them like brothers.

From the kitchen came Manuel's voice, cracked with emotion. "I'll help—whatever you want me to do, just tell me and I'll do it!"

"Me too!" blurted Ana.

"We can't give up now!" Sonia cried.

"Bueno," Javier added, still wrestling with his emotions. The others laughed softly.

"Let's do the leaflet, then," José suggested. "Maybe it will bring the people together. . . ." He straightened up and pushed himself beyond his feelings, focusing upon practical questions, anxious to seize the moment and make something of it. Arching an eyebrow, he said, "First we have to write it, then we need to find a place to print it. The union won't do it, that is for sure."

Antonio blinked as his mind raced beyond the words he was about to say. "That's no problem. I can get it done somewhere."

José began to see the pieces of the puzzle fit together. But there was one part missing. And they had passed that way before. Did he dare raise the same question? he wondered. Would it kill everyone's enthusiasm? Maybe it was better to leave things as they were, to have everyone united again, even if another defeat was inevitable. Maybe . . . no, we have to try, he thought. Oh, Rosa! You are so right! And how wonderful that *you* would be the one to know!

"There is only one problem," José said. "Who is going to pass the leaflet out?"

Sonia summoned together her courage, moved by the moment. "Let's all do it! We might be late for work, but let's all pass it out!" The organizers nodded their heads with silent acceptance, turning to see where the others stood. All agreed in an unspoken vote of confidence—all were prepared to do what had to be done, regardless of the consequences. All but Antonio.

"I don't think that would be a good idea," he said. The other organizers were stunned. "Anyway, you won't have to be late for work. You don't even have to pass the leaflet out. I know someone who can do it for you."

"You do?" Javier asked. "Who?"

"Me."

37

Early the next morning, workers approached the gate to the Mersola factory, lunches and newspapers in hand. They rubbed their eyes, yawned and shuffled toward the plant, haunted by a sense of foreboding, dreading what lay ahead.

But things were not as they expected. They were greeted by Antonio, who handed them leaflets written and mimeographed the night before. What is *he* doing here? they wondered. And who are the other two with him—calling us *compañero*, their eyes as bright as Jesuit priests?

"Brothers and sisters—you've been sold out!" Antonio declared. "What is more—you have been cheated. Pero la lucha continúa! But the struggle continues!"

The guards watched Antonio, Ana, and Manuel from their shack. What in blazes is going *on*? they asked. What *is* this? Everyone knows what happened to the union. And didn't that smart-ass beaner get fired? Man, Mr. Mersola will want to know about *this*!

One of the guards fumbled with an instamatic camera, taking pictures of the trio, waving undeveloped photos in the air like valuable evidence. When a worker dropped a leaflet, another guard rushed out of the shack and fell upon it, convinced it was subversive in nature, though he could not read a word of Spanish.

"Better bring it to the old man right away!" one guard ordered a subordinate. "It looks like there is going to be trouble!"

"Yes, sir!" the guard answered. He bolted down the walkway toward the factory, photos and leaflet in hand, prepared to engage any resistance he might encounter along the way.

Ana and Manuel distributed the leaflets with conviction—a trait that did not go unnoticed among the workers. But under the menacing glare of the guards, Ana grew faint and her hands began to tremble.

"What's wrong?" Antonio asked.

"La chota," Manuel explained. "It's the police. I think she is worried about the police."

Antonio glared at the guards in their shack. "Don't worry about those guys," he reassured them. "They won't hurt you. Honest. They just *think* they're cops."

Meanwhile, inside the factory, much of the excitement returned from the days before the election. Though no one dared defy the foremen, there were clandestine meetings everywhere.

In one such gathering, a middle-aged Mexican silently read the leaflet. A number of workers who could not read studied his face, as though somehow his expressions would reveal to them the contents of the manifesto.

He took a deep breath and turned to them. "It says some big shots in the union sold us out," he explained. He paused and read the next sentence to himself, his lips forming every word. "And it says Mersola cheated in the election—that he brought in his own people to vote." As he moved on to the next paragraph, he nodded his head in agreement and the workers around him turned to each other with anticipation. "That's right what it says. It says we have to stick together, now more than ever— and that we should never give up fighting for our rights."

"Es ciérto," several workers agreed. "That's true."

"El *patrón!*" an old woman whispered, and the workers quickly dispersed, hobbling off to their stations though the morning buzzer had yet to sound.

A foreman rounded the corner, talking to himself in a state of agitation. He spotted the leaflet, abandoned by the workers in their haste, and stopped in his tracks to read it. "Son of a bitch!

I thought we were finished with this shit!"

He searched the area, looking for a clue that would reveal who had been there moments before, already planning their punishment. But the workers were going about their business as usual, showing no emotions, least of all fear. So the foreman raced off to share the evidence with his peers. A nervous twitch tormented him along the way as he rehearsed the words he would say: "Sons of *bitches*! *Motherfuckers*! Goddamn *communists*!"

The foreman soon met up with his comrades who were in the middle of their morning ritual, sipping coffee and ridiculing their wives. He interrupted them and launched into a harangue, reciting the words he had practiced with perfect cadence; his announcement was eagerly received, like news from the front. Soon all the foremen were leaning over his shoulder in an effort to read the leaflet.

"Let *me* see that!" one insisted.

"Goddamn agitators!" said another. "Fucking liberals!" chimed in a third.

"The old man will want to see *this*!" the cleverest among them proclaimed.

Together the foremen marched off to present the plant superintendent with what they had uncovered, snatching the leaflet from one another, each anxious to get credit for the discovery. When they arrived at his office, they translated the Spanish into an English version that, in their interpretation, sounded like a call to arms.

"I'll be damned!" the plant superintendent declared. "Good work, boys! The old man will want to see *this*!"

The plant superintendent stormed off to the controller's office, carefully following the chain of command. He thrust the leaflet into the controller's hand, adding his own personal touch to its contents, which neither of them could read.

By the time a dog-eared copy of the leaflet reached Amerio

Mersola, the factory gates had been locked and secured, extra guards had been summoned to duty, and the local police had been notified of "imminent danger" at the plant.

But all the orders were soon countermanded by Amerio Mersola; he was already aware of the leaflet and its contents. Before the controller had entered his office to present him with proof of an impending insurrection, Mersola had placed a personal call to Don Brady. Brady, at home eating his breakfast, had assured him that the leaflet was the work of one man—a former employee carrying out a personal vendetta. Not to worry, he had said, he knew who it was—and the individual in question would never bother Mersola, or anyone else, again.

The controller sheepishly returned to his office, whereupon he called the plant superintendent and scolded him for overreacting. The plant superintendent in turn summoned the foremen.

"I don't know what's going on, boys, but I was told we're overreacting. Nothing's changed. That's the word from the old man. We're supposed to stick to the original plan."

"What do you mean?" a foreman asked.

The plant superintendent leaned back in his chair and lit a cigar. "I mean—go out there and get those sons of bitches!"

The foremen charged out of the office and into the gray haze of the factory just as the morning buzzer sounded. They went for the organizers, certain they would be engaged in mass agitation. But the four of them were hard at work, having foreseen the foremen's reactions the night before.

Javier paused briefly to check his watch. In a pantomime of concern, he turned to the foremen: "You're *late!*" The foremen stared at him as if he was standing on his head. Confused, they wheeled around and made a beeline for the superintendent's office, where they sought additional counsel.

For the first time in days, the workers laughed. They slapped their thighs with open palms and snapped their wrists in the air with delight. Javier ran an instant replay in his mind, freezing frames of the foremen's expressions, turning up the volume as the workers laughed, their voices like the cheers of a crowd.

But the laughter soon died out, overcome by shadows and the drone of a hundred machines. People settled into their work, women tying their hair back with bandanas as they always did, men finishing cigarettes and gulping down the last of their coffee. The air became heavy, and they could feel it leaning on their backs.

The workers did what they were paid to do. They fashioned leather and cardboard and cloth into shoes to be sold in exclusive department stores—shoes they could never afford, shoes that retailed for more than a week's wages. They worked with the knowledge that every movement they made in the factory belonged to Mersola. Still—though he profited from their labor, though he directed their hands and owned their time—Mersola did not control their minds. And their thoughts wandered.

The foremen returned from their session with the plant superintendent, having been chastised for their lack of backbone and reminded of the need to stick to "the plan." They quickly resumed patrols of the factory and all its enclaves, carefully scrutinizing the faces of workers, gauging their mood. And they could see a change from the day before: the fear had all but vanished. If only there was a way to bind people's *minds* to their work! they thought. But that was impossible. These people are easily distracted and as simple as children. Still, in time they will learn, the foremen reasoned. They will learn—in time.

As the morning wore on, the workers had time—not of the sort to solve complicated problems, but time nonetheless. And though they did not contemplate the classics of literature or analyze tenets of philosophy, they had time to consider what had happened to them, what the company and union officials had done. They figured things out, for the most part, and made sense of it all. And somehow the load they carried became lighter, thanks in large measure to the leaflet written by the organizers.

Still, no words could easily fill the emptiness the workers felt having lost the union drive—though failure was not a new experience for them. In truth, their very lives were built upon the rubble of defeat. It was part of their history, ingrained in their culture, etched in their psyche. But it was one thing to be accustomed to defeat and quite another to believe it possible to win. It was the expectation of *victory* that had shattered their spirits. And it would be a long time—if ever—before they believed in themselves, or anything, again.

Yet as they labored, the leaflet called to them, speaking with their voice, in their language. As morning became day, people wondered: *Was* there really something worth fighting for?

At 8:30, the foremen and supervisors were summoned to a meeting. The workers knew where they were going and why. They took advantage of their absence to talk about the organizers at the gate, about what was happening in the factory, and, most of all, about the leaflet.

At 9:30, the foremen returned. Backed up by managers and executives rarely seen in the factory, they increased the scope and intensity of their campaign. One by one, workers were pushed to move faster, to produce more in less time. Men were followed into bathrooms, foremen timing their bowel movements, counting off seconds like coaches at a track meet. Women who made the mistake of speaking to neighbors were ridiculed and belittled for "trying to do a man's job," instead of being at home "where they belonged."

It was not long before the terror tactics began to take a toll. Workers dared not pause to light a cigarette, much less leave their stations for a drink of water. It seemed that every time they turned around, a foreman or supervisor was there ready to find fault with their work, their pace, their attitude. And there was no end to it.

One executive set out to educate the foremen in advanced management technique. For twenty minutes, he watched a woman as she worked—a woman who had made thousands of shoes without fault, a woman who, unbeknownst to him, had been a vocal critic of the union drive. The executive analyzed her every movement—the layout of her setup, the angle of her elbow, the number of steps between functions. Alterations were instituted in every aspect of her job, though the executive knew nothing of production. Nevertheless, he persuaded her to adapt to the changes, anxious to see his ideas put into practice. Finally, when she approached the breaking point, he left her, content to have imprinted production with his signature, impressed with the adaptability of the human hand.

The executive smiled wryly at the foremen. "*That's* how it's done, boys," he said. Though the foremen knew the changes he had implemented would cut production, they were impressed. They had been taught a valuable lesson: they had learned how to bind workers' minds to their labor.

The foremen and supervisors moved on to the cutting-and-heel department. Sonia knew better than to take note of their arrival. She put on her street face, as hard as concrete, as expressionless as a parking meter. Mersola's men bantered back and forth, attempting to provoke her. But Sonia would not fall for it. She knew better.

Across the aisle, Rosa could not take her eyes off them. She was concerned for Sonia, well aware of what she had been through the past few weeks. Her anxiety did not go unnoticed; the management team quickly abandoned Sonia for an easier target.

Pete remembered the last time he had confronted Rosa, under similar circumstances. He saw an opportunity to get even—to repay her for all the times she had rejected his advances. More than that, he saw a chance to make a name for himself among the supervisors and executives. Without hesitation, he stepped out in front of them, planting his feet firmly on the cement floor, striking a threatening pose. Rosa tried to conceal her apprehension. But it only made matters worse.

As Rosa concentrated on her work, Pete visually undressed her until she sat naked in the dim factory light. It was a thrilling display of machismo for the other managers, who projected their fantasies like holograms.

"I bet Antonio has his hands full with *her!*" Pete chortled in English. "*Both* hands!" Pete fondled imaginary breasts and smiled.

The men grunted their approval, their laughter laced with depravity. Emboldened by their response, Pete wiggled his tongue about rapidly, his eyes bearing down upon Rosa.

Rosa glanced up in time to witness his vile display. She did not attempt to disguise her revulsion.

"What's the matter, baby?" Pete asked her in English. "Cat got your tongue?"

"I guess you have to join the union before you get any of that *snatch*," one of the Anglo supervisors said. "Then you have a meeting every night!"

Mersola's men laughed their nervous belly laughs and licked their lips, excited by the atmosphere of gang rape.

"Too bad, Pete—guess you're not her type," an executive snorted. As the members of management laughed, Pete grew tense and angry. And, more than the others—*because* of the others—he began to lose control.

"Rosa," he cooed with mock affection. "Antonio te paga sueldo de sindicato? O solo cobras el mínimo?"

All machines in the department stopped.

The Anglo managers laughed nervously. "What did he say?" one asked.

"He asked her if Antonio pays her union wages, or does he only pay her the minimum."

Rosa's eyes burned. She leaped up from her bench, pointed

an accusing finger and said, "You're *sick*! You *are*! You're not a man! You're nothing but a company *dog*!"

The men stopped laughing, though they did not understand a word Rosa had said. Sonia marched across the cement floor to Rosa's side, ready to do battle. One by one, other workers joined her.

A foreman stepped into the gathering crowd and waved his arms. "All right, all right everyone," he said in Spanish. "Get back to work! This doesn't concern you!"

The executive with the masterful grasp of management skills became unglued. "Tell them to get back to work!" he cried, his voice quivering. "I *said*—get back to work!" the foreman shouted in English for the executive's benefit.

Word spread about the confrontation. A wave rolled across the factory; machines stopped and workers set their tools down; they abandoned their stations and rushed to witness events firsthand.

"I'm *warning* you—things are going too far!" the foreman said. "This doesn't *concern* you! So you'd all better get back to work, if you know what is good for you!"

José and Javier arrived at the scene, amazed by what they saw.

A shaft of light beamed down on Rosa and Pete from a window in the ceiling. Dust flickered and shadows clung to their features.

When his foreman spotted Javier in the burgeoning crowd, he lost it. "And *you*, you fucking asshole! Get the hell *out* of here!"

"Vete a la chingada," Javier replied calmly, joining the others near Rosa. "Go to hell."

Pete was livid. The veins on his forehead stood out like blue fingers, accentuated by the bright shaft of sunlight.

"Listen to me, Rosa," Pete said. " I don't want anything bad to happen to you. Don't do something you will regret. I mean it! *Think* about it! You're making a big mistake. This thing has gone too far!"

Rosa stood her ground.

Intimidated by the presence of so many workers, Pete took a deep breath. "Okay, Rosa. This is your last chance. Let's go to my office and talk things over."

Still, Rosa did not budge.

"I *said*—let's go to my office—*now!*"

"No!" Rosa answered, jutting her chin out in defiance. In the sharp light of the sun, she was as dignified and relentless as an Aztec warrior.

"Don't you *dare* answer me in that tone of voice! You fucking *wetback!*"

"That's *it!*" Rosa pulled off her smock, threw it on her workbench, grabbed her purse and marched to the door.

"Come *back* here, puta!"

Javier, who had been jockeying for position among the crowd, forced his way to where Pete stood and confronted him, chest-to-chest, nose-to-nose. Javier looked Pete in the eye: "One more word from you and I'm going to kick your ass." Pete's legs buckled and all color evaporated from his face.

The workers stood by and watched; fires burned and glass melted in their eyes. It was a defining moment in their lives, and they knew it. Ghosts of past generations called to them— Don't just stand there! *Do* something! José heard the voices; he whirled around, overcome by their number, moved by their single-heartedness. And he did not hesitate to answer: "That's *it!* Enough! Vamonos! Let's go! Huelga!"

Sonia echoed his call: "Vamonos! Strike!"

Workers marched toward the door en masse, shouting, "Huelga! Huelga!"

Throughout the factory, people picked up the chant until the building trembled. Javier stepped back from Pete and smiled, joining the sea of people as they stormed toward the exit.

Rosa was already out the front gate, waiting at her bus stop, when she heard the chanting. She turned to look just as the first strikers poured out the factory door, José and Sonia in the lead as they cried, "Huel-ga! Huel-ga!"

The workers from the Mersola factory formed a giant picket line, but Rosa hesitated for a moment and bit her lip. She thought about her children at home and what the future held for them. Tears ran down her cheeks and she smiled: "Lo hago por ustedes, mis hijos. I do this for you, my children." She raced toward her compañeros and joined the picket line.

An autumn wind warned of a gathering storm, but the workers looked to the sky and laughed. At long last, their time had come. Rosa thrust a clenched fist above her and it felt good. She was not afraid. Nor was she alone. With the wind behind her and her friends at her side, she added one more voice to the hundreds of others thundering against the looming walls of the factory, chanting "HUEL-GA! HUEL-GA! HUEL- GA!"